ONCE WERE PACIFIC

"A Maori Bartering a Crayfish," drawn by Artist of the Chief Mourr
Tupaia, 1769. British Library, Add. 15508, f. 11. Copyright the Britisl

Once Were Pacific

· · · ·

Māori Connections
to Oceania

Alice Te Punga Somerville

University of Minnesota Press
Minneapolis
London

See page 249 for information on previously published material in this book.

Every effort was made to obtain permission to reproduce material in this book. If any proper acknowledgment has not been included here, we encourage copyright holders to notify the publisher.

Published by the University of Minnesota Press
111 Third Avenue South, Suite 290
Minneapolis, MN 55401-2520
http://www.upress.umn.edu

Library of Congress Cataloging in Publication Data

Te Punga Somerville, Alice.
Once were Pacific : Māori connections to Oceania / Alice Te Punga Somerville.
Includes bibliographical references and index.
ISBN 978-0-8166-7756-6 (hardcover : acid-free paper)
ISBN 978-0-8166-7757-3 (pbk. : acid-free paper)
1. Māori (New Zealand people)—Ethnic identity. 2. Oceania—Ethnic relations.
3. Indigenous peoples—Oceania—History. 4. Māori (New Zealand people)—
Migrations—History. 5. Oceania—Emigration and immigration—History.
6. Regionalism—Oceania. 7. New Zealand—Relations—Oceania. 8. Oceania—
Relations—New Zealand. 9. Māori (New Zealand people)—Intellectual life.
10. New Zealand literature—Māori authors—History and criticism. I. Title.
DU423.E85T4 2012
993'.00499442—dc23
2011052486

Printed in the United States of America on acid-free paper

The University of Minnesota is an equal-opportunity educator and em/

20 19 18 17 16 15 14 13 12   10 9 8 7 6 5 4 3

For the Hakas, Hulas, and Haka-Hulas of Glen Innes:
especially Jessie, Johnny, LeRoy, Joseph, Rhuben,
and Te Morehu.

For Matiu Island: it's good to be home.

E kore au e ngaro
He kākano i ruia i Rangiātea

TRADITIONAL

What belongs to water belongs to blood. . . .
Whole families have journeyed here,
they continue the line.

ROBERT SULLIVAN, "i," *Star Waka*

Contents

Ngā Mihi: Acknowledgments

A FEW YEARS AGO, I asked my Nana for a specific book, and she gave me the family copy of Te Rangihiroa's *The Coming of the Maori* instead. I wonder now if this gift was a challenge or prophecy. My whānau has always been my strength, inspiration, and accountability: Nana and Grandad, Mum and Dad, Auntie Jill and Uncle Mike, Daniel, Amy, Rose, the uncles and aunties, the Te Punga cousins, Loraine and John, Betty Finlayson, the broader connections of hapū and iwi, with special mention of Terese. Ko Te Ātiawa te iwi, ko Waiwhetū te marae. I am compelled to offer a special tribute to Auntie Nanie for the chance to reconnect and to my sister Megan and nephew Matiu for everything.

This project has been supported by a range of institutions and people: major funding for the research was provided by the Royal Society of New Zealand through a Marsden Fast-Start Grant (2006). At Victoria University of Wellington in Aotearoa New Zealand (VUW), I received financial support for this project from pro-vice chancellor (Māori) professor Piri Sciascia, the Faculty of Humanities and Social Sciences, a New Researcher Grant, and the University Research Fund. This joins funding and institutional support from Fulbright, Cornell University, and the University of Hawai'i–Mānoa over the course of my doctoral studies. I have enjoyed collegial and institutional support from VUW, Cornell University, and the University of Hawai'i–Mānoa in the United States and from the Warawara Department of Indigenous Studies at Macquarie University in Australia. Chris Dean from the VUW research office encouraged and supported my Marsden application and so was the first person to hear me describe this project and also the first to believe in it. I am especially grateful to the support and aroha from Te Kawa a Māui and Te Whānau o Te Herenga Waka at VUW.

Other institutional support has come from various archives and libraries and their magnificent staff: VUW, especially Nicola at the Beaglehole

Room; the National Library; the Alexander Turnbull Library; the University of Auckland; Auckland Public Libraries, Hutt Libraries, and the Auckland City Council Archives; the State Library of NSW; the ANU library; the National Library of Australia; University of Hawai'i's Hawai'i-Pacific collection; Kamehameha Schools library and archives; the Bishop Museum Archives; the Mission Houses Archive; the Yale University archive; and the special collections at the University of Birmingham. To Ngāti Mutunga, for permission to conduct research about Te Rangihiroa, ngā mihi.

I have received a great deal of enthusiasm and inspiration from my students, especially the 2008–2011 classes of Pacific Literature at VUW and postgraduate students with whom I have had the pleasure to explore the amazing world of Māori literature. I was supported with practical research assistance from Arini Loader, Gemma Browne, Megan Pakau, and Ronnie Pakau; each is a promising researcher in his or her own right, and I look forward to hearing more from all of them.

Thank you to my academic supervisors and mentors at Cornell University during my doctoral studies (Biodun Jeyifo, Angela Gonzales, Elizabeth De-Loughrey, Laura Brown) and at the University of Auckland, where I wrote my master's thesis (Terry Sturm) and where I first fell in love with English (Witi Ihimaera, Albert Wendt, Michael Neill). I can only hope that your combined influence is visible in these pages—it is certainly felt and appreciated. Special tribute goes to the late Professor Terry Sturm, whose guidance, wisdom, high expectations, and generous aspirations secured me on this path. I wish I had thanked you kanohi ki te kanohi when I had the chance.

I owe a great debt to friends, peers, and mentors and their respective whānau, who have provided a wide and deep layer of warmth and support—intellectual, emotional, and physical. Ngā mihi nunui: Alyssa Mt. Pleasant, Andy Mackenzie, AnnaMarie Christiansen, April Henderson, Aroha Harris, Brandy Nālani MacDougall, Brendan Hokowhitu, Cecilia Tuiomanufili, Chad Allen, Chris Andersen, Dominique Eugene, Erina Potter, Hokulani Aikau, Hugh Karena, Jacob Tamaiparea, Jeani O'Brien, Jo Mossop, Jo Smith, Jolisa Gracewood and Richard Easther, Joost de Bruin, Ka'imipono Kahumoku Ka'iwi and Walter Kahumoku, Karin Speedy, Kate Hunter, Keith Camacho, Ku'ualoha Ho'omanawanui, Lehua Yim, Lisa Brooks, Lydia Wevers, Maria Bargh, Marie Cocker, Meegan Hall and Peter Adds, Michelle Elleray and Anne Lyden, Michelle Trudgett and Ness Garcia, Nadine Attewell, Noelani Arista, Ocean Mercier, Pala Molisa, Paul Meredith, Rachael Barrett, Rawinia Higgins, Robert Warrior, Robert Sullivan, Selina Tusitala Marsh, Sophie

Druett, Tasha Williams, Te Ripowai Higgins, Teresia Teaiwa, Tim Groves, Vince Diaz, Vernice Wineera. My writing groups, Agraphia, the Toihuarewa Write-on-Site team, and Writers Block, kept me on the job, and the members of the "Let's kick ATPS's butt until she publishes her book!" Facebook group provided a supportive and mortifying final push near the end.

Many of the ideas in this book have been shared at conferences, symposia, and other venues, and I have relished the feedback people have generously provided: University of Utah; NAISA at Oklahoma, Georgia, Minnesota, and Tucson; the University of Hawai'i and East West Center; ACRAWSA in Adelaide; SPACLALS in Sāmoa; the Pacific History Association in Dunedin and Fiji; BYU-Hawai'i; the MELUS, ACLA, and MLA conferences; AIS and English at Cornell University; Te Tumu at University of Otago; Manu Ao; Te Pouhere Kōrero and He Rau Tumu Kōrero hui for Māori historians; Ohio State University; Harvard University; UCLA; Pacific Studies and the Stout Centre at VUW; and the University of Auckland French Department.

Huge thanks go to the University of Minnesota Press, especially Jason Weidemann and Danielle Kasprzak. Your decision to take a risk on a book by a Māori scholar from the other end of the world, and the encourage-ment and skill you have applied to its production, means that this book will have the opportunity to travel like an oceangoing waka: as sturdily as possible and with navigators and maps already well aligned. Special thanks go to Mum, Rose Heinrich, Arini Loader, Jo Smith, Rawinia Higgins, and April Henderson, who helped with the manuscript in the last week before the deadline.

Finally, I acknowledge Māori writers who write in English. In some ways, this first book is a feathered korowai, assembled row on row on row. Any beauty in this cloak is because of the feathers you have contributed, and any gaps or unevenness or bits of loose stitching are entirely my own fault, a humble and always-learning weaver of such things.

This book is dedicated to some rangatahi and an island.

Māori and the Pacific

We met with about half a Dozⁿ Cloth Plants, being the same as the inhabitants of the Islands lying within the Tropicks make their finest cloth on: this plant must be vary scarce among them as the Cloth made from it is only worn in small pieces by way of ornaments at their ears and even this we have seen but very seldom. Their knowing the use of this sort of Cloth doth in some measure account for the extraordinary fondness they have shew'd for it above every other thing we had to give them, even a sheet of white paper is of more Value than so much English cloth of any sort what ever.

James Cook, Philip Edwards, and J. C. Beaglehole,
The Journals of Captain Cook

FOR MĀORI AT UAWA IN 1769, the usual European trade goods and trinkets that had been prepared for exchange by the Europeans on board the *Endeavour* were trumped by large sheets of tapa recently acquired in Tahiti. Although we might be tempted to delve into this moment of "first-encounter" for so-called precolonial, first-contact descriptions of Polynesianness and whiteness, the Māori preference for tapa over European cloth signals an alternative simultaneous series of connections. As they interacted with navigator–explorers Tupaia and Cook, Māori communities drew on existing narratives of connection and exchange with the broader Pacific. So, indeed, did the visitors: those on board the *Endeavour* recognized that a few scrawny trees on the North Island of New Zealand were the same as those from which communities all around the "Tropicks" made tapa by beating the bark of a specific tree into flat strips that might be glued together to make larger sheets, dyed and decorated, or left unadorned. In New Zealand's rather more chilly climate, the aute (as the paper mulberry tree is known to Māori) was unable to flourish, yet the process of beating the bark into cloth was retained, and Cook noticed that the cloth was "worn in small pieces by way of ornaments at their ears." Cook describes the "extraordinary fondness" Māori showed for tapa; why did Cook describe this dynamic as "fondness," and for whom is this fondness "extraordinary"? Surely it would be difficult to put into words the "extraordinary" scene in which the evidence supporting generations-old claims Māori had made about mythically large expanses of tapa, and all of the related claims of migration, navigation, and earlier origins around Te Moananui a Kiwa, materialized before them.

Tupaia was among the first of thousands of Pacific people to jump on a Western ship. Hailing from Ra'iatea[1] but boarding the *Endeavour* at Tahiti, he accompanied Cook throughout the Pacific, and is among the first Indigenous Pacific people to produce texts on European paper. Tupaia drew not only his famous map of Polynesia[2] but also a scene depicting a very special interaction: a moment of exchange in which a European person extends a piece of tapa and a Māori person extends a koura, or crayfish.[3] At times this painting has been accompanied by captions that imply that the European man holds out cloth or paper ("An English Naval Officer Bartering with a Maori"[4] or "Maori Bartering a Crayfish"[5]), but the original caption, "A Maori Exchanging a Crayfish for Tapa Cloth with Joseph Banks at Uawa New Zealand 1769,"[6] and Cook's own use of "paper" as well as "cloth" for tapa emphasize a rather more messy moment of encounter. The richness of this triangulated moment—Māori, European, and Raiatean holding crayfish, tapa, and paintbrush, respectively—both underpins and compels this book.

Certainly Māori once were Pacific. A series of complex and impressive ocean journeys were undertaken over the last five thousand years in an unparalleled and unparallelable feat of navigation and curiosity. The last legs of those deliberate journeys were across unprecedented distances: to Hawai'i, Rapanui (Easter Island/Isla de Pascua), and Aotearoa.[7] As Hirini Moko Mead puts it, "there is honor in being part of the peoples of Polynesia and knowing that we have relatives spread across the great Pacific Ocean."[8] Similarly, in 2009, Tate Pewhairangi described the seventy-fifth anniversary of Te Hono ki Rarotonga, a meetinghouse opened in 1934 as a manifestation of connections between Rarotonga and Tokomaru Bay:

> We are honoured that our "cousins" from Te Moananui a Kiwa attended the festivities. Our reo is similar, and our tikanga and ancient stories are also very similar.[9]

Likewise, the poet Robert Sullivan describes Māori as people "of waka memory" and "of seagoing / and waterborn descent." These configurations of Māori connection with the Pacific do not merely describe historical links but also engage ongoing connections between "relatives." No singular narrative can account for all the entities, events, people, and places involved; articulations of the waka (canoe, vessel) journeys are many, layered, nuanced, and contested. As Māori archaeologist Peter Adds puts it, on arrival to our large, cold islands, these Pacific people became specifically Māori.[10] Once we arrived in Aotearoa, we began to recall Hawaiki, the warmer homeland from which we had physically departed and to which we would spiritually return after death.[11] Hawaiki is a consolidation of our Pacific origins, and around Polynesia this mythical homeland bears versions of the same name. Whereas this Pacific is recalled in some specific spaces, however, our location (both on the cold islands of Aotearoa and in the nation-state of New Zealand) has shaped how we articulate who we are. Although Māori are ethnically Polynesian and Aotearoa is clearly a part of the Pacific region, within the New Zealand national space, *Māori* and *Pacific* colloquially refer to two distinct communities: *Māori* are Indigenous, whereas *Pacific* refers to those migrant communities from elsewhere in the region. It can feel like we *once* were Pacific but are no longer, and this book explores the ways in which the relationship between Māori and the Pacific has been articulated over a long period of time and in multiple sites.

There Was an Island

I spend a lot of time with various relatives on a mostly uninhabited island that sits in the middle of Te Whanganui-a-Tara, Wellington Harbor, the large bowl of water around which the city of Wellington is wrapped. The island, which takes a forty-minute stroll to circumnavigate, is a twenty-minute ferry ride from Wellington and a ten-minute ferry ride the other way from Petone, or Pito-one, the place from which my relatives watched the first Europeans sail into our harbor. When we are standing on Matiu Island, we are standing on (at least) two stories, two narratives, two explanations for who and how we are as Māori.

When we are on Matiu, we are in the mouth of a fish. Before the North Island was given its descriptive, poetic, and creative English name, it had another name that we still use: "Te Ika a Māui." This name is derived from the original fishing up of the island by Māui, the trickster demigod figure who pops up all around the Pacific. Māui took his grandmother Murirangawhenua's jawbone and fished up te ika, the memory of which is still encoded in the name for the various parts of the fish. One end of the island is called "Te Hiku o te Ika," the "tail of the fish," and Wellington is located at the other end: "Te Ūpoko o te Ika," the "head of the fish." Māui's hook went into the mouth of the fish, which (according to my relatives) is our harbor. This is a story of firstness: as long as there has been a fish, there have been us. When we introduce ourselves to other Māori people, we name the mountains, lakes, rivers, and harbors to which we are related so they know who we are. We are standing in the mouth of a fish on which our people have always lived, and on this basis, we are Indigenous.

When we are on Matiu, we are also standing on a memorial to a female relative. Kupe and his family were living in Hawaiki, our ancestral homeland, and traveled south in pursuit of an octopus. (Some people give other reasons for this trip.) They followed the octopus into very cold waters and ended up in Aotearoa, which was so named because of its appearance—a "land of a long white cloud"—when approaching from across the sea. Te Whanganui-a-Tara, my harbor, was used as a haven while they were here, and the island in its center offered a particularly lovely place of refuge. Kupe and his entourage left Aotearoa and went back to Hawaiki and told everyone about this cold but amazing (and enormous!) place they'd found. As he left, Kupe named the two islands in the harbor after two of his beloved female relations, "Mākaro" and "Matiu." When we introduce ourselves to other Māori people, we name the waka on which our relatives traveled to Aotearoa from Hawaiki so they know who we are. Matiu Island is an important memorial to the voyage of Kupe and to the predicted migration of Polynesians (and, more broadly, Pacific people) to our islands of Aotearoa, as manifested in the naming of the islands in my harbor after younger female relatives. When we stand on Matiu, we are standing on a memorial to our collective voyaging from across the ocean we know as Te Moananui a Kiwa. On this basis, we are migrants; we are Pacific.

Yet, because of our location on Aotearoa and in New Zealand, other articulations have been urgent. There is a third story about Matiu that explains its contemporary official name of "Matiu/Somes." This story is about Matiu's history as Somes Island. Somes Island is geographically useful in the same way that Alcatraz is useful: as a close but separate island near a major city, it offers (at least in theory) an easy place to keep things and people.

After "the Crown . . . assumed ownership of Matiu in 1841 or thereabouts without the consent of or any consultation with Māori, and without making any payment,"[12] Somes was used for various kinds of internment: for new migrants to New Zealand; for Japanese, Germans, and Italians; for people with particular illnesses; for conscientious objectors; and so on. Later, it was an area of quarantine for incoming animals of all kinds, and still later, it served as a different kind of quarantine area: a wildlife sanctuary for species that are no longer able to thrive on the disease- and pest-ridden North and South islands. Ironically, Matiu/Somes is now a refuge for native species that are threatened by the very livestock and methods of farming that entered New Zealand through the island in the first place. Matiu/Somes is doubled, bicultural: Māori and non-Māori, Indigenous and non-Indigenous.[13] The slash between Matiu and Somes in the official name of our island simultaneously separates and connects. Our own narratives about this island, which are tied to Matiu rather than to Somes, exist in endless relationship with this third, colonial narrative.

Once Were Pacific

If we once were Pacific, what are we now? The book title *Once Were Pacific* clearly plays with the titles of Duff's 1990 novel and Tamahori's 1994 film, *Once Were Warriors*,[14] and so directly refers to, and inverts, dominant ideas about Māori before interaction with Europeans. Such narrow representations draw, of course, on a mythical precolonial "once" that ventures back not to another time but to timelessness. The title *Once Were Pacific* suggests that although we have been understood as warriors, we have also been pacific in its original sense of being calm; our histories cannot be restricted to monolithic characterizations and narratives. Additionally, Māori scholarship, writing, politics, and discourse have tended to focus either on the occupying nation-state of New Zealand or, recently, on particular articulations of (fourth world) Indigeneity.[15] Directly engaging the title *Once Were Warriors* foregrounds the circulation of texts by and about Māori. The unfamiliar idea that Māori once were Pacific is juxtaposed with the familiar claim that we once were warriors. The project of decolonization in which all Indigenous people are engaged demands the grappling with, not the erasure of, colonization; it is about re-remembering.

At specific moments, we have articulated ourselves as Pacific people: when, why, and how? In some ways, it seems odd to claim that Māori have not retained a strong sense of connection with the Pacific when the migrations to Aotearoa are always already recounted and memorialized in many spaces. Indeed, it is almost paralyzing to reflect on the vast and multiple ways in which Māori people "of waka memory" have articulated, and continue to articulate, connections with the Pacific. At times this project has felt like a ridiculous attempt to describe something that is always going to be far larger than what is accountable in a single book. Vernice Wineera published the first collection of poetry in English by a Māori woman when her collection *Mahanga* came out in Hawai'i in 1978, and she later wrote a poem that includes the following lines:

> This island
> Is the tip of an underwater volcano
> so large it is disorienting
> imagining all that mountain beneath you.[16]

Once Were Pacific is a tip that can barely hope to indicate the bulk of the mountain beneath. Even to get its head above water, it depends on all that it does not manage to represent in its own pages. The presence of Pacific pupils at Māori boarding schools, Pacific players on Māori sports teams, Pacific soldiers in the Twenty-eighth Māori Battalion of World War II, and the appointment of Māori people to Pacific governmental roles (from Te Rangihiroa as medical officer to Niue and the Cook Islands in the 1910s to Georgina Te Heuheu as minister of Pacific Island Affairs in 2008) all demand further consideration. Specific moments of encounter in more recent times, such as the second South Pacific Festival of the Arts held in Rotorua in 1976, ongoing activist connections in New Zealand and around the Pacific region, the collaborative carving effort of a large pou in Manukau City, and countless others, would provide a rich space for reflection and demand recognition as well. This project, which is "so large it is disorienting," is merely a starting point, "the tip of an underwater volcano"; while humbled by being a mere tip, it is also compelled by the underwater volcano. Ultimately, I hope, *Once Were Pacific* will provide space for conversations alongside those we are already used to having: about Māori, about writing in English, about Māori writing in English, about Indigeneity, about the Pacific. The urgency and significance of this book are derived not from the singularity of the Māori–Pacific connections it describes but from the mountain of those various connections that have been obscured.

Once Were Pacific is about the intersections of Indigeneity and migration. It turns to creative works (broadly defined) produced by Māori in Aotearoa and around the Pacific, and by other Pacific people based in New Zealand, and asks, How do Māori and other Pacific people articulate their connections at the levels of region (New Zealand as a part of the wider Pacific) and nation (Māori and Pacific communities in New Zealand)? How does the distinction in New Zealand between Māori and Pacific blur the complexity of historical and contemporary connections? How do Māori articulate and negotiate the rather difficult intersection between discourses of migration (we came from Hawaiki on waka) and claims to Indigeneity (we've always been here)? Claiming that we once were Pacific does not undermine or delegitimize national or transnational discursive formations that seal Māori into one of two possible relations—with the state or with Indigeneity—but rather suggests that the Pacific is a rich and significant additional context for Māori articulation and scholarship. Indeed, this book implicitly asserts that Māori exist outside, beyond, and between any narrow fads of framing, stereotype, or representation. Despite a dominant differentiation between Māori and the Pacific, then, this book keeps turning back to those scraps of the Pacific that are still visible. On seeing the tapa on Cook's and Tupaia's ship, Māori response was primarily one of recognition and reconnection. For Māori—for us, for me—these moments in which Māori and the Pacific are reunited suggestively complete the cycle that started when our ancestors navigated their way to Aotearoa generations ago.

Connections, Disconnections

Māori and Pacific people connect differently at the levels of region and nation. Because of the histories of migration mentioned earlier, Māori are both geographically and genealogically a part of the Pacific region. We presently make up around 14 percent of New Zealand's total population (we numbered 565,329 in the 2006 census[17]), and in addition, an estimated one in five Māori people live outside New Zealand. However, as a result of recent histories of political and physical mobility in the region, Māori relate to the Pacific in the national space as well. Over the second half of the twentieth century, as migrants from other places in the region made their homes in New Zealand, and echoing the production of the local identification of Māori over time, a new Pacific identification emerged here. Colloquially, migrants from elsewhere in the Pacific are often known by a local umbrella term: *Pasifika* (a transliteration of *Pacific* also spelled "Pasifica," "Pacifika," "Pacifica," and "Pasefika"), and in this book, Pasifika refers to New Zealand–based non-Māori Pacific people. Although there are obvious problems with lumping together culturally and linguistically distinct groups with a single term, a strategic amalgam can create visibility and the grounds for collaboration.

At present, Māori–Pasifika connections are deeply inflected by the colonial project within which Māori and a number of Pasifika communities are rather tightly bound. A combination of factors has led to the Pasifika community making up 6.9 percent of the New Zealand population, but the foundations were laid by two forms of colonialism in the region: specific colonialism, where New Zealand officially colonized Sāmoa (1920–62), the Cook Islands (1901–65), Niue (1901–74), and Tokelau (1926 to present), and broader impacts of colonialism in the Pacific, whereby disparities in the region and the usurpation of Māori land and resources led to New Zealand becoming a destination for economic migrants. In the postwar period, Māori communities were moving to New Zealand's cities at the same time as the first sizeable migrations from elsewhere in the Pacific arrived there—and often in the same suburbs. Māori and Pasifika people have had to scramble for the few resources available to them in the area of employment (competition for work, particularly in the areas of unskilled, semiskilled, and trade labor, still persists today) but also in the areas of education, housing, health care, and so on.[18] Alongside this dominant movement of Māori and people from around the Pacific toward urban spaces, in the 1960s and 1970s, some specific Pacific groups were sent to rural and town areas to work in laboring, forestry, and agricultural jobs, through which they had opportunities to interact with local communities. Māori communities were efficient and effective in including Pacific migrants, both formally (rituals of welcome, provision of practical support, and cooperative political activism) and informally (intimate relationships and friendships), until the more numerically significant arrivals from elsewhere in the Pacific simultaneously prevented this kind of local incorporation and enabled some Pacific communities to produce viable community organizations of their own.

Māori–Pasifika connections are marked by discourses of relationship and reconnection but also of disjuncture. For example, we might consider familial prohibitions on marriages or partnerships with the other, informal prejudice, ethnically drawn rivalries between youth gangs, and so on. Compounding this, Pākehā racism has tended to lump Māori and Pasifika together in a way that flattens out differences and further marginalizes all communities involved. Surely a focus on Māori–Pasifika connections should also attend to the rather embarrassing genealogies of suspicion, derision, and competition between our communities. They certainly provide a counterpoint to Pacific-centered discourses that echo and sometimes explicitly draw on Albert Wendt's and Epeli Hau'ofa's visionary framings of an Oceania whose insistently regional focus allows little room to problematize the relationships between Indigenous and immigrant Pacific peoples in particular spaces. Except for occasional popular and mainstream references to race-based violence in the wake of specific incidents, the articulations of disconnection (or indeed connection) between Māori and Pasifika communities are literally off the mainstream record, and so deciding to publicly discuss them in this book feels like a rather risky, invasive, and even duplicitous act. And yet, the complex patterns of prejudice that inflect Māori–Pasifika relationships at the national level can also shape Māori articulations of connection with the Pacific region, and a project that focuses on connections demands a frank and complex exploration of disconnections too.

This book argues that Māori and Pasifika communities are drawn into the logic of New Zealand–specific prejudices as long as they insist that their primary relationship is with the New Zealand nation-state. Recalling the two names of our island in Wellington Harbor, the multiplicity inherent in the name "Matiu" can be diminished by the presence of the alternative name, "Somes." On one hand, tāngata whenua (Indigenous or local people; here the people responsible for Matiu) may subsume Pasifika communities under the category "not Indigenous" (Somes) given that Pasifika communities are not Indigenous to the current configuration of the New Zealand nation-state.[19] On the other hand, migrant communities can tend to focus on their relationships with the visa-granting nation (Somes) rather than other, Indigenous, coexisting nations that occupy the same land. (Indeed, the public ferry that carries visitors to the island continues to refer only to "Somes.") This stalemate can be paralyzing for our discussions of Māori–Pasifika connections, and yet I believe this is the very reason that this kind of project *should* be undertaken. Indeed, it is in these moments and modes of Māori articulation with the Pacific that the nation-state is relegated to one strand of a matrix of relationships within which tāngata whenua operate.

Writing in Place

Any book is a product of place: one always writes somewhere, and I am writing in a discipline, in a university, and in Aotearoa. Throughout *Once Were Pacific,* arguments will return to the place of place, from this point right here through until place is given the final word in the epilogue. The roots of this book lie partly in a chapter of my doctoral dissertation, written in the lands of the Cayuga Nation (upstate New York) and the Kanaka Maoli (Hawai'i), but more particularly, the roots of *Once Were Pacific* are embedded in this place. One specific point of genesis for this project was an interaction in Hawai'i when someone mentioned that he was pleased that there was another Pacific Islander in the English department that year; I replied, "Awesome—who is it?" before realizing that the person was talking about me. In that moment and that place, a Māori person was unproblematically Pacific Islander, but Māori and Pacific Islander are distinguished in New Zealand to the extent that I had not recognized myself when I had been spoken about.

Who was that Pacific Islander in the English department? For my part, I have mobility in my blood: I am a member of the Te Punga family, and our tribal connections are primarily to Te Ātiawa. After living in Taranaki on the west coast of the North Island since arriving across the Pacific Ocean from Hawaiki many generations ago, we migrated farther southward to the Wellington area—to the land around the harbor in which Matiu Island is located—in the early nineteenth century. Although that is our home base, we have been moving ever since, as individuals and in small family clusters. I was born here in Wellington, but when I was five years old, my immediate family moved to Auckland, where I attended a school in which almost all the kids were Pacific (Māori and Pasifika). Although one tends not to notice these things when one is small, on reflection, I can see how all of this affects who I am today and, importantly, why this is my first book. There are many stories to be told about Māori writing in English and many places to tell them. I have felt some urgency around telling this particular story—Māori articulations of connection with the Pacific—because it helps answer questions that were in the air I breathed growing up and because the relationship between Indigeneity and migration is so crucial to Indigenous creative, cultural, political, and theoretical activities in the present.

I write as a practicing academic, a scholar, a researcher, and a teacher. Though there are many spaces in which these roles may be filled, I choose to work in a university. However, this book (and this scholar) sits alongside, and seeks neither to ignore nor detract from the multiple ways in which Māori migration across the Pacific is remembered, articulated, and mobilized in whaikōrero, waiata, ruruku, karakia, haka, and visual arts. *Once Were Pacific* is not about waka traditions or Māori involvement in the revival of Pacific navigation,[20] but it takes for granted that people of waka memory affirm and share those memories in spaces outside as well as inside the university. Plenty of people who are well versed in the topic of waka traditions and the history of voyaging in the Pacific occupy scholarly halls, library bookshelves, and paepae.[21] In important ways, for example, this book seeks to sit alongside a large gathering that was hosted by Ngāti Kahungunu on the eastern coast of the North Island in November 2008. Relatives of Ngāti Kahungunu and of the other Tākitimu-derived iwi (tribes, nations, people) based around that part of the island poured into the area from around the Pacific: most obviously from the Cook Islands, from where the Tākitimu had departed for Aotearoa, but also from Sāmoa and beyond. In a press release, Ngāti Kahungunu iwi chairperson Ngahiwi Tomoana describes the festival as

> a celebration and development initiative in the rebuilding of rela-
> tionships of indigenous peoples across Aotearoa, the Pacific and
> the Hawaiiki nation. We encourage all families and communities to
> celebrate our past, our present and our future in Aotearoa and the
> Pacific by participating in the festival.[22]

Over the course of five days, descendents of Tākitimu celebrated their connections and shared stories and cultural products. Wānanga and other learning opportunities enabled the connections to be communicated and debated during the festival. I hope this book will provide space for other kinds of conversations alongside those we are already having about Māori, about writing in English, about Māori writing in English, about Indigeneity, and about the Pacific.

Once Were Pacific has regional and global roots but has been written in Aotearoa. If I lived elsewhere—indeed, when I did live elsewhere—the questions that would matter would be differently configured to the ones I ask in this book. This book asks questions that are important *here,* and yet writing from and in a specific place is not necessarily the same as parochialism. This book seeks to speak with, rather than for, others; it also seeks to refrain from speaking *at* others. Although I have provided cultural and linguistic translations at some points throughout the book to offer hospitality to a wider readership, this is not a visitor's manual or travel guide. I anticipate that the tight focus of *Once Were Pacific* on Māori will, rather than produce barriers to consideration of its arguments in allied contexts, ultimately enable more robust extrapolation of its claims beyond Aotearoa. The specificities of the discussion will better enable connection rather than separation. As I write about the dynamics of connection and borders between Māori and Pasifika people during the 1970s Dawn Raids, for example, I cannot help but think about other borders as they are negotiated in the present day in relation to the designations "Indigenous" and "migrant." Or, to extend the previous example, in Hawai'i, a Māori person may well be a Pacific Islander, but is a Hawaiian?

Within the world of academia, this book is located at the intersection of particular approaches and fields, and a central aim of the book is to produce new readings of existing texts to explore how Māori (and some Pasifika) writers already explore connections with the Pacific. It seems worthwhile, for the sake of the interdisciplinary readership of the book, to spend some time reflecting on its disciplinary terrain. *Once Were Pacific* centers Anglophone literary studies,[23] broadly defined, with one hand on interdisciplinarity while keeping a firm view on Māori, Pacific, and Indigenous studies. Literary studies emphasize the place of creative texts in the broad range of Māori articulation; it infuses my approach to a wide range of texts rather than simply restricting my focus to texts or genres that look and feel a particular—literary—way. Poetry, fiction, plays, films, TV, music, and so on take their place alongside journalistic writing, visual texts, scholarly work, historical writing, archival texts, performances, songs, chants, and beyond. In addition, paying attention to the means of creative production cannot help but (re)narrate broader publishing, literary, and creative contexts. I am interested in Māori *articulation* of connections with the Pacific rather than in establishing (or proving) whether or why those connections might exist; this is not a history as such or a book about waka traditions, although both are present throughout. Concurring with Thomas King that "the truth about stories is that's all we are,"[24] I take for granted that we cannot account for history outside of discourse; any language we use itself bears the mark of the histories we describe. Crucially to my politics as well as my disciplinary training, focusing on articulation foregrounds the extent to which our worlds are themselves produced by language. Articulation is about how and perhaps why rather than what; texts are engaged not only with the description or representation of things (communities, histories) but with their very *production*.[25]

Although a critically uneven but vibrant conversation about Māori writing in English has taken place for as long as that writing has been produced, little sustained formal critical attention has been published. Even sixty years after Kohere's 1951 *The Autobiography of a Maori*,[26] arguably the first published single-author creative monograph in English by a Māori writer, there are only five published book-length treatments of (English-language) Māori literature,[27] of which only three focus solely on Māori texts (specifically fiction), and none was written in New Zealand or by a Māori scholar. The predominant focus on Māori writing in English has been on Māori connections with Pākehā and privileges the New Zealand national literary context, and though some work in the field of Pacific literary studies smoothly assumes that Māori are in the Pacific, this book applies some pressure to the naturalization and limits of that inclusion, not to disprove or undermine it but to more carefully elaborate its terms. At the same time, conventional national and regional histories have tended to overlook moments of Māori–Pacific connection such as those investigated in this project. Tracy McIntosh's exploratory "Hibiscus in the Flax Bush" and two pages of Donna Awatere's *Maori Sovereignty* seem to be the only critical pieces published about these connections.[28] At the same time, Anglophone Indigenous studies, within which Māori studies is most obviously and most often located, has not tended to focus on migration and diaspora,[29] with the clear exception of scholars whose work treats Hawaiian and Chamorro communities on the U.S. mainland.

Whereas the verticality of Indigenous relationships with non-Indigenous communities is widely explored, horizontal modes of Indigenous–Indigenous connection have enjoyed far less critical consideration. My research focuses on *Indigenous* "movement and cultural traffic," to borrow a phrase from historian Tony Ballantyne, who advocates for work that explores "the forms of movement and cultural traffic that linked colonies in the 'periphery' together" rather than the many postcolonial narratives that reinforce the center–periphery relationship between London and the colony.[30] Although Ballantyne's focus is on predominantly European movement between the settler colonies, this project is both Indigenous centered and comparative, departing as it does from research into Indigenous–European or black–white interaction but also from research that focuses entirely on a singular

Indigenous community. Within the New Zealand national space as well as in the region, I am interested in how Māori and other Pacific people talk about each other. This does not cut out the European gaze completely, but it certainly sidelines that gaze and produces spaces where its power is decentered.

An Extraordinary Fondness

Let's return to Tupaia's painting and reflect on the moment in which a Māori, a Raiatean, and a European stand in close proximity. The triangulated relationship between Māori, Raiatean, and European that is both represented and recorded in the painting offers a productive structure for this book. Although there are many links between the two parts of the book, the relationship between Māori and the Pacific looks different when one is looking at the region (part I) or the nation (part II).

In part I, *Once Were Pacific* turns to focus on the realm of the tapa that is extended for trade, exploring the ways in which Aotearoa is articulated as part of the broader Pacific region on the basis of cultural and geographic proximity. Starting with three specific instances—an individual, a tourist attraction, and a literary form—the first chapter interrogates the ways in which Māori are present in Pacific spaces. Next, as a significant departure from existing accounts of Māori writing in English, in chapter 2, the project includes in its scope Māori writers who live and publish outside New Zealand and who have specific ties to the Pacific such as Robert Sullivan (based for some time in Hawai'i, published in New Zealand), Vernice Wineera (lives and published in Hawai'i), and Evelyn Patuawa-Nathan (published in Fiji). This is the first critical treatment of the latter two writers and the first to look at Sullivan's work in this way. Chapter 3 focuses on Witi Ihimaera and Hinewirangi, two Māori writers based in Aotearoa who have written about Māori as a part of the regional Pacific. Part I concludes by reflecting on the impact of cultural and historical differences as well as proximities in the region.

Part II turns to the realm of the koura, or crayfish, which is reciprocally extended; this section foregrounds Māori–Pacific connections as they are elaborated and negotiated in the national context of Aotearoa New Zealand. An Aotearoa-based Pacific focuses on the national boundaries of New Zealand and recognizes that communities from all over the Pacific—including Māori—interact with one another within those boundaries. Indeed, because it is subsumed by the nation-state of New Zealand, which is host to large diasporic Pasifika communities, Aotearoa is in very particular ways the site of a Pacific microcosm. After considering a series of collaborations between Māori and Pasifika communities in chapter 4, chapters 5 and 6 treat Māori and Pasifika texts that engage Māori–Pasifika relationships, respectively. Given that the majority of Māori and Pasifika people in New Zealand live in relatively close proximity in urban areas, and given the appearance of haka hulas (children of mixed Māori and Pasifika relationships),[31] it is curious that the relationship between Indigenous (Māori) and immigrant (Pasifika) communities is rarely treated in Māori cultural production. Chapter 7 turns its attention to three performed texts (two plays and a television series) that explore Māori–Pasifika disconnections by mobilizing the story of Romeo and Juliet.

Finally, the book concludes by stepping out further from the painting itself and turning its attention to the production of the text: to Tupaia and to his use of the paintbrush, the third item that is being held in the moment of encounter depicted in his painting. The paintbrush provides an opportunity to ask a series of questions: who's looking at whom? Who gets to paint or, in this case, write? What parameters shape the conception and mobility of a text? Which cultural, political, and economic configurations inflect this project and its publication in an Anglophone and American academic context? The conclusion considers the significance of the gaze and means of production that ultimately inflect all articulations and reflects on the stakes and implications of the project of *Once Were Pacific,* not to limit the project but to more carefully articulate its possibilities. A key disciplinary aim of *Once Were Pacific* is to carefully respond and contribute to contemporary literary studies. Rather than pitting itself in opposition to the fields of New Zealand, Pacific, Indigenous, and Māori literary studies as well as postcolonial and ethnic literary studies, this project seeks to extend and broaden that scholarship, and the final section of the book gestures toward the implications of the project for those fields. In line with the call from Indigenous studies to consider the broader political and institutional contexts of research, it is necessary to be self-conscious about the present project. *Once Were Pacific* closes by considering the potentially negative extrapolation of an argument by which—at its possible extreme—"Indigenous bodies" might be recoded as "migrant bodies." Ultimately, *Once Were Pacific* argues for a kind of regional identification—Tomoana's "Hawaiki nation" perhaps—that emphasizes rather than distracts from Indigeneity.

Perhaps this—all of this—is something along the lines of what Tupaia saw when he depicted the trade between Europeans bearing tapa and Māori bearing koura. In her discussion of Cook's voyaging around the Pacific,[32] Salmond rightly comments that we will never know the extent and nature of the conversations between Tupaia and specific Māori communities with which he conversed. With a rather different conviction, Banks, the European depicted in Tupaia's painting, recalled later in his life that the picture focused on him. Walking a fine line between the unrememberable and the misremembered, *Once Were Pacific* looks at Tupaia's sketch and reads it in terms of the complicated dynamic of Māori–Pacific connection it implies: a symbolic reunion of those Mead describes as "relatives spread across the great Pacific ocean." I like to imagine Tupaia recognizing the significance of that moment in which Māori acquired the first *new* influx of material culture from one of their ancestral homes—tangible affirmation of oral traditions and cultural practices that had been passed down through generations of isolation from the rest of the Pacific—and choosing that as the image to record for posterity.

Tapa: Aotearoa in the Pacific Region

> ... I am taking my place
> on this vast marae
> that is the Pacific
> we call home.

Vernice Wineera, "Heritage,"
Into the Luminous Tide

Beads and nails were good currency for fish and sweet potatoes, but curiously enough large sheets of tapa obtained earlier at Tahiti were the best trade articles and were valued more highly by the New Zealanders than anything else the English could offer.

Ernest Stanley Dodge, *Islands and Empires*

IN TUPAIA'S PAINTING OF EXCHANGE between Māori and European men, the European extends a piece of tapa recently acquired in Tahiti. The plant from which tapa is made, the paper mulberry tree *(Broussonetia papyrifera)*, which Māori know as aute,[1] could not thrive in Aotearoa's colder climate, and so the production of the cloth had all but diminished there. However, the moment Māori reconnected with the tapa, and indeed, the moment Tupaia chose to represent that scene with the new technology of European paint, Māori were reglued into the Pacific region. Although moving south of tropical Polynesia did not mean that Māori had literally left the Pacific as such, the ongoing physical connections had died down over the past few centuries. An Aotearoa-inclusive Pacific considers the geographic region of the Pacific and notices that Aotearoa is a part of that area on the basis of cultural, linguistic, genealogical, and geographic proximity.

In part I, the regionality of the Pacific is to the fore. Whereas the con-figuration of Māori and Pacific in the national space will take center stage in part II, here we retain a regional focus. As a significant departure from New Zealand–centered accounts of Māori writing in English, this project includes in its scope Māori writers who live and publish outside New Zealand, many of whom articulate specific ties to the Pacific. The complicating factor is that around "the region"—that is, outside New Zealand—Māori tend to be considered a part of the Pacific anyway.[2] Why does Aotearoa's place in the Pacific region even require attention when we note that there is a Māori village in the Hawai'i-based Polynesian Cultural Centre (PCC) because of shared "Polynesian" ancestry and culture and that the inclusion of Māori literary and critical texts in the Pacific Literature syllabus at the University of the South Pacific is unmarked? Although exploring the presence and position of Māori in the Pacific has urgency—or indeed, makes any sense—only within certain national borders, and though some texts and critical discussions do articulate Aotearoa as part of the Pacific region,[3] this book focuses on the basis of that inclusion, especially in the present moment, which is marked by legacies of colonialism and migration.

Part I is the realm of tapa, and I am using "tapa" as a generic name to describe the cloth that has a vast number of production techniques and names across the Pacific. Tapa is simultaneously regional and specific. Although the paper mulberry plant itself is found around the region, having been carefully and painstakingly carried in seed form as a part of the progression of migration across the ocean, and though most of the processes of collecting, preparing, and finishing the bark bear strong relation to each other, the cloth produced in every region of the Pacific is distinctive. Hawaiian kapa has watermark patterns stamped into it, Fijian masi is stenciled, and Samoan siapo is made in long strips that are glued together, to describe but a few examples. The continuities of plant and process are not undermined but are instead quietly distinguished by discontinuities that have developed in each specific place. As a metaphor, tapa provides an opportunity to reflect on cultural (including scientific, philosophical, material, architectural, legal, artistic, spiritual, and social) and genealogical continuities across the Pacific and simultaneously to observe local specificities. Like for tapa, there is no regional name for the Pacific Ocean: Māori may call our ocean Te Moananui a Kiwa, but others have other names and memories of the great expanse. Our present and recent modes of circulation, mobility, and connection compel us to create a singular entity—tapa, Pacific—by using a singular word. Though masi is not the same as kapa is not the same as hiapo, when they are understood as versions, or perhaps iterations, of each other, we have the opportunity to draw connections that may lack prominence in any single example.

In Aotearoa, the meaning of *tapa* is twofold: it describes those shreds of paper bark worn as ornaments in memory of much larger sheets long ago and far away, but it also (and more dominantly) refers to sheets of the cloth brought in from around the Pacific and especially from those places with which New Zealand has a history of specific relationship. While Māori are certainly included under the Pacific umbrella (small scraps of tapa), one is far more likely to hear "Pacific" and think of those places from which

Pacific migrants to New Zealand came (large sheets of tapa). The uneven familiarity of these two meanings echoes the prominence of the idea that we once were Pacific. In Aotearoa, the aute struggled to grow because the paper mulberry is best suited to the warm temperatures of tropical Polynesia. Indeed, it only remained in a small number of particularly warm locations: the Far North, Hawke's Bay, and the East Coast of the North Island. Despite the predicament of climate, however, the aute was still meagerly present when Europeans arrived at Aotearoa to stay.

Each discussion of the Pacific imagines a different version of the region. According to some, we once were Oceanic. *Oceania,* which appears in the subtitle of this book, can be discursively traced through Wendt in 1976[4] and Hau'ofa in 1993[5] to the successive explosion of its use. Even though it is an English term that belies a degree of colonial infiltration and complicity, *Oceania* can be conceptually traced—as they both argue—back through countless generations.[6] Wendt's essay "Towards a New Oceania" famously opens by claiming the region *as a region* and outlining the reasons for his decision to turn from "fact" (he had completed a master of arts degree in history) to creative articulation:

> I belong to Oceania—or at least, I am rooted in a fertile portion of it—and it nourishes my spirit, helps to define me, and feeds my imagination. A detatched/objective analysis I will leave to the sociologist and all the other 'ologists who have plagued Oceania. . . . Objectivity is for such uncommitted gods. My commitment won't allow me to confine myself to so narrow a vision. So vast, so fabulously varied a scatter of islands, nations, cultures, mythologies and myths, so dazzling a creature, Oceania deserves more than an attempt at mundane fact; only the imagination in free flight can hope—if not to contain her—to grasp some of her shape, plumage, and pain.[7]

The essay continues to praise Oceania by advocating, as well as turning to, creative written works to grapple with the similarities, possibilities, and colonial histories of the region. In 1993 the Fiji-based Tongan academic and writer Epeli Hau'ofa extended the concept of Oceania in his essay "Our Sea of Islands,"[8] one of the most influential and widely read pieces of Pacific scholarship, in which he demonstrates that local principles and cosmologies can radically shift the terms by which we know ourselves and each other. "Our Sea of Islands" reapproaches the concept that marks the broadest parameters of this area of study—the region itself—on its own terms and thereby recenters Indigenous knowledges of the Pacific. Rather than accepting the smallness and isolation the West associates with the region, "islands in a far sea," Hau'ofa claims that the Pacific is "a sea of islands"[9] in which people construct their world by their very inhabiting, and traversing, of the ocean:

> The contemporary process of what may be called world enlargement that is carried out by tens of thousands of ordinary Pacific Islanders right across the ocean . . . mak[es] nonsense of all national and economic boundaries, borders that have been defined only recently, crisscrossing an ocean that had been boundless for ages before Captain Cook's apotheosis.[10]

He proposes that because Pacific people have always occupied and traveled around the Pacific, the ocean has always been a part of the experience and worldview of Pacific people and so is itself meaningful space rather than a watery gap. This argument collapses the European binary of sea and land, transforming Pacific space from the smallest to the largest in the world, and he renames it "Oceania."

Aotearoa is necessarily and inextricably a part of Hau'ofa's Oceania because Māori are Oceanic seafarers. Hau'ofa writes about Māori navigation (albeit, or perhaps significantly, in parentheses) as an example that challenges the externally proposed model of population dispersal by "accidental drift":

> (Only blind landlubbers would say that settlements like these, as well as those in New Zealand and Hawai'i, were made through accidental voyages by people who got blown off course—presumably while they were out fishing with their wives, children, pigs, dogs, and food-plant seedlings—during a hurricane.)[11]

His configuration of Oceania has significant implications for the reading of Māori texts because Aotearoa is visible when someone looks at the place with "Oceanic" eyes rather than treating New Zealand as a white (or an empty) metropole to which Oceanic people migrate. The construct of Oceania has deep, complex, and politically explosive implications for the ways in which any scholar might approach the field (or, to use a better metaphor, ocean) of study. Oceania proposes a dynamic regional sensibility that enlarges and puts pressure on contemporary structures of nation and region. Although I am using the term *Pacific* throughout this book, the subtitle names Oceania to affirm that *Once Were Pacific* both grows out of and elaborates the Oceanic scholarly and cultural project as well as to take advantage of the dual association Oceania has with the region and the people of the region.

If Māori are Pacific, Māori literary studies must therefore be connected to Pacific literary studies.[12] In some ways, the field of Pacific literary studies has come about as a local incarnation or manifestation of English literature and language teaching. In other ways, the line between Pacific literary studies and Pacific studies is blurred,[13] not least of all because Pacific scholar–writers, such as Albert Wendt, Epeli Hau'ofa, Vilsoni Hereniko, Teresia Teaiwa, Steven Winduo, Sina Va'ai, Regis Stella, Haunani-Kay Trask, and Konai Helu Thaman, have contributed many of the now foundational texts of Pacific studies. (This phenomenon of critics also being involved in literary production is so common that Steven Winduo gave them a name: "Pacific Writer Scholars.")[14] Many non-Indigenous scholars have also worked with the texts produced in the Pacific since the beginning of the field, and many scholars of Pacific literature turn to aesthetic and cultural frames already in the region before writing.[15] For example, Wendt's 1996 essay "Tatauing the Post-colonial Body" took Pacific literary studies in a new—and yet not new at all—direction, insisting as it did on the dynamic relation between this critical endeavor and the cultural, aesthetic, and political contexts from which the texts come.[16]

Fiji-based Subramani's landmark 1985 text *South Pacific Literature* remains the only book-length study produced within the region to attempt to speak to and for the whole Pacific. Certainly Subramani's contribution to literary studies in the Pacific deserves greater attention than it presently enjoys, but here we focus on his articulation of the relationship between Māori and the region:

> The literatures of Australia and New Zealand form the fifth region. The literatures of Maori and Aboriginal peoples share common motifs with literatures of other Pacific regions. But they ought to be viewed as belonging to the mainstream of Australian and New Zealand writing.[17]

Subramani excludes Māori and Indigenous Australian literatures on the basis of "belonging to the mainstream," which he believes overrides shared "motifs" and is unhelpful for elaborating the relationship between Māori and Pacific literatures or people. (Interestingly, this exclusion does not extend to the book's cover, which includes, among other icons, the stylized illustration of a Māori carving.) The three major edited collections of Pacific literary criticism are Sharrad's *Readings in Pacific Literature,* Goetzfridt's *Indigenous Literature of Oceania,* and Hereniko and Wilson's *Inside Out,* which came out of the 1994[18] conference on Pacific Literatures held in Hawai'i.[19] All include Māori texts in their scope but tend to focus on diasporic movements from the independent Pacific to New Zealand, Australia, Hawai'i, and the U.S. mainland, which means that a Pacific critical and political gaze in this direction has often focused on a metropole (New Zealand) more clearly than on a Pacific nation (Aotearoa).

A great deal of Pacific literary studies scholarship exists in journal articles (in the journals *Mana* and *SPAN* but also elsewhere), book chapters, conference proceedings, theses, and introductory essays to anthologies and critical collections. Although the surprisingly poor commitment to Pacific literature from many universities around the region is disheartening, a number of scholars are now engaged in the study of Pacific literatures, both within and outside the discipline and departments of English. The critical and institutional interventions made by the previous generations of Pacific literary scholars are being continued and expanded by a new wave of researchers and writers such as Ku'ualoha Ho'omanawanui, Ka'imipono Kaiwi Kahumoku, AnnaMarie Christiansen, Brandy Nālani MacDougall, Noenoe Silva, Selina Tusitala Marsh, Juniper Ellis, Liz DeLoughrey, Michelle Keown, Susan Najita, Chadwick Allen, Emelihter Kihleng, and Craig Santos Perez. All these scholars—and this is certainly not an exhaustive roll call—extend both the range and sites of Pacific literary studies and are committed to projects covering a vast constellation of concerns: comparative, national, regional, disciplinary, interdisciplinary, Indigenous, migrant, diasporic, and more.

Part I comprises three chapters, each of which considers a specific way in which Aotearoa is a part of the Pacific region. In chapter 1, three configurations of Māori people in Pacific places allow us to focus on the structures by which Māori are included in the region. First, it examines Te Rangihiroa (Sir Peter Buck), the medical doctor, politician, military serviceman, and

anthropologist of the early twentieth century who explored Māori connections with the Pacific through his scholarly work on the region and
whose decision to spend his last two decades in Hawaiʻi exemplifies the
continuation of Māori mobility throughout the region. Next, the chapter
examines Māori presence at the PCC, a commercial visitors' attraction in
Hawaiʻi. The PCC has cultural, religious, and educational purposes beyond
its commercial enterprises, and all of these have produced certain kinds
of Māori engagement in (often literal) performance of the "Pacific" over a
number of decades. Finally, the chapter proposes the literary anthology as
a crucial space in which articulations of the "Pacific" as a region are both
produced and extended. I argue that although Pacific literary studies has
tended to focus on individual writers and texts, paying attention to anthologies enables a different kind of regional literary analysis. Holding together
an individual, a tourist site, and a specific form of publishing might feel like
a stretch, but this combination enables us to consider the sheer range of
means and contexts by which and within which the relationship between
Māori and the Pacific is produced.

Chapter 2, "Pacific-Based Māori Writers," foregrounds the work of Vernice
Wineera, Evelyn Patuawa-Nathan, and Robert Sullivan, three writers who
are based and/or published in the Pacific outside of New Zealand. Wineera
and Sullivan are (or have been) based in Hawaiʻi, and Patuawa-Nathan is the
only Māori writer published by the Fiji-based South Pacific Creative Arts
Society. Following on, chapter 3 considers the small number of Māori writers based in Aotearoa who have written about Māori as a part of the Pacific
region and focuses on Ihimaera and Hinewirangi, who enjoy differing levels
of fame and critical attention and whose work has not previously been read
side by side. Chapters 2 and 3 both extend the writers, texts, and modes of
reading that currently dominate discussions of Māori writing in English.
Including Māori writers outside Aotearoa in a discussion of Māori literary
studies has been one of the great pleasures, and will be one of the major
interventions, of this book. Finally, in a concluding section, I propose some
possibilities of regional analysis.

This realm of tapa, the region, points directly to historic navigational feats
that produced a new group of people, Māori, living on these cold southern
islands. Māori planted and then nurtured the aute over these centuries, despite an inhospitable climate. Writing about the aute in his 1923 discussion
of Māori clothing, Te Rangihiroa cites Colenso's 1880 words:

I once saw this plant growing in an old plantation at the head of the Kawakawa River in the Bay of Islands—that was in 1835. There was, however, but one small tree left, which was about six feet high, with few branches, and not many leaves on them, it appeared both aged and unhealthy, and it soon after died. On my finally leaving the Bay of Islands in 1844, to reside in Hawke's Bay, I heard of some aute trees still living at Hokianga. I wrote to a chief of my acquaintance there (EM Patuone), who kindly sent me several good cuttings; saying (in a letter) that the plant there was nearly destroyed by the cattle of the Europeans. Unfortunately . . . I lost them all.[20]

Te Rangihiroa follows with an observation that "the plant is now extinct in New Zealand."[21] This tragic final turn of events for the aute was therefore brought about by the introduction of European farming. Although a focus on the New Zealand state and its machinery for redress and partnership has been urgent and essential for Māori since the nineteenth century, the same alienation of land that loudly undermined Māori sovereignty also quietly and literally killed off one of the modes by which Māori had intentionally retained a connection with the Pacific. Although it would have been easy simply to let it die out in this temperate environment, the aute was deliberately cultivated and the technology associated with turning its bark into paper was maintained, a mnemonic device to recall living and moving across the Pacific region, and these chapters explore the extent and modes by which this continues to be recalled. This careful maintenance of the aute plant and tapa production in Aotearoa provides an explanation for the remarkable moment described by Cook's crew of an unexpectedly rapturous Māori response to the great sheets of tapa they encountered in 1769.

CHAPTER 1

Māori People in Pacific Spaces

AOTEAROA IS CLEARLY a part of the geographical region of the Pacific, and Māori are Polynesian and therefore culturally connected with other Polynesians and, beyond that, the whole Pacific. But where does connection take place? What does it look like? How is it articulated? What is the relationship between individual and collective connections? On what basis are Māori present in a Pacific space? Taking three specific but disparate instances of Māori people in Pacific spaces provides an opportunity to consider the range of ways in which Māori connect with the Pacific. First, this chapter considers the singular figure of Te Rangihiroa, a Māori anthropologist whose career took him to Hawai'i in 1927 to take up a position at the Bishop Museum, the major Pacific research institution that he directed for the last two decades of his life. Te Rangihiroa was a man and scholar of the Pacific, and his mobility was enhanced by his Pacificness when he was in the anthropological or scholarly field but was limited by an external imposition of understandings about his Pacificness when he unsuccessfully applied for U.S. citizenship. Moving closer to the present, but still with a focus on Hawai'i, the chapter considers the Māori village installation at the Polynesian Cultural Centre (PCC), a Mormon-run Polynesian visitor attraction on O'ahu. Balancing long-standing ties between Māori and other Polynesian Mormons, on one hand, and texts produced for a predominantly non-Pacific tourist audience, on the other, Māori presence at the PCC sits at the intersection of agency, self-representation, performance, and domination. Finally, the presence of Māori texts in Pacific anthologies gestures toward the place of politics and cultural negotiation in the production of literary products. While literary collections have had a unique role in the production of Pacific writing, the stakes of selection and inclusion have been central to their development. Language is central to the policing of borders, either by compulsory repatriation or unsteady admission in each of these examples. In each of these situations, Māori are neither uncomplicatedly Pacific nor wholly not Pacific. Each case emphasizes, instead, that Māori articulations of the Pacific are deeply rooted in the specific: inflected by contextual factors of time, place, history, and intention.

Te Rangihiroa: A Māori Man in the Pacific

Te Rangihiroa, also known as Sir Peter Buck, was a member of the group of Māori scholar–politicians prominent in the early twentieth century.[1] His parents, Ngarongo-ki-tua and William Henry Buck, were Ngāti Mutunga and Irish, respectively. His grandmother Kapuakore was an important feature of his childhood whose impact resonated throughout his life. Educated at Te Aute, a significant Māori boys school at the time (his 1897 speech about Parihaka to the Te Aute Students' Association was his first publication),[2] Te Rangihiroa studied medicine in university and then enjoyed careers in public service, parliamentary politics, and the military (World War I), before he eventually moved into the field of anthropology. He spent the last two decades of his life based in Hawai'i, and although he was engaged in administrative work, heading the Bishop Museum for much of that time, and some teaching at Yale University and the University of Hawai'i, his long-standing and impressive legacy is his formidable commitment to research (after his 1910 thesis, he published numerous books, chapters, and articles[3]). Despite his impressive career in Hawai'i and beyond, in New Zealand, we tend to focus on his domestic exploits. To take a fairly crass example, the Wikipedia entry for Te Rangihiroa describes only his New Zealand–based activities, and the description of his career (and life) peters out after his 1920s public service work in the area of public health.[4] Therefore, in at least one version of the popular imaginary, the last thirty years of his life, and indeed his last career, with all its Pacific as well as scholarly dimensions, remain obscured.[5] At the same time, his 1949 book *The Coming of the Maori*[6] is often acknowledged as a (or even *the*) foundational text for the discipline of Māori studies.

Reflecting on Te Rangihiroa's connection with the Pacific and, in particular, his connection with other Pacific people enables us to imagine both him and the region a little differently. We might notice, for example, his activities in the then-colonies of the Cook Islands and Niue while he was based there as a medical officer.[7] This could in turn foreground the occasion of his visit to Sāmoa, during which he was quickly identified as the Tulafale ("talking chief") of a visiting group of anthropologists. His ability to speak a Polynesian language produced a kind of cultural and social fluency as well. Indeed, his Polynesianness at times trumped his scholarly position from the perspective of the communities he visited. In Sāmoa, he attended an 'ava ceremony that was intended to welcome the group of visiting foreigners. According to Condliffe, however, on recognizing Te Rangihiroa not merely as a scholar but as a relative, the hosts quickly changed the type of 'ava they would serve: instead of offering the variety of 'ava that is used to welcome new visitors, they offered 'ava uso, which is reserved for reunion between long-lost relatives.[8] This act, securely located within Samoan epistemologies and hosting practices, reframed the entire encounter: Te Rangihiroa became the central member of the visiting party, and others were merely peripheral. Finally, we might notice that Te Rangihiroa's last public outing in 1951 was to chant at the dedication of a restored medicinal heiau.[9]

As well as being a man of the Pacific, Te Rangihiroa was a scholar of the Pacific, and his scholarly work was both premised and focused on drawing connections between various Polynesian communities. Te Rangihiroa's work in the Pacific strove at least in part to stitch Polynesians into the broader racial maps that circulated at the time: as well as writing about Pacific peoples and Polynesia, he taught a courses at Yale in 1933 and 1934 called Native Races of the Pacific and later taught a summer course on Polynesia at the University of Hawai'i at Manoa. From the perspective of the present, it can be easy to forget that the ethnography and anthropology (and linguistics) in which he worked were considered to be sciences in less social ways than they are today. Working with prevailing theories about race and people, linguists and ethnologists attempted to sketch scientifically rigorous explanations for how different people were connected,[10] and many of the methodologies on which Te Rangihiroa depended for his work included the precise physical measurement of human bodies and implements. Though these methodologies and their uses are regarded rather dubiously today, at the core of Te Rangihiroa's research was the racialization of people of the Pacific. He was extremely well versed in Polynesian languages and material culture and spent a great deal of time concentrating on a small number of specific Polynesian communities: Māori, Sāmoa, Mangaia, Kapingamairangi, and Hawai'i. He spent years producing detailed sketches, believing strongly in actively participating in research, and was not satisfied that he was able to write about an item until he could construct it himself. This elongated the work, and yet it also meant that he had a deep and clear understanding of how things were constructed in their layers. His academic work was highly recognized: he received honorary doctorates from Rochester (1939), New Zealand (1939), Hawai'i (1948), and Yale (1951), and he received British and Swedish knighthoods in 1946. In 1952 he posthumously received the Huxley Memorial Medal, the highest award from the Royal Anthropological Institute. Because Te Rangihiroa is both an object of study and a scholar in this field of research, his own contributions to scientific literature about Polynesians (and, more broadly, the Pacific) ultimately shaped the ways in which he himself is understood.

In the late 1930s, Te Rangihiroa applied for U.S. citizenship as a gesture of gratitude for the professional opportunities that country had extended to him, and the outcome of that application emphasizes the limits but also the traces of individual agency when it comes to Māori identification with the Pacific. Although Te Rangihiroa did not apply for citizenship to depart from his identification as Māori, his being Māori, and therefore Polynesian, rendered him ineligible for U.S. citizenship. His application was not therefore an intentional articulation of being Pacific, but his Pacificness was produced for him by the U.S. government, and he responded by recognizing the implications of becoming Pacific in this context. Despite his unsuccessful appeals, which he later abandoned, Te Rangihiroa recognized that if he was Pacific on the basis of being Māori, then he needed to consider his experience in relation to other people also understood as Pacific.

The connection between his scholarly work and location in Hawai'i was not disconnected from broader relations between Hawai'i, then a territory of the United States, and the U.S. nation-state. He was in Hawai'i in an in-between phase, having arrived in 1927, a mere twenty-nine years since the formal U.S. annexation and a full twenty-two years before statehood, when Hawai'i would be fully incorporated into the Union. The Bishop Museum was the Pacific branch of Yale University,[11] serving as an important outpost for the vibrant field of Pacific-related research that occupied many of the disciplines in the early twentieth century, when U.S. scholarly interest in the Pacific was tied to U.S. economic and political extension into the same region. Indeed, the Bishop Museum, and Te Rangihiroa, who was its director throughout World War II, provided cultural training for U.S. military preparing to participate in the Pacific War. His role in this training has since been questioned as people have grappled with his complicity with U.S. imperialism and militarism in the Pacific, for which the activities during World War II laid an additional foundation. On May 5, 1948, Te Rangihiroa wrote a letter from Hawai'i, where he lived, to his good friend Eric Ramsden,[12] in which he explained how this bid for naturalization has failed:

> With regard to the matter of American citizenship you have my authority to say that it is definitely abandoned by me and that any rumors to the contrary are incorrect. To recapitulate, I could not become an American citizen under the . . . law for an applicant has to be over 50% Caucasian. The Polynesians are classed as Orientals in spite of anthropological evidence of their Caucasian origin so I could only show 50%.[13]

When his application for U.S. citizenship was declined, Te Rangihiroa occupied a position that was dramatically contradictory: he applied because he occupied an elevated educational and occupational position; he was rejected because he occupied a subjugated racial position. The story of his application for citizenship became rather exciting after his rejection. His many friends in high places started to agitate for the United States to reconsider.

Specifically, in 1943, the two houses in the Hawai'i territorial government issued a joint resolution about Te Rangihiroa's declined application for citizenship, calling on the United States to grant Te Rangihiroa citizenship and for the resolution itself to be forwarded to the president, Congress, and Senate:

> Whereas, Peter Henry Buck, for many years an honored resident of Honolulu, Territory of Hawaii, a British subject, part white and part Polynesian, in every way qualified for American citizenship except that he is ineligible for naturalization under presently existing law; and
> Whereas, said Peter Henry Buck is thoroughly imbued with the principles of democracy, is attached to the Constitution of the United States, and is desirous and ambitious to become a citizen of the United States . . .[14]

Echoing Te Rangihiroa's own commentary about U.S. citizenship law ("either an individual is good enough personally or he isn't"), the resolution describes his personal contributions to Hawaiian society, to the United States, and to the academy. The idea of color-blind citizenship, in which his achievements trump the racial limits placed on that citizenship, is summed up in the final phrase of the resolution, which argues that citizenship is "fitting" because of "his outstanding services to the country of his adoption and the high esteem in which he is held by all who know him throughout the scientific and educational world."[15] Despite his individual merit, however, Te Rangihiroa was marked by a racial category that compulsorily threw his lot in with all other Polynesians. Near its end, the resolution engages with the problem of racialization:

> Doctor Buck is the son of a distinguished Irish citizen of New Zealand and a Maori chiefess and is therefore half Irish. He is of Caucasian and Polynesian blood. Polynesians themselves have Caucasian origin.[16]

No further elaboration of this point is supplied, and given the detailed treatment of the rest of the information provided in the resolution, this seems particularly blunt.

Whereas one might focus on the category of "Polynesian" as the primary racial configuration when Te Rangihiroa's application for citizenship is refused, actually, this refusal was about whiteness. To be clear, the place of race in U.S. citizenship law was rather complex in this period. In 1790 Congress restricted U.S. citizenship to "white persons," and this general rule remained in place until 1952.[17] In the meantime, several individuals attempted to access citizenship by arguing that they were, in fact, white and therefore satisfied that race requirement. Haney Lopez notes that fifty-two "racial prerequisite" cases were heard between 1878 and 1952, including two by the Supreme Court:

> Seen as a taxonomy of Whiteness, these cases are instructive because they reveal the imprecisions and contradictions inherent in the establishment of racial lines between Whites and non-Whites.[18]

Hawaiian, Chinese, Japanese, Burmese, and Filipino attempts were declined, whereas Mexican and Armenian cases were successful. The courts were unsure what to do with Syrian, Arab, and Indian applicants. Over the course of these cases, the boundaries of citizenship, allied as they were to whiteness, were interrogated: "Whites [were] a category of people subject to a double negative: they are those who are not non-White."[19] To gain U.S. citizenship,

Te Rangihiroa needed to gain recognition of whiteness or, to follow the logic as Haney Lopez puts it, recognition that he wasn't "*non*-White."

Two distinct approaches developed to determine whether a particular group was white: common knowledge and scientific evidence. The scientific approach drew most heavily on ethnological work, such as that by Keane, which stated that

> the Maori of New Zealand, the Tongans, Tahitians, Samoans, Marquesans and Ellice Islanders, and Hawaiians . . . are an Oceanic branch of the Caucasic division.[20]

Te Rangihiroa's own scholarly work is implicated here; extending various discussions of race around the British Empire,[21] much of his research concurred that Polynesians are racially Caucasian. However, in 1923, *United States v. Thind* had marked a movement away from the slippage between white and Caucasian.[22] Despite this uncoupling of the whiteness required for citizenship from Caucasian in *Thind*, Te Rangihiroa's own case—at least in the words of the territory of Hawai'i—depended on his being Caucasian.[23] The resolution attempts to clarify that: "He is of Caucasian and Polynesian blood. Polynesians themselves have Caucasian origin," suggesting that Te Rangihiroa does in fact satisfy the race requirements of U.S. citizenship by being "Caucasian and [Polynesian-which-is-Caucasian]."[24] In some ways, then, the resolution puts a dollar each way on Te Rangihiroa's relationship to U.S. citizenship: on one hand, citizenship should be attached to deeds rather than race; on the other, he can be understood as white for the purpose of satisfying a racist citizenship requirement.

While an argument for citizenship on the basis of merit is an individual matter, an argument about race is prescriptively and unavoidably about the collective. Te Rangihiroa was refused citizenship because Māori once were—and still were—Pacific. There is a sharp distinction between Te Rangihiroa's relationship with the United States as a result of his own personal transnational mobility and the position of other Polynesians in American Sāmoa (and Hawai'i) for whom the United States was an invading power that had "moved to them." Te Rangihiroa's is not a singular case in which an individual is categorized through the racial logics of a single nation but rather is caught in the much larger racial crossfire between the United States and its colonies in the Pacific:[25]

> I agreed with Roosevelt and held that a more comprehensive
> act should be passed to admit Samoans and other Polynesians
> to American citizenship. Under the present act, the Samoans in
> American Samoa cannot become American citizens. A bill is being
> brought before Congress now to allow people of the Pacific to
> qualify.[26]

U.S. imperialism is the backdrop for his application for U.S. citizenship, and Te Rangihiroa recognized the link between his situation and unsuccessful American Samoan attempts to gain U.S. citizenship.[27] That Polynesians were understood by the United States as "Oriental" at the time (the official reason that his individual application was declined) is not easily extricated from the production of the Pacific as an "American lake" in the U.S. imperial imaginary at the time, which squished together "Orient" and "Pacific."[28] Ultimately, Te Rangihiroa withdrew his application when he was offered a knighthood from the British Empire instead, but this episode in applying for citizenship still illuminates the ways in which imperialism can shape Māori articulation of connections with the Pacific.

Te Rangihiroa's Māori-ness was understood as Polynesianness not only in the context of U.S. citizenship law; he was understood primarily as Polynesian in scholarly spheres as well. In 1951 Te Rangihiroa accepted an honorary degree from Yale University during its 250th anniversary celebrations. In the citation from the Yale ceremony, he is described in glowing terms:

> First among those who know the peoples and cultures of the
> Polynesian world, medical doctor, warrior, ethnologist, author and
> poet, you have brought many races of people to greater under-
> standing and peace.

He was given the honor of being the invited respondent to address the ceremony on behalf of himself and the other twenty-four doctoral recipients and did so according to his own terms and in the Māori language. More specifically, Te Rangihiroa responded with a traditional navigation chant. This unique individual, who navigated several racial, national, and regional designations, ultimately drew on his Polynesian—his Pacific—lineage and all of the cross-Pacific migration that entailed at the moment he articulated his position in the academy as a Māori scholar and as a scholar of the Pacific.[29]

first draft of a waiata tangi (for Te Rangihiroa)

Alice Te Punga Somerville

it's hot here:
without electric fan, open window, bare legs
i'd be lying in the dark, heavy limbed and drowsy

as it is, i can feel an ache of warmth at the back of my neck
where hair falls in a tight curtain around an already moist little nook
i'm lying on my tummy, skin pressing into a warm patch of blanket
working on the first draft of something i'll never finish

although warmed milk and sheets are supplied at nighttime
to wide-awake children in the islands of our births
warmth has the opposite effect here:
it's too hot to fall quickly to sleep tonite

i visited your whare "Te Pātaka o Pīhopa" today

before heading to the archive in the back of the building
i walked through front doors, up stairs, over carpet
to greet the small Māori display at the end of the mezzanine

laid a handful of leaves beside the whakairo there
quietly sang to them under my breath,
a small one-sided karanga
surprising the other occupants more than the other visitors

wondered if you used to visit these cabinets too
if you looked across the carpet as i did and felt them looking back,
appraising,
gluing feet to floor and tumbling body into air,
all at the same time

walked along corridors you paced for years,
a precise producer of catalogues:
a scientist working with the test-tubes and bunsen burners of culture

before it was embarrassing to treat people like lab rats,
to steal things and ideas for safekeeping on airconditioned shelves

the relief it must have been to return here after your last trip home,
but also the grief:

did you visit the whakairo more or less after your final wrenching?
does spending time with those things of our own provide solace or
discomfort?
do things behind glass feel enclosed, cut off, pristine, or do they keep
you company?

e te rangihīroa

still hot, still sticky:
was it like this the night you died?

i wonder if you felt more at home as your body turned cold after
last breaths

i wonder if your wairua found a path to follow to hawaiki,
departing as it did from this wrong end of our marvellous watery
hemisphere

"All Those Islanders of the Sea!": Māori at the Polynesian Cultural Centre

The PCC is the state of Hawai'i's most popular paid visitor attraction: at present, about a million people visit the PCC each year. A kind of "theme park"[30] located on the opposite side of O'ahu from Waikiki, the PCC provides visitors with the opportunity to spend a day circulating around cultural villages, shopping, eating, watching films, participating in various cultural activities, listening to talks in each village, partaking of a luau for dinner, and finally, attending the "night show" song and dance extravaganza. The PCC is run by the Church of Jesus Christ of Latter-day Saints (LDS) and is a twin institution to the regional religious undergraduate college Brigham Young University–Hawai'i (BYU-H), which was opened in 1955 as Church College. According to the PCC Web site,

the Church of Jesus Christ of Latter-day Saints opened the Polynesian Cultural Center, considered one of the world's most successful
cultural theme attractions, on October 12, 1963, to help preserve
and perpetuate the more ideal aspects of Polynesian culture, and to
provide work opportunities for students at the adjoining Brigham
Young University–Hawaii.[31]

Although the PCC is managed and partly staffed by full-time employees,
most of the performers, guides, and service workers are students of BYU-H,
who in turn come from all around the Pacific region as well as from Asia,
Africa, Europe, and the continental United States.

The relationship between performance, Indigenous bodies, money, and
the tourist (read colonial) gaze at the PCC is certainly complex. Critical
work on the PCC has often focused on exploitative, romantic, inauthentic,
neocolonial, and inappropriate aspects of cultural performance and cultural
representation at the site. Certainly it is possible to argue that the PCC represents the conspicuous cultural consumption of the European-imagined
Pacific in which stylized and decontextualized cultural performance is offered as a commodity to tourists who seek to interact with a Pacific—and
specifically, a Polynesia—that never existed in the first place. Webb has
gone to some length to explore the PCC as a simultaneously tourist and
Mormon space:

> Onto the tourists' expectations of Polynesian simplicity of which
> the villages, the *tohua,* and the night show are variations, the PCC
> grafts a Mormon allegory. Fundamentally, then, the PCC is Mor-
> mon art, but it is also undeniably tourist art.[32]

However, this analysis fails to account for uses of the PCC by people who
are not tourists: the same physical venue that offers the night show to paying
guests each evening, for example, is used during the day for cultural performances of different kinds. Polynesian community groups and local schools
use the venue for performances to their own families and group members.
The venue is also used for Whakataetae, a kapa haka competition at which
Māori from around Hawai'i and the continental United States gather each
year;[33] the Samoan community enjoys an annual knife dance performance
and competition there; and so on.

Though it would be simplistic to characterize the various approaches to the PCC as either attacking or defending the site, in this context, I position my own consideration of the PCC within the company of scholars such as Wineera, Aikau, and Kester,[34] who are interested in teasing out the complexities—including the contradictions and sometimes surprising possibilities—of the site. Vernice Wineera, for example, focuses on the affective ties of PCC employees to their workplace, and despite her own strong personal links with the PCC, she concluded her doctoral dissertation with an expression of surprise at the extent of employees' agency in negotiating various roles at the site.[35] Similarly, Hokulani Aikau explores the roots of the PCC's linking of cultural performance and fund-raising when she considers the early efforts of the Laʻie community to achieve financial independence and fund their own building and community objectives.[36] Furthermore, though it is possible to cynically decry, for example, the "prostitution" of Māori culture at the PCC and the exploitation of Māori student labor in a Mormon-owned business venture, it seems important to recognize that hundreds of Māori students (both from Aotearoa and beyond) have the opportunity to afford and achieve university degrees at BYU-H because of that income source. The difference between Māori students working at the PCC to support their studies at BYU-H and Māori students working at McDonald's to support their studies at my home institution would seem, at least on some levels, to be somewhat negligible.

What is a Māori village doing at an LDS–Polynesian tourist site in Hawaiʻi anyway? At this point, it is helpful to backtrack a little to the specific connection between Māori and the LDS Church. Māori are included in the Mormon Church in particular ways through LDS cosmological understandings of the Pacific and specifically of Polynesia. These views are well described in a number of treatments elsewhere, including in Hokulani Aikau's doctoral dissertation and forthcoming book and in R. Lanier Britsch's *Moramona*.[37] Aikau points out that there have been Pacific Mormons as long as there have been Mormons in Utah. The LDS mission to Hawaiʻi began in 1850 (around the time the Church was settling into Utah) and was originally directed toward white people. Soon after arriving, however, the missionary George Cannon had a prophetic dream "in which the Lord spoke to him telling him that the Hawaiians were of the House of Israel."[38] Cannon's dream suggested that Hawaiians—and, by extension, Polynesians—are lost descendents of the original pre-Indian communities based in the United States that are at the core of LDS teachings.[39] One does not have to believe the dream on its own terms to recognize its historical impact: it shifted the gears for

Mormon theology but also for the LDS mission to Hawai'i and the Pacific. Hawai'i occupies a unique place in the LDS Church, and in 1919, the first temple outside the United States was dedicated in O'ahu at La'ie (Hawai'i was a twenty-one-year-old territory, not a state, of the United States at the time). Religious migrations from around the Pacific began shortly after, particularly as Pacific Mormons sought to fulfill religious obligations that could only take place at a temple. In 1955 Church College opened (this later became a four-year college and was renamed BYU-Hawai'i). Pacific students were a dominant community at Church College and have continued to be so at BYU-Hawai'i.

The impact of Mormon missions on Māori communities has been widely felt, especially in the Far North and on the East Coast of the North Island. In 1947, Elder Matthew Crowley, an American Mormon who had lived in New Zealand for some time, recognized the effort required by the Māori saints to undertake religious pilgrimages to the Hawai'i temple. He praised their devotion and proposed that they build an appropriate house and organize cultural performances that would be a "double blessing": accommodation and an income to cover the costs of travel for the Māori visitors and a tourist attraction to La'ie. His proposal is recounted in *Hands across the Water—the Story of the PCC*:

> Let some of the Maori Brethren come to La'ie and build a carved house for them and other Maoris to stay in while doing their temple work. Already many tourists were drawn to La'ie by the Temple; such a dwelling would attract even more. And—why not go one step further? Maoris loved to sing and dance. They could earn money, perhaps enough for their passage home, by putting on a program of Polynesian entertainment.[40]

The plan was intended to benefit Māori as well as the La'ie community and, more indirectly, the LDS Church. The pairing of temple work and entertainment for visiting community members on religious pilgrimages was later rearticulated as an opportunity for students at BYU-H to financially support their education and participate in the preservation of culture.

The idea that the Māori performance could be joined by contributions from other communities was introduced at this point: according to *Hands across the Water,* President Clissold replied, "What a wonderful idea! And if the Maoris can do it, why not the Samoans and Tongans?"[41] That "the

Maoris" should be the instigators and models for this kind of enterprise became central to Elder Crowley's dream for the place:

> I hope . . . to see the day when my Maori people will have a little village at Laʻie with a beautiful carved house. Oh, how they could teach you Hawaiians how to do beautiful carving and wonderful decorative work in their meeting houses. The Tongans will have a little village out there, and the Tahitians and Samoans—all those islanders of the sea![42]

At the time, Hawaiians were understood by many commentators to have compromised their own culture beyond repair. (This echoes Te Rangihiroa's first reactions to Hawaiʻi, where he was an early proponent of this idea of Hawaiian cultural degeneration until he lived in Hawaiʻi for several years and was so struck by the robustness of the Hawaiian people that he spent his last years completing a mammoth book on their culture.)[43] In this context, the comments about Hawaiʻi are condescending but perhaps not surprising. What is unfortunate, however, is the apparent inability or refusal of the LDS Church to recognize a link between its perception of diminishing Hawaiian culture and its own part in the acquisition of Hawaiian land and the capitalization of the Hawaiian Islands. Crowley's dream that "all the islanders of the sea" would perform and gather together finally materialized as the PCC, which was opened in October 1963 on the basis of a specific dream by Elder Crowley and with a dual focus: the ability for students to earn money for study and the so-called preservation of Polynesian cultures. The PCC was reopened in 1976 with the addition of Marquesas (1975) and a bit of refashioning all around. Just as Aikau notes that as long as there have been Mormons, there have been Pacific Mormons, we can also add that as long as there has been a PCC, there has been a Māori village.

Māori presence at the PCC is tied to the success of the LDS mission to Māori. The physical construction of the Māori village at the PCC was dependent on visiting groups and individuals, and in an oral history interview in 1982, Laʻie resident Barney Christie emphasized the significance of Māori mobility around the LDS networks.[44] Epanaia Whaanga (Barney) Christie was from Nuhaka (b. 1921), but his great-grandparents Hirini and Mere Whaanga had traveled to the temple in Salt Lake City and were buried in Utah. His own father had been nine when he was taken to the United States, and he grew up and was educated there (at the University of Utah) before moving back to New Zealand in 1918. Christie worked on a canoe that had been intended for King George's visit, but the King died, so the canoe was never completed. However, thirty years later, he brought it to the PCC, where no one knew how to rework a canoe until he made contact with an old carver, Bill Whautapu, who helped him. In 1972 Christie was asked to work in the Māori village of the PCC: he traveled to Hawai'i in 1973 and returned to continue carving there in 1975. In the BYU-H archives, Christie's interview about his life in and around the PCC is accompanied by similar interviews with people such as Joe and Millie Te Ngaio and John Elkington. These personal narratives make up an important, site-specific history of Māori connection with the PCC and of Māori diasporic experiences and deserve further sustained research.[45]

The Māori space at the PCC is simultaneously a marae and a performance-oriented village.[46] The marae was opened with support of the Te Arohanui cultural group, a New Zealand–based group that formed specifically for the task. Te Arohanui had a nucleus of thirty members and started at Temple View (the location of the Mormon temple near Hamilton in New Zealand) in 1956. The group had to pay its own fares, but that did not stop 136 members from touring. After being farewelled at Whenuapai by a group of five thousand people, including the prime minister, Te Arohanui conducted a performance tour through the United States, then spent six weeks at PCC helping to finish the physical plant of the village. Finally, the group performed in the opening night ceremonies of the PCC. This huge commitment from New Zealand–based Māori individuals and communities has had long-standing effects on the PCC as well as on individual members of the group. The marae is kept warm by the multigenerational Māori community in La'ie and surrounding towns: that community is itself a transnational combination of Hawai'i-born, Aotearoa-born, and elsewhere-born Māori. Some members of the marae community are permanent, such as community members of La'ie and nearby Hau'ula (some Māori families have lived in and around this part of O'ahu for multiple generations), while some are more transitory, such as Māori students who travel from New Zealand to BYU-H for education. The presence of Māori leadership has been important to the marae, and from the beginning, the village had a designated "chief."

That the PCC is located in Hawai'i is not inconsequential for the inclusion of a Māori space among its villages. Whereas in New Zealand, "Māori and Polynesian" is common shorthand for "Māori and non-Māori Polynesian" (in which "Māori" cannot logically be "Polynesian"), the presence of Māori in the "Polynesian" Cultural Centre is easily normalized in Hawai'i. Paying careful attention to the language used to describe the Māori village provides one way to track the place of Māori at the PCC and the ways in which this in turn articulates with the relation between Māori, the New Zealand state, and the international tourist audience. A recent (undated) pamphlet welcomes the visitor to "explore seven ancient Polynesian island villages in one beautiful Hawaiian day." Whereas the other villages are consistently called by a vernacular name, including Tahiti (which is officially Polynesie Francais) and Hawai'i (which, if the same rules were to apply to this village as to the present "New Zealand" village, would be called the "United States" village), copywriters have tried a range of ways to describe the Māori village. The village itself has not changed a great deal, but the language has shifted according to a range of factors: time, place, writer, and reader.

A 1969 booklet called *Polynesia in a Day* includes a map with a "Maori area" (the language of "villages" appears in the 1971 updated version of the booklet) and notes "Haere mai/Maori village."[47] The booklet emphasizes the diversity represented across the Polynesian region, and Aotearoa is used as an example of one extreme:

> From tropical Samoa to a Maori village in temperate New Zealand
> is a contrast that adds zest. The change brings you into a marvel-
> lous realm of carvings, weaving and color.[48]

A description of the waka carved by Barney Christie, which was located on the PCC's lagoon, highlights the relations between Māori and New Zealand in imperial terms:

> Floating in the lagoon nearby is a royal Maori canoe—literally
> royal for it was intended as a gift to the King of England on a visit
> to New Zealand which however he never made.[49]

The slippage between "royal Maori" and "literally royal" suggests that from the point of view of some visitors (and perhaps the American PCC management), the "King of England" seems as much a relic of tradition as the Polynesian cultures represented at the PCC.

The problem of describing a Māori village that represents people from a place more commonly known by its English name (New Zealand) has meant that copywriters have negotiated an ongoing tension between accuracy and accessibility of meaning. A 1975 pamphlet describes the village as "Maori" on the map but "Maori New Zealand" in a written portion. An early (undated but post-1975) brochure for the PCC lists the Māori village as "Aotearoa":

> The Maori welcome you with *kia ora* (key-ah-OH-rah). Because *Aotearoa,* as the Maori call their New Zealand homeland, has a temperate climate, the styles of dress and architecture are quite different from the other Islanders.

From 1982, a twenty-four-page booklet titled *This Is Polynesia* includes a Māori carving on its front page, and the Māori village is called "Aotearoa," with "New Zealand" in much smaller print alongside:

> Greeting word: "Kia ora." The Maoris are Polynesians of New Zealand and they call their homeland Aotearoa, or the Land of the Long White Cloud.[50]

Advertisements in 1984 describe the Māori village variously as the "New Zealand" and "Maori New Zealand" village, but a map lists it as "Aotearoa"; in 1985 "Maori New Zealand" had been retained; and in 1986 they were back to "Aotearoa." A pamphlet from 1987 put a dollar each way: on the map, the village is "Aotearoa," but later in the brochure, it is "Maori New Zealand." A full-size booklet from the same year, however, notes "Aotearoa (New Zealand)" on the map and "Aotearoa (New Zealand)—The Land of the Long White Cloud" in the text. By 2000 "New Zealand" is back, and on the map, "New Zealand" is accompanied by "(Aotearoa—Maori)" in much smaller print. A recent pamphlet marks the return of Aotearoa-free "New Zealand": an interesting return, given that the villages themselves are described as "ancient Polynesian island villages" and "New Zealand" is not a very "ancient" name. The Wikipedia listing for the PCC lists the Māori village as "Aotearoa (present-day New Zealand)."

The shifting name attributed to the Māori village emphasizes the instability of the terms involved at the PCC. Despite the Māori village being central to the physical conceptualization of the PCC since its beginning, it struggles to maintain a fixed position linguistically. The PCC desires to represent cultural ("ancient") Polynesia and not the national, political Pacific. For example, the coexistence of a Tahiti village and a Marquesas village is only made possible through ignoring the fact of French imperialism, which includes the islands in the same conglomerate.[51] However, visitors to the center are likely to have heard of "Tahiti," and so the meaning of the village is clear from its vernacular name. The same could be said, as I have already argued, for "Hawai'i." "Aotearoa," conversely, is not a widely known name (or at least, outside the Indigenous world): on one hand, it makes the village appear to be more "Polynesian" when it has a Māori name, but on the other hand, it obscures the meaning for most visitors. Because the PCC by definition has no interest in non-Māori New Zealand culture, in this singular site in Hawai'i, unlike at home, Māori get to occupy the space of "New Zealand" all by themselves. The slipperiness of the name for the Māori village, then, produces possibilities as well as limits to cultural representation when that culture is removed from its occupying nation-state in every way but in name.

Our Sea of Anthologies: Māori in Collections of Pacific Literature

Do Māori texts belong in Pacific anthologies? The regional Pacific is not merely reflected in but produced by Pacific literary texts and institutional configurations. The lineup in any Pacific literature course or anthology clearly indicates a particular view of what might be included in the "Pacific." The course Special Topic: Pacific Literature was a first for Victoria University of Wellington (VUW) in 2008. Despite Albert Wendt's presence at VUW as a student in the 1960s, an institutional commitment to Pacific studies as a discipline, and a sizeable Pacific student community, a course focused on Anglophone Pacific literature had not yet been offered. When designing this course, my desire to expose students to a wide range of texts meant that four of the seven texts we read were anthologies: *Whetu Moana, Niu Voices, Vārua Tupu,* and *'Ōiwi 3.*[52] In just four books, my students and I could access a huge variety of creative texts and, in the introductions, readable, short, clear critical texts. Anthologies have shaped the literary navigation of the region. Commenting on the collection of writing from Francophone Polynesia, *Varua Tupu,* Oscar Temaru writes, "We all belong to the Pacific, as brothers, sisters, and cousins, and it is significant that we are able to travel freely across the reef, physically and through the imaginations of our artists, and get to know one another again."[53] Pacific anthologies become waka: taking on things and travelers, dropping them off in new places, accruing value and meaning from the diversity of their cargoes.

A literary collection is, rather obviously, the result of collecting. In his introductory notes to the vast five-volume anthology of Māori writing, *Te Ao Mārama*, Witi Ihimaera describes the collection as "a marae where our writing will stand, to reflect the times, and to show others a little of what we were like during a crucial decade."[54] Barbara Benedict, writing about the rise of the English-language literary collection in the eighteenth century, describes editing as an act of "gathering together":

> Both the terms "anthology," derived from the Greek for a collection of flowers, and "miscellany," meaning a dish of mixed fruits designate a collection: literally, a gathering together of objects, in this case literary works.[55]

Benedict argues that the appearance of the new genre of the literary collection during the historical period in which various other forms of collecting were also on the rise is no coincidence. Indeed, the practice of literary collection is closely allied to the specific mode of European colonial expansion that was fanatical about collecting, categorizing, and cataloging plants, animals, ideas, materials, and people. The opportunity to "gather together" writing from a range of sources to produce a nuanced and multivoiced perspective on a time or place is particularly helpful in a regional anthology of the Pacific, a region whose immense diversity compelled Wendt to describe it as "so vast, so fabulously varied a scattering of islands, nations, cultures, mythologies and myths, so dazzling a creature."[56] Indeed, the anthology seems an important tool in a region crisscrossed by Indigenous, indentured, enslaved, settler, colonizing, and transient peoples, let alone the multiplicity inherent to a region that covers one-third of the earth's surface, with over twelve hundred Indigenous languages. While creative texts by non-European writers appeared around the Anglophone world from the 1950s, and collections of creative works by white Anglophone writers appeared earlier in settler countries such as New Zealand, Australia, Canada, and the United States, nonwhite writers were seldom included in those anthologies.[57] Partly because access to the white publishing world was difficult, and partly because a large number of factors led to a greater proportion of short pieces by Indigenous and other nonwhite writers, literary collections were crucial to the development of national and regional literatures. It is perhaps ironic that this distinctly colonial mode of collecting, which underpinned most

Pacific–Europe relationships and from which the Pacific has suffered a great deal, produced a genre that has served the Pacific so well.

But do Māori texts belong in these Pacific anthologies? The Pacific produced in anthologies is demarcated as much by absences as by presences. Anthologies are about time and place, but they are also about selection: someone does the "gathering." According to Māori writer Paula Morris, who edited *The Penguin Book of Contemporary New Zealand Short Stories* in 2009,

> there's some creativity, I guess, in selecting, and interpreting. I like the intellectual challenge presented by writing an introduction. A creative challenge too, like writing a book review—reading, thinking, structuring and argument. Choosing words precisely. Trying to engage a reader. Drawing lines in the sand![58]

Editing is as "creative" and "fictional" an act as any of the creative pieces contained in the resulting anthology, and an anthology is securely located in subjectivity and politics. The politics of editorship has significantly inflected—even shaped—the parameters of Pacific writing. Non-Indigenous editors produced the first collections of Pacific literature (e.g., New Zealand–based Bernard Gadd's 1977 *Pacific Voices: An Anthology of Writing by and about Pacific People*[59]), and their selections tended to include European writers resident in the region and strikingly fewer Indigenous writers than the later anthologies. A London-based publishing company's request that Pākehā New Zealander C. K. Stead edit *The Faber Book of Contemporary South Pacific Stories*[60] (to be part of a series of anthologies of short fiction by Australian, Caribbean, Latin American, Canadian, and gay writers) sparked off a series of events that foregrounded the stakes of anthologizing in the region.

While the Faber anthology has been treated elsewhere (most fully in Hereniko and Schwarz's "Four Writers and One Critic"[61]), it is worth outlining here because it so neatly and horrifyingly demonstrates the politics of Pacific anthologies. The episode is now recognized as a remarkable line drawn in the sand of Pacific literature in 1994. Just before the anthology entered the final phase of publishing, Albert Wendt, Witi Ihimaera, Patricia Grace, and Keri Hulme withdrew their work. These writers, who between them form a mammoth constellation in the landscape of Pacific short fiction (and indeed, of Pacific literature in general), staged this withdrawal to protest Stead's editorship. This eleventh-hour withdrawal had two major effects: the anthology was guaranteed a much-diminished place in the literary scene, and Stead wrote an extremely prickly and defensive response to the situation titled "A Note on Absences," which followed the introductory essay. This protest emphasized the problems of continued Eurocentrism in the treatment of Pacific literatures and the significance of anthologies as spaces of production and contestation in the region. Certainly Wendt (or Ihimaera) would have been a more appropriate editor for the collection, and even if Faber didn't realize this, presumably Stead would have. To put the timing of the publication in context, when the Faber anthology appeared in 1994, Wendt's *Lali* was fourteen years old and had enjoyed numerous reprints, Ihimaera's coedited collection of Māori writing *Into the World of Light*[62] was about the same age, and the first volume of Ihimaera's Reed-published multivolume anthology *Te Ao Mārama* had come out in 1992. As well as implicitly sidelining the achievements and capacity of these two as editors,[63] the Faber anthology also failed to recognize that Wendt's and Ihimaera's earlier work as anthologists in the 1980s was instrumental in providing the opportunity for writers in the Faber collection to enjoy recognition in the first place.[64]

However, this is not the only possible reading of the story. For the purposes of the present discussion, it is significant that three of the four writers who withdrew their work were Māori (Hulme, Grace, and Ihimaera), and being Māori had actually excluded them from Wendt's anthologies to date. Indeed, whereas Indigenous and other nonwhite writers around the Pacific found themselves left out of national collections and regional Pacific anthologies produced by white editors, these collections tended to include Māori writers. Though Stead's editorship was certainly problematic, neither *Lali* nor *Nuanua* included Māori writing. The positive impact of Indigenous editorship of Pacific anthologies, at least at that time, was at the cost of Māori and Hawaiian writers. While Wendt's view of the region, collecting on the basis of country of origin, made many states visible, it obscured others, including Aotearoa. Certainly it would be ungenerous for Māori writers to bemoan their exclusion from Pacific anthologies that provided the only possible means of publication for writers from many places around the region. After all, Māori have other publishing opportunities available to them. Although some Pacific nations have had success with self-publication,[65] anthologies of Pacific literature bring together these literatures with others and make possible their mobility to other places.[66] The need for anthologies is exacerbated by the size of various Pacific nations and, thus, the size of their writing communities, readership, publication infrastructures, and distribution networks.[67] At the same time, texts from the larger Pacific nations that have managed to publish and distribute collections at the national level—Aotearoa, Hawai'i, Papua New Guinea, and Fiji[68]—also benefit from being brought into relationship with other Pacific texts and readerships.[69] Suffice to say that the scope and shape of the regional Pacific are reconfigured in each anthology, and the place of Māori is relitigated each time.[70]

One of the important functions of the anthology is to create a sense of "us." Tusiata Avia introduces a chapbook collection, *Fika: First Draft Pasefika Writers*: "These writers individually and collectively have contested the quiet space, the empty page, and allowed something bigger than themselves to be made."[71] In whose interest is this community building carried out? Obviously the implied present members of the community and their contemporaries are crucial, but Ihimaera extends this to a witnessing, testimonial, historical role:

> an opportunity to say to the present, "This is how we are,"—to say to the future, "This is how we were."[72]

Ihimaera produces community by using the inclusive plural pronoun *we* ("how *we* are . . . how *we* were"), whereas Wendt oscillates between the singular and the plural in the introductions to his anthologies. His 1980 introduction to *Lali* was a version of his essay "Towards a New Oceania," which he had written as an introduction for *Mana*, volume 1, number 1, in 1976. After *Lali* opens with a description of its title, a new paragraph starts with Wendt's now immortal words "I belong to Oceania," echoing precisely his 1976 opening. The first pronoun, then, in Wendt's introduction to *Lali* is personal and singular: "*I* belong to Oceania."[73] As in the earlier essay, the plural pronoun appears in the second paragraph:

> In spite of the political barriers dividing *our* countries, an intense creative activity is starting to weave firm links between *us*.[74]

In the introduction to *Nuanua*, again Wendt uses the plural pronoun, and although he later speaks from his individual position ("for me"[75]), he starts the anthology with an assumption—and thereby the production—of a "we":

In many of our Pacific languages nuanua means rainbow . . . the
richness and variety of our literature, both oral and written.[76]

One of the effects of the inclusive plural pronoun is its implicit recognition
of a Pacific readership: the "our" might be a Pacific "our" on whose behalf
Wendt writes, or it might be an "our" in which a Pacific reader is included.
As a Māori reader, I find that many discussions about my home and my
region are written like tourist brochures. By what is explained, translated,
omitted, and not known, I know that the writer doesn't have a reader like me
in his mind as he writes. So although I am a Māori person—a person from
Oceania—when I read discussions of Pacific literature, I am often forced
to peer over the shoulder of the expected reader: the white reader from
the metropole. For this reason, I love rereading these introductory essays
and feeling included in Wendt's "our." It's quite a radical act when Wendt
finishes the introduction to *Lali* by writing about "the warmth and love of
our mother, the Pacific" because in that phrase—in which the phrase "our
mother" connects him and me and others who share "our mother"—he
simultaneously makes me visible and forces the non-Pacific reader to read
over my shoulder instead.

The question of whether Māori texts belong in a Pacific anthology is
remade in this context: who is the "we" in a Pacific anthology? Why do I,
as a Māori reader, imagine myself to be included in his "our"? If we wish
to credit Wendt with the production—or at least the foregrounding—of
a regional consciousness, what is the scope of the region implied by his
"we"? Barbara Benedict describes the anthology-produced community
("something bigger than themselves") in this way:

> Because of their cooperative means of production and multiple
> authorship, anthologies are material expressions of a kind of
> community, and their format also directs readers to understand
> them as vessels of a common enterprise, even while registering the
> independence of each author. . . . Often the community is in fact
> created by or for the anthology itself, rather than serving as the
> basis of it.[77]

Each time a region is produced by a collection, borders are marked out in
introductions and implied through the selection of texts. One of the problems
of collection in the Pacific is the difficulty of producing criteria by which

writers and communities are admitted or omitted. So Wendt's anthologies have not collected writing by white writers, and yet to protect the collections in this way, it becomes very difficult to include, for example, Fiji Indian writers and Māori writers in the same collection. After all, *Lali* and *Nuanua* include Indigenous and non-Indigenous writers from Fiji on the basis of their deep affiliation to a country that's a part of the independent Pacific, and *Whetu Moana* includes Māori writers on the basis of our affiliation with Polynesia, which is incapable of recognizing later arrivals from outside the region. *Whetu Moana* bears the mark of its triple-Aotearoa parentage (Wendt is based in New Zealand; Sullivan and Whaitiri are both Māori) and collects on the basis of Indigenous ancestry rather than nation-state. Importantly, this approach produces the conditions for reading diasporic alongside Aotearoa-based Māori writers.

It seems that, at least for the time being, Māori texts belong in Pacific anthologies when they are Polynesian anthologies. Paradoxically, or perhaps just unexpectedly, the use of *Polynesia*—a term often derided for its colonial origins and connotations—enables a rather radical re-viewing of Aotearoa and Hawai'i. When the Pacific is made up of all the independent nations in the region, a huge range of countries are included in its scope, but others drop out. *Whetu Moana* looks at the homelands of Māori and Hawaiian people, and rather than seeing the white nations of New Zealand and the United States, it sees the configurations of those places outside colonialism: Aotearoa and Hawai'i. Perhaps this is a manifestation of Wendt's rather brilliant formulation of postcolonial in his introduction to *Nuanua*: a way of looking at New Zealand and Hawai'i "outside/beyond colonial."[78] Using the term *Polynesia* as the central tenet of collection excludes those parts of the Pacific that aren't in Polynesia, then, but it also enables two particular communities to be included alongside work from places we'd expect to see represented in a Pacific anthology: welcome, Māori and Hawaiian writers.[79]

Māori People in Pacific Spaces

Te Rangihiroa's ideas about the Pacific changed over his lifetime. When he first went to Hawai'i, he was disparaging toward the Hawaiian people, whom he considered to be extremely compromised and whose cultural legacy he believed to have already passed. After two decades living on O'ahu, he had shifted in his thinking so that his last book, a mammoth undertaking, was about Hawaiian arts and crafts. In the context of this chapter, the remarkable feature of this story is not that Te Rangihiroa had the capacity to conduct such a shift in his thinking, although that is impressive in its own right, but rather that it points to the possibility of genuine negotiation in the relationship between Māori and the Pacific. Te Rangihiroa was more than equipped to make an intellectual assessment of Hawaiian culture when he arrived, but he had the wisdom, rigor, and curiosity to recognize that simply ticking off a set of categories will only provide a superficial observation. His ideas changed because he was in Hawai'i, interacting with Hawaiians, drawing and redrawing lines over the course of over twenty years in their company. Although a book like this could simply decide on a policy or formula by which all things Māori might be determined to be Pacific, Te Rangihiroa—and the PCC and Pacific anthologies—remind us that it is through the lived, negotiated, ongoing, and specific interaction between Māori and the Pacific that articulations of connection, or otherwise, have any meaning and, indeed, any possibility of change.

Māori people in Pacific spaces cannot help but foreground the layers of connection, reconnection, and disconnection between Māori and the Pacific. Although these three examples—Te Rangihiroa, the PCC, and Pacific literary anthologies—are dramatically distinct, they all gesture quite directly toward the significance of historical, cultural, economic, religious, and creative contexts in this negotiation. Furthermore, these three examples remind us that the relationship between Māori and the Pacific is multimodal and multigenerational: in each iteration of the relationship, different pressures and motivations affect the stakes and limits of connection. Each of these Pacific spaces has a life at the regional level, and it is worthwhile recalling that Māori also spend time in Pacific spaces within the national context—and although these connections are bordered and configured differently, they are a worthwhile comparison. Later in this book, for example, the inclusion of a Māori village at Auckland's annual Pasifika Festival provides a significant and contrasting counterpoint to the Māori village at the PCC.

Each moment of connection and each articulation of being Pacific or being Māori is itself a site in which the relationship between the two is re-called and maintained. Furthermore, each of these three disparate examples affirms that the extent to which Māori are part of the Pacific depends on the specific context within which the relationship is negotiated. Te Rangihiroa was a Māori individual in Pacific geographic, scholarly, cultural, and racial spaces; Māori people at the PCC are in a Pacific performance, religious, and economic space; and Māori texts in various anthologies are present in particular Pacific literary, cultural, creative, educational spaces. In each case, the relationship between Māori and the Pacific has implications for the production and maintenance not only of the category "Māori" but also of the category "Pacific." The biographer of Te Rangihiroa cannot help but consider his work to be Pacific work; the visitor to the PCC will unconsciously include Māori in a lineup of Polynesia; and the reader of *Whetu Moana* will take for granted that alongside poetry from Sāmoa, Tonga, Niue, Hawaiʻi, and the Cook Islands, there will be poetry from Aotearoa. What some of that Māori poetry might look like is a story for the next chapter to tell.

· CHAPTER 2 ·

Pacific-Based Māori Writers

A GREAT DEAL OF ENERGY, both contemporary and historical, has
been expended on exploring the historical migration of Māori people
through the Pacific to Aotearoa. The Māori poets Vernice Wineera, Evelyn
Patuawa-Nathan, and Robert Sullivan all write about and demonstrate
journeys in which Māori start at Aotearoa and venture out into the region.
Vernice Wineera and Robert Sullivan are two very different poets: one
older, one younger; one woman, one man; one from lower North Island
iwi, one from iwi based at the northern and southern ends of Aotearoa;
one with long-standing residence in Hawaiʻi, whose link to Aotearoa derives its strength from emotional connection, and one who was there for a
comparatively short time, with a view to returning home. Evelyn Patuawa-
Nathan is the only Māori writer published by the South Pacific Creative
Arts Society (SPCAS) in Fiji.[1] Originally from the north of the North
Island (Kaihu valley), she wrote her collection while living and teaching
in Sydney. Māori writers based outside Aotearoa negotiate their ongoing
membership of Māori and iwi communities in different ways to those based
in Aotearoa, and it is unfortunate for the writers, but also for a potential New
Zealand (including Māori) readership, that with the exception of Robert
Sullivan, who mostly publishes with Auckland University Press, diasporic
Māori writing is virtually inaccessible in New Zealand. As a result, the first
two collections of English-language poetry by Māori women (Wineera's
Mahanga and Patuawa-Nathan's *Opening Doors*) are impossible to buy and
rarely acknowledged; it is only when the Māori connection with the Pacific
is explored that their work becomes visible.

"Ocean of Possibilities": Vernice Wineera

In 1978, the first book of poetry in English by a Māori woman was published.
The first published work of Māori creative nonfiction had appeared in 1951
(Rewiti Kohere's *The Autobiography of a Maori*); the first book of poetry

in English by a male Māori writer had been Hone Tuwhare's *No Ordinary Sun* in 1964; and the first books of fiction by a Māori man (Witi Ihimaera's *Pounamu Pounamu*) and by a Māori woman (Patricia Grace's *Waiariki*) appeared in 1972 and 1975, respectively.[2] It remained for a Māori woman to publish a collection of poetry in English. However, when Vernice Wineera's *Mahanga: Pacific Poems* was published in 1978, it did not as loudly enter the list of firsts as the others had.[3] To be frank, if the poetry had been published but was a little ho-hum in terms of poetic quality, this quietness around its publication might be understandable, but Wineera's collection is packed full of rich, lively, compelling poetry. The themes of the collection are wide ranging: family, maternity, childhood and children, location and place, teaching and knowledges. Wineera's ongoing residence in Hawai'i prevented her publication from being hooked into the worlds of New Zealand literature by the usual means of literary geography, and this has dropped her out of the dominant Māori literary horizon as well.[4] Ironically, this distance from New Zealand and from Aotearoa may be precisely what enabled her to achieve publication in 1978, when Māori women poets at home could not.

Inside the front cover of *Mahanga*, bibliographic notes suggest the multiple spaces in which Wineera and her work had already circulated: her poetry had previously appeared in *Te Ao Hou* (Māori), *Marae* (Māori), *Kula Manu* (a Brigham Young University–Hawai'i student–staff creative magazine based in Hawai'i), and *Ensign* (a Mormon creative writing journal). *Mahanga* is subtitled *Pacific Poems,* and in the preface, Wineera is described as "a sensitive, soul-searching Pacific poet" as well as "of Maori, English, and French ancestors."[5] In her own introductory poem, she writes,

> The Maori has always been an artist and
> poet, and I hope herein to convey in
> English my respect for Maoritanga and
> the Polynesian heritage which enriches my
> twentieth-century life.

Even though the slippage between Pacific and Polynesian is rightly contested, what I am interested in is the inextricability of the specific term *Māori* ("The Maori," "Maoritanga") from the regional configuration of the Pacific ("Pacific poet," "Polynesian heritage"). The year after *Mahanga* was published, Wineera edited a literary collection, *Ka Po'e o La'ie,*[6] in which her writer's statement echoes Wineera's articulation of the "Pacific heritage" described in *Mahanga* and looks forward to the "vast [Pacific] marae" from a yet unwritten poem we will explore later:

> My Polynesian heritage is the vital element in my work. I see the Pacific as an extended marae that is rich in culture and experience and I want to express this in poetry that will reveal the universals in human experience.[7]

Wineera's work oscillates between an Aotearoa-consciousness and a Pacific-consciousness, perhaps because she is a diasporic writer based in Laʻie, Hawaiʻi. Rather than journeying out from Aotearoa to consider the rest of the Pacific, Wineera's poetry journeys home from one part of the Pacific (Hawaiʻi) to Aotearoa.

Mahanga includes a number of poems about Aotearoa, and these often imagine returning home through memory or physical travel. In "Toa Rangatira," Wineera reflects on a visit to her home marae and articulates the possibility of ongoing connection with Aotearoa and "Maoritanga":

> "I am home," I said
> to a whip of playful wind
> that trailed my words
> and flung them
> at the wide-eyed tekoteko.
> He gave no sign
> save that carved out
> of defiance.
> Nor would he prance forth
> to lay at my feet
> the fern-leaf symbol.

The speaker of the poem literally speaks—"I am home"—but the agency lies in the many entities that make up this "home": the wind and the tekoteko.[8] Whereas the speaker's actions are simple and passive ("I said," "my words," "my feet"), the wind and tekoteko are more active and described through physicality: the "playful wind" "trailed" and "flung" the speaker's words; the tekoteko is "wide-eyed" and capable of "sign," "prancing" and "laying."

The reciprocal relationship between the speaker and the entities of home—visible, as in the tekoteko, and invisible, as in the wind—is initiated by the speaker's return and utterance but requires response.

Lest we read this as a withheld response and therefore draw conclusions about the impossibility of continued connection when residing as far away as Hawai'i, we might look more closely at the way in which the "I" of the poem describes the inaction *as action*. The voice of the speaker has been wrested away, and yet she does not understand herself to be voiceless. Rather than the wind rendering her silent, it "playfully" repositions her "words," first quietly "trailing" but then "flinging" them at the tekoteko. In this act, then, the wind supports her claim—"I am home"—by carefully and forcefully repositioning it. Reading this poem alongside Apirana Taylor's well-known 1979 "Sad Joke on a Marae" is immensely compelling because they both focus on a self-proclaimed dislocated individual engaged in the act of approaching a familial marae. In both poems, the claim of ignorance expressed overtly by the poem's speaker is simultaneously undermined by the speaker's knowledgeable articulation of what is not apparently known. The speaker betrays her knowledge about the tekoteko, anticipating specific action—"pranc[ing] forth to lay at [her] feet the fern-leaf symbol"—even as she recognizes that the tekoteko himself is not forthcoming in this instance. Also in both poems, the reciprocal relationship between the marae (especially the tekoteko and other whakairo) and the individual is unmediated by the presence of other people. [9]

In her poems about Hawai'i, Wineera focuses on the ocean itself, and her descriptions of the Pacific waterscape are particularly rich. Prophetically supporting Hau'ofa's not-yet-written essay "Our Sea of Islands," she writes about the ocean as a being: multiple, lovable, active, promising. In "Watching the Limu Pickers," for example, she describes "the sea's unruffled skin." [10] Her longer reflection on Pacific voyaging in her description of the launch of an oceangoing waka, "Hokule'a," describes an "ocean of possibilities," "an ocean of hospitality," and "an ocean of welcome," countering the idea that the vastness of the ocean is either threatening or empty space. Indeed, this relationship with the ocean comes out of intimate and affectionate connection between people and the ocean: "knowing already the fragility / of the sea's soft skin." Both poems focus on ocean-related activities: subsistence in the case of gathering limu (edible seaweed) and navigation in the case of Hokule'a. At the same time, the position and voice of the poet are slightly outsider in these poems; in both, the speaker deliberately and mindfully watches rather than participates.

In "Pacific Note," the ocean is central to the poet's worldview. This is a significant intervention in Māori writing because ocean-centricity (as opposed to land-centricity) is uncommon in writing by Māori based in Aotearoa, perhaps because the sheer size of the islands has led to an affinity with geographies and metaphors of land more so than water and perhaps also because—at least until the Seabad and Foreshore Act 2005—Māori have needed to defend themselves from a Crown that was more intent on alienating land than ocean. The poem starts with the production of an "us"—a Pacific "us"—whose common denominator is the ocean:

> It is a curious fact
> that some of us have
> lived all of our lives
> at the ocean's curled edge
> —have breathed with every breath
> we ever took, salted air.

"Our" shared ocean-centrism is underscored by comparison with "others / living out their days / without ever comprehending this fact." The ocean provides the basis for a collective, relational identification between those who share a relationship with the ocean in this way. Furthermore, the "edge" of the ocean marks it as presence rather than absence, which undermines the view of the Pacific as an empty space (available for atomic testing, available for South Sea fantasies, producing no texts or theories worthy of studying in world literature or postcolonial literature courses). The presence of the ocean as an entity produces the sense of an oceanic identity, despite the lack of interest that continental people have in the Pacific as a region and the unique perspectives of its people ("and should they / ever confront it, would shrug, / and say something like / 'so?'"). The poet sharpens her insight into her "Pacific" perspective by attempting to imagine living on a continent: "I would suffer from / claustrophobia." This fear of claustrophobia directly reverses a common continental perspective on living on islands.

The ocean both manifests and produces history ("For where would I hear / the surf's steady song / rolling out of the depths / of time?"), an idea that anachronistically reminisces Caribbean writer Derek Walcott's famous poem "The Sea Is History." Rather than being overwhelming, the vastness and depth of the ocean (both in time and space) is a constant toward which the poet returns to refocus after petty human interactions:

> And how would I stand
> week-long wrangles
> among my like-kind,
> without the evening
> joy-giving
> tranquillity
> of wind,
> sand,
> rock,
> sun,
> pacific,
> ocean?

The ocean is not solely a body of water but a framework for all the elements; sand, rocks, and the sun are included in the "ocean," just as the islands are included in Hau'ofa's Oceania. The poem produces the history of the Pacific's naming as a pun, drawing attention to the original denotative meaning of the term *pacific* as a parallel to *tranquillity*. However, despite Magellan's external observation of a passive and "calm" (pacific) ocean, the ocean itself is the active agent, and the calm (the pacific-ness) is something that is sought—and attained—by the Pacific "I."

A more explicitly Māori position is asserted in "Heritage,"[11] in which the speaker of the poem challenges the reader to engage in the very individualized and intimate act of literalizing the "marks" of Maoriness by carving them onto skin. The poem directs the reader to "take," "carve," "let," "rub," and so on, and thereby the reader is commanded to apply the tattoo to the face of the poet. The poet is aware of the various and reciprocal ways she is represented as Māori—"Carve upon my face the marks / of Maoritanga"—and elaborates the complexity of Māori representation and creative production. Although the poem is readable in multiple ways, I am most interested here in how a poem so invested in specifically Māori representation ends with the words "I am taking my place / on this vast marae / that is the Pacific / we call home." In important ways, the poem resonates with Wendt's essay "Tatauing the Postcolonial Body" because both turn to a specific localized practice and history of tattoo to engage with questions of representation, literacy, and aesthetics at the local and regional levels.

One reading of the poem would identify the tattoo as a metaphor for representation in all forms, and from the very first word of the poem, "take," the reader is forced to actively participate in, and therefore become complicit with, the act of tattooing as well as the creative production of the poem. The first instruction to the reader is to pick up certain implements and prepare them for an unknown use:

> Take the sharpened pipi shell,
> piece of paua, bird bone,
> razor blade if you like.

The reader is directed to choose from instruments used for cutting, and although the first three are natural elements, the razor blade is not from the same series. Indeed, whereas the shells[12] and bone are all remnants of other lives, the razor blade is manufactured and rarely associated with life. Turning the decision over to the reader about which tool to pick up—"if you like"—is at once a false gesture (the voice of the poet completes the poem regardless) and recognition of agency about the forms of representation with which people choose to engage.

After selecting a tool, "Carve upon my face the marks / of Maoritanga" reveals the act on which the rest of the poem depends. The task is impossible partly because it is an arresting idea to carve someone's face as she stands in front of you. The reader is trapped: having selected a tool, the choice is to "carve" or walk away. If the reader "carves," the process will be bloody and cause massive pain—and risk of death—for the speaker of the poem. However, walking away will be difficult because the poet has spatially located the reader at no more than arm's length from the "face," which reinforces their mutual proximity. Likewise, when it comes to representation, one must decide whether to engage, and risk causing deep, irreversible, and possibly irreparable indentation, or not to engage, and thereby render the poet—the subject, the object—invisible. "Carving" also seems impossible because the application of the moko is highly ritualized, so the poet forces the reader to assume a specific expert role that (most) readers would know themselves to be unable to occupy and that is dependent on the person being tattooed for instruction. In a literal sense, once the "face" is cut, the speaker will have a difficult time providing instruction; likewise, any attempt at representation cannot help but be inflected by the always already shredded and bleeding language available.

Comparing the "marks / of Maoritanga" to "the moko of the old women / wrapped in blankets round the cooking fire" historicizes the art of tattoo but also links the wearing of moko to ancestry. In this way, collective memory is a form of self-representation. Significantly, the poet does not compare herself to the "old women" but instead compares her "marks" to their "moko." Rather than placing herself in the same position as the women, she elaborates a link between the processes of acquiring such "marks"; the strict comparison is between her "blood" and their "moko":

> Let the blood spurt
> and dribble down my chin
> like the moko of the old women

Her "blood" may literally "dribble down [her] chin" and thereby mimic the appearance of tā moko, but "blood" could also refer to whakapapa in which tā moko portrays specific genealogical meaning.[13] A further reading is possible when we consider the double meaning of *moko,* which is most likely to be understood as "tattoo" in the context of this poem and yet is also a widely used affectionate shorthand for *mokopuna,* or "grandchild." In this case, the poet is claiming her place as a descendent of the kuia—a "moko of the old women"—as well. The speaker's acquisition of moko is simultaneously about genealogy and inherited familial position and thereby underscores the slippage between past and future that is central to the whole poem and that provides the foundation for a vision of Māori connection to the Pacific region that is not restricted to historical migration.

Having selected a tool and "carved" the "face" of the poet, the poem continues through the process of applying a tattoo. Although the rest of the poem deserves much closer attention, it is worth noting the suggested link between writing and tattoo: "Rub the juices in the wounds, / Charcoal, vegetable dye, India ink." The act of "carving" becomes a tattoo when it filled with an appropriate dye, a painful process that will ensure that the "marks / of Maoritanga" are legible across time. As with the sharp tool, the reader is offered a choice of "juice," and again the precontact technologies are joined by "India ink," which explicitly gestures toward the act of writing.[14] The poem shifts in pace as the poet coaxes the reader to "make beautiful the design" with aesthetic and artistic forms sourced from a distinctively Māori cultural context. After "the old women," the poet acknowledges her koroua (grandfather) and a "proud cloak," "karanga," "nose flute," and "tekoteko" as other Māori forms that engage and embody memory and inheritance. Identifiers from Māori and non-Māori worlds add to the pattern "carved" onto the skin:

> Cut statistics on my face:
> name, age, place of birth, race,
> village, tribe, canoe.

Like "razor blade" and "India ink," "statistics" jolts the imagery of the poem, but this time the word is co-opted by the poet. "Statistics" includes the details of "age, place of birth, race" required for legitimacy in the context of the state, but the "statistics" of "village, tribe, canoe," invisible to the European statistician, provide the mechanism by which citizenship can be determined and elaborated in the Māori world. Like the karanga, the tekoteko, and "the moko of the old women," this second series of "statistics" requires and makes visible another kind of literacy.

The poet also explains why the tattoo must be applied: "Carve deeply, erase doubt / as to who / I am." The existence of doubt—acknowledged for the first time here—suggests that this act of representation is not innocent but is underpinned by an existing "doubt / as to who / I am." "Doubt" is linked to the face-without-moko, suggesting why the memory of "the old women" is so warm and why the poet insists on being "carved." That the doubt is not mentioned until the ending section of the poem could suggest that the doubt is less important to the poet than the "marks / of Maoritanga" named much earlier, or it could suggest that after splitting the "skin, membrane" and rupturing the barrier between self and other, a deeply held sense or fear of "doubt" can be revealed.

Until its final turn, the poem could have been written by a Māori poet based anywhere and with little interest in asking whether we once were Pacific. However, Wineera closes the poem not by further introspection or by an appeal to a Māori cultural space or, indeed, to a New Zealand national space but rather by turning the focus back out to the broader Pacific region:

> . . . Lacerate
> my legacy upon me
> where all who read will perceive

>   that I am taking my place
>   on this vast marae
>   that is the Pacific
>   we call home.

These last lines clarify the main purpose of the moko for which the poet has dictated instructions. More than this, though, it affirms that the moko is dependent on legibility and literacy: like the readers of things written with India ink, those "who read" moko draw on specialized skills. The poet assuming her "place / on this vast marae / that is the Pacific" does not depend on these reading skills, or even on the moko itself, but the moko—her "legacy"—provides a text by which her act of "taking [her] place" can be understood.

Because Wineera's articulation of Māori connection with the Pacific is intimately tied to her location in Hawai'i and her career-long commitment to regional activities, this turn to the Pacific is not a deflection but a deeper center; indeed, describing "the Pacific" as a "vast marae" is a particularly rich image. Certainly it reframes the Pacific region according to a specifically Māori spatial concept. A marae is a meeting space that is linked to connection, belonging, negotiation, and specific roles and rituals carried out by those for whom that marae is "home." Finally, the focus of the poem shifts here from the reader to the speaker. Whereas the first act of the poem is the reader's ("take the sharpened pipi shell . . ."), the poet ("I am taking my place") and the collective ("the Pacific / we call home") conduct the final actions of "taking" but also "calling."[15] However, to extend this a little, the Māori concept of the "marae" is itself a pan-Pacific (certainly pan-Polynesian) idea. That the Pacific is a "vast marae" gestures toward the great marae Taputapuatea, located in Opoa on Ra'iatea (yes, Tupaia's own home island and the Rangiātea in the epigraph to this book), which was the central space for spiritual and intellectual exchange and from which major acts of Polynesian exploration and ongoing navigation took place. If the "vast marae" is Taputapuatea, the "we" of Wineera's poem ("this is the Pacific / *we* call home"[16]) includes all of those who link to that marae, that is, all Polynesians. Wineera does not lessen the specificities of Māori identification because of her region-focused sensibility, and vice versa, and in this way, she confirms that "the Pacific / we call home" is simultaneously regional and specific.

"Holding Back Ocean Barriers": Evelyn Patuawa-Nathan

Evelyn Patuawa-Nathan is the only Māori poet published by the SPCAS. Like Wineera's *Mahanga,* her collection contains an explanatory subtitle: *Opening Doors; a Collection of Poems by the Maori Poet Evelyn Patuawa-Nathan.*[17] Patuawa-Nathan was an active member of the early Māori writing scene; the introductory notes mention that she worked with Harry Dansey and Hone Tuwhare in trying to set up "a Maori Writers Society," which was unsuccessful but is now manifest in the organization Te Hā.[18] Patuawa-Nathan lived in Sydney at the time of publication, and much of the poetry in *Opening Doors* deals with Australia, the Tasman Sea, and Aotearoa. Indeed, very little of the book explicitly engages Pacific connections at all, with the exception of "Omamari," which draws attention to migration histories, and yet her collection's inclusion in the SPCAS series absorbs the work into the scope of Pacific writing.

In "Omamari," the ocean is figured as a place of mobility and circulation, historicizing and normalizing Māori migration:

> At dusk, with the tide running out
> and gulls leaving the cliffs
> in noisy packs
> to worry uncovered flotsam,
> then, history stirs me.

The temporal in-betweenness of "dusk" parallels the spatial in-betweenness of the shore, and Patuawa-Nathan places this luminal time in the context of multiple currents and trajectories: "the tide running out," "gulls leaving the cliffs," "uncovered flotsam." The in-betweenness is reinforced in the second stanza:

> And again on windy mornings
> at first light
> while a heavy surf
> pounds the shore line

"Again," the spatial liminality of the "shore line" finds a parallel in the temporal cusp of "mornings / at first light,"[19] and the lines between these zones are both reinforced and blurred: "windy mornings" and "heavy surf / pound[ing] on the shore line." Rather than a generalized "stirring" of (or by) "history," the speaker is reminded of the specific history of her ancestral waka[20] and this specific place:

> ... I remember that
> my ancestral canoe,
> Mamari,
> foundered
> on this beach.

That the "history" is a memory of an "ancestral canoe" collapses the dominant limits of "history" to include memory and "ancestral" entities. The movement in the poem is tidal: the "surf / pounds the shore" while "gulls leav[e] the cliffs . . . to worry uncovered flotsam," while her "ancestral canoe" is described as having "foundered" on that beach. This zone of messy yet cyclic encounter complicates the relationship between land and sea (again, like Wineera, this anachronistically echoes Walcott and Hau'ofa), and this is where "history" emerges. To the speaker of the poem, history is not a structure or overlay by which she frames the place she is in but rather is itself an agent. History is a constant by which the speaker is "stirred," placing the speaker in the same category as the "flotsam." For Patuawa-Nathan, as for Wineera, the sea is at once text, agent, and mnemonic device, recounting and prompting recognition of Pacific connections.

Also like Wineera, though, Patuawa-Nathan foregrounds the struggle between being home in the Pacific and being home in Aotearoa. "In the Beginning" relates the story of a young Māori man, Manu Te Waaka, who moves to Australia ("Living in King's Cross") and whose homesickness and tortured exploration of his sexuality get him involved in drugs that ultimately prove fatal. The discoveries and freedoms associated with distance from home enable an exploration of sexuality beyond the normative restrictions of (at least some sectors of) the Aotearoa-based Māori community:

> He changed his life style,
> changed his sex,

had hormone shots,
became cosmopolitan
and very very chic.[21]

Manu Te Waaka's individual freedom and expression provides him with

Moved with a crowd
of other transvestites
absorbed in their own particularity
Walked with ease in a
society that accepted
the fates of the extraordinary[.]

Sydney is associated not only with freedom and community but also with mobility ("moved," "walked"), implying that Aotearoa is linked to stagnation or incarceration. This oscillation between homesickness and the imagined impossibility of meaningful return is echoed in Patuawa-Nathan's poem. The beginning of Manu's demise is due to homesickness ("he . . . needed to dull the worries / of family ties left behind"), and yet reversing its effects by returning home is also impossible:

Home-sickness was not stronger
than fear of returning
to face humiliation
and intolerance.

His "fear" of "humiliation / and intolerance" literalizes the meaning of *homesickness* in which home is the source of sickness, and so he seeks healing by staying away from, rather than returning to, home.

However, the ending of the poem, although relieved of explicit moral judgment, suggests that this healing from homesickness is impossible. Although the narrator seems to be a dispassionate third-person observer through most of the poem, merely listing off a series of events ("In the beginning," "he became," "He changed," "Worked at," "Moved with," etc.), the relationship between the narrator and Manu is clarified near the end of the poem. Although Louise's "fear" of "humiliation / and intolerance" keeps her from "returning," she ultimately ends up being taken care of by relatives ("other Northerners"[22]) in death. At this point, the narrator enters the narrative of the poem and claims a familial connection to Manu, "descendent of Northern chiefs":

> We followed the coffin,
> myself and other Northerners . . .
> we found
> an elder to perform
> traditional rituals.

After death, Manu is relieved of the burden of mobility and his "fear of returning" to Aotearoa; instead, "other Northerners" move toward him. His final migration is in his casket as he travels with, rather than to, his relatives. In death, then, both communities are present, and Manu–Louise is claimed by both of them: "friends of Louise," who "dressed up / a sad funeral into a / gay wake" and thereby affirm sexual identity, and "Northerners" who affirm genealogical location.

At the moment of death, then, Louise is finally buried in Australia but is oriented outward toward "the sea":

> He rests now in the cemetery
> at Botany
> On a hill overlooking the sea.

Despite "overlooking the sea," Louise is buried far from "the North." The fast pace of the poem, with short lines in long, narrow stanzas, is abruptly arrested by this squat, separate stanza. In death, then, Louise gets to "rest" from struggle for the first time. Alongside the articulation of sustained—if foreclosed—longing for home, the decision to identify as Māori in Sydney is tricky. When "Manu te Waaka" becomes "Louise Santos," the new name suggests an alternative brownness that secures a new gender identity but deflects attention away from being Māori.[23] Certainly it is tempting to suggest that shedding the name "Manu" (literally, "bird") symbolically clips wings and secures Louise as an exile. At the same time, the poet consistently uses the pronoun *he* ("he rests") despite Manu having become Louise over the course of the poem; it appears that after death, Louise's gender identity is reassigned by those who bury her. The burial "at Botany" returns our attention to the place of the ocean in Māori identification. In death, the diasporic exile Louise is still (and ultimately) foreclosed from returning home physically yet remains oriented toward home as represented in the poem, Pacifically enough, by "the sea."

"I Meant This to Be a Poem about Aotearoa, So Forgive Me": Robert Sullivan

Robert Sullivan (Ngāpuhi, Kai Tahu) lived in Hawai'i for a year in 2001–2 and returned to live there with his family in 2004. He has since returned to Aotearoa in 2010. After his first two collections, *Piki Ake* and *Jazz Waiata*, he worked on the feat of *Star Waka*, a collection of 101 poems (100 in the book and 1 on the cover) and 2001 lines. Published in 1999, this number of lines peeks over the new millennium and, thereby, the space and time beyond popular focus:

> IN 101 POEMS
> STROKING Y2K
> STANZAS PEOPLED WITH STARS AND WAKA
> AND SEA STROKING PAST TWO THOUSAND LINES[24]

Paying close attention to the detail of numbering evokes the precise mathematical foundation of navigation. Each poem retains internal integrity in terms of topic and form, and yet they are all tied into a broader structure in very particular and carefully counted ways. This reminds us of navigation, then, but also of whakapapa, a reference reinforced by the "peopled" poetry along with the image of "lines," which refers to lines of poetry but also lines of whakapapa. The slippage between poetry and genealogy, produced by the word "lines," suggests that poetry itself might function as a form of genealogy. Next came *Captain Cook in the Underworld* (2002), the lyrics for an opera that Sullivan was commissioned to write, in which he brings together two major explorers of the Pacific: Māui and Cook.[25] Rather than Cook and his voyages being understood as singular and precocious, they are tied into a broader context of navigational feats around the Pacific. Likewise, while each written poem marks a shift in perspective or time, the dominant narrative is located at the level of the whole book rather than at the level of each poem. Rather than demonizing Cook, Sullivan subsumes him through incorporation into a Pacific-derived story that is under the creative and metaphoric control of the Pacific. The collection *voice carried my family* came out in 2005 and is another kettle of fish. Structured by four sections rather than by an overarching logic, the collection roams in very specific ways between Aotearoa and Hawaiʻi, and it foregrounds a range of ways in which that roaming is both prophesied and underpinned by earlier connections and feats of navigation. In three consecutive collections, then, Sullivan explores three distinct ways of articulating Māori connections with the Pacific: the originary[26] and ongoing telling of the waka traditions; the founding stories of Pacific exploration at the regional level, with a dual focus on Cook and Māui; and reflection on the multiple sites and spaces of Māori contact with the Pacific, including late-eighteenth-century European and Polynesian navigators and more recent formulations.

Before focusing on *voice carried my family,* we will return for a while to *Star Waka,* which has been treated elsewhere[27] and is taught widely, and which demands consideration as a predecessor to *voice* in the context of this discussion. *Star Waka* centers Māori voyaging *out* from Aotearoa; otherwise, it would be called by vaka or vaʻa instead of by the Māori waka, which appeared only after Māori had landed in Aotearoa and spent some time reworking the Polynesian language.[28] This is confirmed by the speaker of the poem, "Waka 89," who directly introduces himself as the Polynesian trickster demigod Māui and asserts, "Without me the waka would be a vaka." In his explanatory note to *Star Waka,* Sullivan points out that "each poem must have a star, a waka or the ocean," and in this way, the collection focuses on the voyages but also on the knowledges of navigation and the wider context in which those make sense. Although *star, waka,* and *ocean* are interchangeable, the ocean is silent in the title of the book and in the first poem, "He karakia timatanga," in which Sullivan repeatedly directs his attention toward star and waka:[29]

> I greet you in prayer oh star oh waka . . .
> and pray for your combination here.
> *He Karakia mo korua, e te waka, e te whetu o te ao nei.*
> Star and waka, a prayer for you both.

Despite not being named in the karakia, the ocean has the capacity to exceed any boundaries and can stand in for star or waka in the other poems.

Sullivan reflects on Māori as ocean people: voyagers, navigators, travelers, deeply embedded in specific land because of, not despite, previous migrations. He draws close connections between Pacific migrations and whakapapa: "what belongs to ocean belongs to blood" ("i"), "we all belong to a waka" ("xxxii herenga waka"), "there is a Kupe in all of us" ("waka 70"). In the final poem of the book, "Waka 100," he writes about "each person / of waka memory . . . / waka names." In the second poem of the book, "i," Sullivan describes the physical act of traveling by waka but also challenges assertions that the art and science of Māori navigation are diminished by affirming the continuation of waka traditions through the ongoing articulation of those journeys. Just as he later writes about the possibility that ahi kā[30] is maintained through linguistic as well as physical occupation of specific space in "Ocean Birth" (treated later), in "i," Sullivan describes the maintenance of voyaging and navigation:

> In ancient days navigators sent waka between.
> Now, our speakers send us on waka. Their memories,
> memory of people in us, invite, spirit,
> compel us aboard, to home government, to centre:
> Savai'i, Avaiki, Havaiki, Hawaiiki, from where we peopled
> Kiwa's great sea . . .

This poem moves across time and space: from the physical–past ("navigators sent waka") to the poetic–present ("speakers send us on waka") and back to the physical–past ("from where we peopled Kiwa's great sea"). Rather than simply producing a one-way process of moving from literal to metaphoric voyaging, Sullivan establishes and affirms an ongoing oscillation between physical and poetic mobility. The poetic–present articulation of mobility is sandwiched between references to historical physical migrations. The "we" of the poem, however, exists across time: while "*our* speakers send *us* on waka"[31] in the present day ("now"), "*we* peopled Kiwa's great sea," demonstrating the understanding that ancestors live on through successive generations. Furthermore, the desire to move is simultaneously derived from "[speakers'] memories" and "memory of people in us": "memories" of historic events (when "we" peopled the Pacific) coexist with "memory" of people from those times (ancestors who live "in us") as it is experienced by "us" in the present. As in Patuawa-Nathan's "Omamari," the act of navigation in this poem is both an historical event and a rhetorical and literary gesture.

Sullivan views the Pacific in *voice carried my family* from Hawai'i as well as from Aotearoa. Rather than seeming confused or disjointed, however, this shifting of perspective is immensely generative: Sullivan newly draws links between Aotearoa, Hawai'i, and the broader Pacific to emphasize connections and disconnections between all. The collection is structured by four sections: "For Gods and Waka," "For Shadows," "For the Ocean of Kiwa," and "For Fires." Whereas the first two sections seem to continue the work of *Star Waka* and feel New Zealand based, the third section, "For the Ocean of Kiwa," has a regional focus and foregrounds the historical figures of Mai and Tupaia, and Sullivan adds Koa and Te Weherua to their memories. The title of this section not only emphasizes the Māori name for the Pacific (Te Moananui a Kiwa) but, like the Māori word *waka* in the title *Star Waka*, also names an originary Polynesian navigator as he is remembered by Māori speakers (Kiwa), and through this name, Sullivan claims the navigation of the Pacific as a Māori activity. The section, which seems to come out of Sullivan's own experience of departing Aotearoa and moving to Hawai'i, is thereby itself a return of sorts.

"The Great Hall," the first poem of the section, describes the position of Māori, and specifically Sullivan, in the representational logic of the settler nation:

> Stained-glass figures: Cook and Marsden,
> a WWI veteran, foundational figures of Canterbury,
> and the launch, launching Cook's caulked vessel—CC
> *in the underworld—*

Sullivan names the dominant masculinist genealogies of any colonial settler nation: explorer ("Cook"), missionary ("Marsden"), soldier ("WWI veteran"), and pastoralist–trader ("foundational figures of Canterbury"). New Zealand is distinguished from other settler nations through the specific details of "Cook" (Englishness), "Marsden" (Anglicanism), "WWI veteran" (Gallipolli and its "birth of the nation" mythology), and "foundational figures of Canterbury" (the nineteenth-century provincial system and the specific alienation of land to produce a primary economy). This settler genealogy, depicted in "stained glass," is fragile and translucent yet fixed and authoritative. The poem reflects on the occasion of his previous book launch and suggests a quiet unease with the same old colonial story:

> Still, I feel like I'm with the *Endeavour*
> making repairs off the Great Barrier,
> fothering the hull with the sails of the story[.]

Although the national story may have produced space for certain kinds of conversation and articulation, including Sullivan's own previous collection ("*CC in the underworld*"), it is not enough: another perspective is craved ("we had . . . a problem, / a problem that scratches the sails as they form their skin / of tar").

This poem, then, located as it is in the beginning of the second half of the collection, marks a shift not only in physical location but also in focus, as Sullivan explicitly seeks an alternative narrative and set of relationships:

> And so I bring a new lens, two, a pair of eyes
> for the mission: Tupaia's, and another pair, Mai's,
> two other pairs: Koa and Te Weherua's. Polynesian eyes
> on Cook's several crews.

Describing the new perspective as the "bring[ing of] a new lens, two, a pair of eyes" suggests a literal, and quite deliberate, decision about perspective. The poet is the agent in the poem: he "brings" the new perspectives rather than simply looking through them or considering them. This is about conscious and purposeful selection of "a new lens" and "pairs of eyes": Sullivan's choices are as careful and productive as the quadripartite configuration of the settler nation from which he has just signaled a decision to shift away. Seeking an alternative genealogy to that offered by the nation as memorialized in a space like "The Great Hall," the poet names Tupaia, Mai, Koa, and Te Weherua as another cast of symbolic ancestors. Reminiscent of the memories and genealogies that move across time and space in *Star Waka*, these "eyes" are marked as historical "eyes" ("Polynesian eyes / on Cook's several crews") at the same time as they are available to Sullivan to become his eyes today both figuratively and, perhaps, literally through inheritance. Because the "eyes" are "on Cook's several crews," however, the meaning of "eyes" extends beyond mere perspective and becomes about witnessing and, perhaps, surveillance. The "Polynesian eyes" do just accompany Cook: they are "on" him and his "several crews," which might include not only his literal crews but all those other figures of colonialism who arrived after. The "eyes" that the poet "brings" make possible a form of intergenerational witnessing, in which "Cook" and his "several crews" are simultaneously under the watchful eye—and thereby in the record—of mobile "Polynesians" not only in their own time in the past but also through Sullivan's own "Polynesian eyes" in the present. The major features of New Zealand colonial–settler history may be fixed in specific and generic "stained-glass figures," but the witnessing of "Polynesian eyes" is just as enduring.

In the final section of the poem, Sullivan moves from the generic "Polynesian" to Māori:

> I looked at the stained glass
> in Canterbury's Great Hall, and noticed
> one unidentifiable Maori at the lowest right
> on whose shoulders stood all the others.

Taking his "Polynesian eyes" to "look" at "Cook's several crews" as represented in "the stained glass," the poet sees something new. Sullivan's decision to shift his focus from the settler nation to the regional Pacific means that an "unidentifiable Maori" becomes visible. Significantly, this decision to name and look at—and literally through—a regional Polynesian genealogy (Tupaia, Mai, Te Weherua, Koa) produces the poet's ability to see this Māori figure for the first time. The "unidentifiable Maori" is not elsewhere in the hall but is found in the very "stained glass" with which the poem began. Indeed, the only "unidentifiable" figure in the hall is this one, the one closest to the poet both in terms of genealogy and physical proximity. Once the Māori figure is finally "noticed," after all the other figures have been identified, the poet realizes that all the others are entirely dependent on the "unidentifiable Maori at the lowest right" after all. This realization shifts the focus of the whole poem, and we step back and realize that all of the weight of the poem rests, concretely and on the page as well as historically and conceptually, on these "shoulders" in the final line.

Much of the book's section "For the Ocean of Kiwa" historicizes and reflects on the configurations set up in this first poem. The poems range from narrating events that are perhaps unknown to many readers ("Koa was 10 years old amid topmasts and mainstays . . . Polynesian"[32]) to considering the ethics and limits of Sullivan's own decision to write about non-Māori Polynesian historical figures ("You're in the public domain . . . but I can't. I just can't take the middle of your throat. / Who would I pay for the privilege?"[33]). The section reinforces the links between contemporary, "recent," historical, and originary migration. The poem "Ocean Birth" journeys around—and centers—the various origin stories of Oceania. The poem starts, appropriately enough, in Aotearoa, and the speaker of the poem retraces the steps to Hawaiki alongside those who journey there after their lives in this physical world have ended:

> With the leaping spirits we threw
> our voices past Three Kings to sea—
> eyes wide open with ancestors.

As the babies of the Pacific (these were the most recently settled islands, according to archaeological and genealogical evidence[34]), a journey into the Pacific is simultaneously a journey home and a journey back in time along the routes of the navigators who brought Pacific people to Aotearoa in the first place. In this sense, the "sea," the "Ocean of Kiwa," is full of "ancestors": those who have journeyed there after passing away here and those people who come from earlier bloodlines and continue to inhabit the islands from which we departed. "Ocean Birth" names the originary stories of Rapanui, Tahiti, Hawai'i, Aotearoa, Sāmoa, Tonga, and beyond to the Lapita people.[35]

After imagining Mai and Tupaia, along with Māori travelers Koa and Te Weherua ("the first Maori ever / to leave Aotearoa that way"[36]), as precedents for his own journey across the Pacific, Sullivan is finally able to talk about Hawai'i. Near the end of the section, "Pearl Harbour" begins "I meant this to be a poem about Aotearoa / so forgive me"[37] and focuses on the process by which the United States overthrew the Hawaiian monarchy and continues to overthrow the Hawaiian people. After considering various mobile Polynesian figures, perhaps the "I" of the poem hoped to identify the "unidentifiable Maori" by writing "a poem about Aotearoa." However, reflecting on the Pacific makes it impossible to write about Aotearoa without recognizing the broader context, starting where Sullivan's own feet are located. For one poem ("a poem about Aotearoa") to morph into the other (a "poem about" Hawai'i), the two places must be rendered substitutable. The boundary between "Aotearoa" and "Hawai'i" is permeable because of "waka memory"—Polynesian whakapapa—but also because of shared colonial experience. "Kuki/Cook" is one example of this shared colonialism, and the slippage between Aotearoa and Hawai'i is further gestured toward in Sullivan's corrective when describing the "Queen":

> . . . arrested the Queen. Not Victoria.
> Nor Elizabeth. Lili'uokalani . . .

The poet's intervention ("not Victoria. / Nor Elizabeth") suggests that the imagined reader will wrongly assume which "Queen" he is writing about. The English Queens Victoria and Elizabeth stand in for the past and present colonial context in Aotearoa; the likelihood that the reader will misrecognize the Queens (the poet "means" Liliʻuokalani, after all) supports the similarity between the two contexts of Aotearoa and Hawaiʻi at the same time as the colonial contexts (Queens Victoria and Elizabeth vs. "Congress . . . Pearl Harbour . . . America") are contemporarily distinct. "Pearl Harbour" articulates the dual position of Hawaiʻi and Aotearoa in relation to one another: substitutable and distinct. For Sullivan, although this is "meant" to "be a poem about Aotearoa," the poem is about Hawaiʻi, and this, in some ways, makes it about Aotearoa after all.

Pacific-Based Māori Writers

What happens when the Māori people travel to the regional Pacific, either through physical mobility, poetic treatment, or place of publication? In her preface to *Ka Poʻe o Laʻie,* Wineera writes,

> One does not stop being Maori or Samoan or Haole because one is now living in Laʻie.[38]

Although this comment is part of a larger point she makes about "the Laʻie experience," in relation to the place of culture in that uniquely heterogeneous town, it also speaks to the relationship between "being Māori" and place. Because Māori are fixed to Aotearoa (through Indigenous claims to land), which is in turn fixed to New Zealand (through the occupation of the nation-state of New Zealand, which covers the same geographical area as that understood as Aotearoa), the Māori person venturing to the Pacific is departing New Zealand. In this way, the Māori person *departs from* an originary home. But at the same time, because Māori genealogies and cultural and linguistic traditions are fixed to the Pacific (and, most locally and especially, Polynesia), the Māori person venturing to the Pacific is retracing migration routes, seeking genealogical and cultural sources and tributaries. In this way, the Māori person *returns to* an originary home. It seems that, at least for these three writers "of waka memory," writing in the Pacific region produces a quite different view of the region from writing by those "of waka memory" in Aotearoa. In this double-directional mobility between departure and return, Wineera's, Patuawa-Nathan's, and Sullivan's poetry not only extends the scope of the Māori literary canon but also— significantly—articulates and challenges our thinking about the relationship between Māori, the Pacific, and Indigeneity.

CHAPTER 3

Aotearoa-Based Māori Writers

I F, TO PARAPHRASE VERNICE WINEERA, one does not stop being Māori when one is living in the Pacific, does one stop being Pacific when one is living in Aotearoa? Although Aotearoa-based Māori writers tend to focus either on Māori connections with Europe or Pākehā, or on Māori-centric configurations, a small group of Aotearoa-based Māori writers have produced texts about Māori as a part of the Pacific region. Interestingly, this Aotearoa-based articulation of an Aotearoa-inclusive Pacific is fragmentary: less like the large tapa sheets writers based outside New Zealand are able to produce and more like the carefully constructed shreds of tapa worn as ornaments and only recognizable if you know what you are looking for through familiarity with that from the "Tropicks." New Zealand stepped up its claim to connection, or at least solidarity, with the Pacific region in the 1980s when, to protect its own nuclear-free values, New Zealand sacrificed defense arrangements with Australia and the United States and Prime Minister David Lange delivered a now famous antinuclear speech in a British debate. The issues of nuclear testing and political configuration in the region were paired by the "Nuclear-Free and Independent Pacific" movement, in which several Māori were players, and their participation consolidated and laid further foundations for activist networks in the region.

A great deal of New Zealand popular music, art, and writing in the 1980s and since has focused on a nuclear-free Pacific and on resistance to weapons testing in the region, and this chapter pays attention to two texts from the period that turned their attention to the politics of the region. Witi Ihimaera's 1987 novella *The Whale Rider* has received huge attention since the popularity of the film *Whale Rider* but has received little attention for its commitment to Pacific regionalism,[1] and Hinewirangi's 1990 collection of poetry *kanohi ki te kanohi*,[2] in which the poet reflects on engagements with Indigenous people in specific places around the world, has received little critical attention at all. Hinewirangi's collection centers the specifically Māori practice of connection named in its title (literally, "face-to-face"), and both texts track the physical journey of an individual—the character Rawiri in *The Whale Rider* and the speaker of the poems in *kanohi ki te kanohi*—away from Aotearoa into the Pacific region, where such face-to-face meetings take place, and then back to Aotearoa with a newfound understanding of what it is to be Māori.

These are not the only Aotearoa-based Māori writers who treat the Pacific region, but they comprise a productive pairing for the reasons I have explained earlier. Hone Tuwhare wrote about his experiences in Sāmoa ("Village on Savaii"[3]) after he worked there and in Papua New Guinea as a boilermaker, and Apirana Taylor's poems in *Whetu Moana* are also about Sāmoa ("The Fale" and "In Samoa at Solaua Fatumanava"[4]). Tuwhare and Taylor both reflect on traveling to Sāmoa and finding their perceptions of life in Sāmoa to resonate with their experiences of Aotearoa. Certainly, although this present discussion does not treat Cathie Dunsford's Cowrie trilogy, of which the first novel appeared in 1994, her writing belongs in a longer discussion of Aotearoa-based Māori articulations of Pacific regionalism. The first book, *Cowrie*,[5] centers on a woman of Māori and Hawaiian ancestry who travels to Hawai'i to connect with her relatives there; the second novel, *The Journey Home*,[6] continues the theme of Māori migration as it narrates the travel of a Māori woman to California for doctoral studies; and the possibilities of alliance in resisting French nuclear testing in the Pacific compose the central narrative in *Manawa Toa/Heart Warrior*.[7] In 1995, many New Zealanders again became active as the French government renewed testing in the Pacific region, and Ambury Hall compiled *Below the Surface*, an anthology that included several Māori writers.[8] The Māori poems in the collection articulate connection with the Indigenous people of Moruroa through references to Rangiatea, linguistic resonance, similar physicality, the ocean and its deity Tangaroa, and histories of militarism.

Whāngārā mai Papua New Guinea: Whale Riding around the Pacific

One of the most widely distributed images of Māori in the last decade is the feature film *Whale Rider*, written and directed by Niki Caro, which was released to global audiences in 2002–3.[9] Based (very loosely, in parts) on Witi Ihimaera's 1987 novella *The Whale Rider*,[10] the film was made with the help of the first batch of New Zealand government funding to support the production of local feature films.[11] Like all widely viewed films about non-mainstream communities, especially films that bear such a heavy burden of representation,[12] much could be said about the representational politics of the movie.[13] This discussion does not focus on the film, but it is worth noting that key differences between *The Whale Rider* and *Whale Rider* are the result of expunging the most innovative contributions *The Whale Rider* makes to Māori writing in English and, in this case, to Māori articulations of connection with the Pacific. Within the context of this chapter, and with a nod to Hau'ofa, whereas the film's Whāngārā might be described as an "island in a far-flung sea," the novella locates Whāngārā and the events and characters of the narrative within a "sea of islands."[14]

Although the narrative of *The Whale Rider* is deeply rooted in the oral traditions and territory of real tribal groups and a real town on the East Coast of Aotearoa, Ihimaera pushes the scope of the story beyond Whāngārā to Australia, Papua New Guinea, nuclear testing sites in the French Pacific, and, ultimately, Hawaiki.[15] This locates very specific Māori-centric events and struggles within a wider regional framework: Pacific connections are reaffirmed when Māori recognize their links with other Pacific people through shared cultural concepts and similar colonial histories. The whale story that parallels the human story in the novel makes the issue of nuclear testing in the Pacific visible and prompts an orientation of political energy toward Pacific (rather than metropolitan[16]) politics. Additionally, in the original edition of the novella, six illustrations by John Hovell track stages of the story with stylized art forms from cultural groups around the Pacific.[17] The navigational capacities of these "Pacific" Māori, at once adamantly Indigenous and confidently mobile, are emphasized by the appearance of an authorial endnote immediately after the text in its first editions: "New York, 14 August 1986."[18]

Kahu's uncle Rawiri narrates the human narrative[19] in *The Whale Rider*, and this generational distance from the main character, Kahu, secures a third-person narration of events throughout the novella and introduces the Pacific context for the events at Whāngārā. In the space of a few pages early in the novel, Rawiri describes his travels outside Aoteaora while Kahu—the future whale rider—is still living with her mother's family:

The next year Kahu turned four and I decided it was about time I went out to see the world.[20]

He travels to Australia and then to Papua New Guinea before returning to Whāngārā, and the expectation he will return is emphasized during his departure at the airport:

> "Give Kahu a kiss from me."
> "Ae," Nanny Flowers quivered. "Ma te Atua koe e manaaki. And don't forget to come back, Rawiri, or else—"
> She pulled a toy water-pistol from her kete.
> "*Bang,*" she said.
> I flew to Australia.[21]

Rawiri spends a year in Sydney, meeting up with relatives and forming a close friendship with his "buddy" Jeff. After a year in Sydney, his older brother Porourangi calls, and Rawiri considers returning home, but his journey is not yet complete. Rather than simply traveling to Sydney to restitch diasporic Māori into the wider narrative of the novel, Rawiri has yet to establish whakapapa connections and historical relationships with other Pacific people.

Porourangi's phone call is not isolated; Rawiri and Jeff both receive calls from family asking them to come home, foreshadowing the different familial directions in which they will eventually be pulled. By this time, Rawiri is living with Jeff, who is not racially positioned until they move to Papua New Guinea together after Jeff's parents ask him to return to their house there:

> Jeff was a friendly, out-front guy, quick to laugh, quick to believe and quick to trust. He told me of his family in Mount Hagen, Papua New Guinea, and I told him about mine in Whangara.[22]

Although Rawiri's description of his friend's background parallels his own, Rawiri is about to discover the difference between residence in the Pacific on the basis of continued colonial exploitation ("his family in Mount Hagen") and identification with the Pacific on the basis of Indigeneity ("mine in Whangara"). Jeff's whiteness is made explicit for the first time when he is summoned by his parents:

> His mother called from Papua New Guinea to ask him to come home.
> "Your father's too proud to ring himself," she said, "but he's

getting on, Jeff, and he needs you to help him run the coffee plantation. He's had a run of rotten luck with the workers this year, and
you know what the natives are like, always drinking."[23]

Jeff's mother's racism collapses all Indigenous people into a singular type
("natives"[24]), and this links the specific situation in Papua New Guinea to
colonial racism globally, including New Zealand, in which Rawiri is himself
a "native." Additionally, the link between Papua New Guinea and a wider
colonial structure is underscored by the crop Jeff's family produces, coffee,
which is consumed by and profits the bourgeoisie both in Papua New Guinea
and its (unofficial, since so-called independence in 1975) colonizing power
of Australia[25] but also throughout the global system of capitalist imperialism
that exploits "native" land and labor to produce cash crops.

As Jeff and Rawiri discuss Jeff's imminent departure, a comment about
loyalty to family[26] prefigures the impossibility of his escape from other
kinds of loyalties, allegiances, and privileges once the two men are in a
more explicitly colonial context:

> "But it looks like all my chickens are coming home to roost," Jeff
> said ruefully.
> "Family is family," I said.[27]

Rawiri decides to accompany Jeff, and while he could have immediately
recognized a "native" identification there, in a romantic moment of regional
Pacific solidarity, "family is family" for Rawiri too. When he announces
his intention to move to Papua New Guinea, Nanny Flowers humorously but problematically calls up a set of racist stereotypes that rival Jeff's
mother's:

> "E hika," she said. "You'll get eaten up by all them cannibals.
> What's at Papua New Guinea"—I mouthed the words along with
> her—"that you can't get in Whangara?"[28]

Later, Kahu repeats this joke to her uncle on his return:

> "Did you like Papua New Guinea? Nanny Flowers thought you'd
> end up in a pot over a fire. She's a hardcase, isn't she!"[29]

For Māori to be Pacific, then, we first need to rethink our exposure to, and participation in, years of racism that has been directed toward Indigenous people from around the Pacific.

Despite Rawiri's apparent equality with his friend in Australia, over the course of two years in Papua New Guinea, Jeff's family redraws the boundaries of their relationship, aided by and responsive to explicit structures of white settler racism and its exclusive institutions such as "the Bridge Club." He first encounters Jeff's family at the airport, where he meets Jeff's mother:

> Although Jeff had told her I was a Maori it was obvious I was still too dark. As soon as I stepped off the plane I could almost hear her wondering, "Oh, my goodness, how am I going to explain this to the women at the Bridge Club?"[30]

Rawiri immediately recognizes her attitude toward him as racism that, for white Australians in Papua New Guinea (as represented by Jeff's family and their "offscreen" community), is tied to skin color. At the same time, his own comment about relative complexion belies his own initial ambivalence toward the Indigenous people in Papua New Guinea ("*although* Jeff had told her I was a Maori"[31]) and Nanny's racial othering ("them cannibals"). Ihimaera does not present a grotesquely simplified version of Aussie racism, and Jeff's father is portrayed as a more complex figure:

> Tom, Jeff's father, was another story, and I liked him from the start. He was a self-made man whose confidence had not been shattered by his long and debilitating illness. But it was clear he needed his son to help him. He was standing on the verandah of the homestead, resting his weight on two callipers.[32]

Although Rawiri describes him with admiration ("I liked him from the start"), this is complicated by the context in which Tom lives and prospers. After all, Tom is actually the opposite of "self-made"; his "success" is directly attributable to the hierarchical system of exploitation in Papua New Guinea to which his status as a white Australian man allows him privileged access. In this case, however, it seems the center cannot hold.[33] Although Tom's physical health was not cited by Jeff's mother as the reason for his "rotten luck" at the plantation, preferring to blame deficiencies on the part of the "natives," Tom leans on "two callipers," crutches that metaphorically undermine his being "self-made." "It wasn't until weeks later that [Rawiri] discovered the [Parkinson's] disease had not only struck at his limbs but also had rendered him partially blind,"[34] an image of colonial decay in which the gradual in-ability to function is accompanied by a (less apparent) degeneration of vision. His blindness could be to the inequalities of the colonial system, although Rawiri's admission that Tom is an ambiguous figure and Jeff's mother's emphasis on visual differentiation racism ("I was too dark") allows that Tom could be increasingly unable to distinguish between "natives" and his own kind, an extension of "going native" as a result of proximity that would be seen as a form of degeneration by the colonizing community. The ability to see becomes crucial later, at the climax of the section, when the difference between the white community and those who are "too dark" is placed in sharp contrast.

Rawiri first articulates his identification with Papua New Guinea when he works on the land. As he describes the work of "putting the plantation back on its feet,"[35] he first identifies himself with Jeff's family and their project of domesticating ("taming") the landscape:

> Putting the plantation back on its feet was a challenge which the countryside really threw at *us*; I have never known a country which has fought back as hard as Papua New Guinea. I doubt if it can ever be tamed of its temperatures, soaring into sweat zones, or its terrain, so much a crucible of crusted plateaus and valleys, and its tribalism. But *we* tried, and I think *we* won some respite from the land, even if only for a short time.[36]

Including Indigenous people ("its tribalism") as a part of the "countryside" is a particularly colonial configuration, and the inclusive plural pronouns (*us, we*) make Rawiri an ally. However, he draws on a particularly Māori view of their effect on the "countryside," and this is the first time he differentiates himself from the colonial project:

> Man might carve his moko on the earth but, once he ceases to be vigilant, Nature will take back what man has once achieved to please his vanity.[37]

Although he is committed to the project of "taming" ("I've always been pretty good at hard work, so it was simply a matter of spitting on my hands and getting down to business"[38]), Rawiri recognizes the "vanity" that will ultimately be undermined by "Nature." Furthermore, because the moko is a form of tattoo that reflects genealogies and histories, labor and the physical structures of the plantation become an expression of identity and history. Echoing Wineera's poem "Heritage," the additional meaning of moko as descendents supports a vision of genealogical as well as economic future in the "tamed" plantation space. Rawiri recognizes, however, that the carving of this genealogy and history will be ultimately resisted by the landscape when "Nature . . . take[s] back what man had once achieved."

Eventually, Rawiri identifies further links between Papua New Guinea and Aotearoa. At first he describes his observations of Papua New Guinea politics as an outsider:

> I used to marvel at the nationalism sweeping Papua New Guinea
> and the attempts by the Government to transplant national iden-
> tity and customs onto the colonial face of the land.[39]

This idea of marking "the colonial face of the land" gestures to the "moko" described in the plantation context, linking the colonial plantation with "the Government" but also implying that their efforts will be futile. ("Nature will take back what man had once achieved"). Furthermore, despite Rawiri allegedly "marveling" at the process of nationalism, the metaphor of "transplanting" suggests that "national identity and customs" are introduced from outside and, in the context of plantations, that the purposes served by their "transplantation" will also be foreign. Rawiri turns to Māori terminology to outline the barriers to this "transplantation" and thereby produces a slippage between Papua New Guinea and Aotearoa:

> First, Papua New Guinea was fractionalised into hundreds of *iwi*
> groups and their *reo* was spoken in a thousand different tongues;
> second, there were so many outside influences on Papua New
> Guinea's inheritance, including their neighbours across the border
> in Irian Jaya; and third, the new technology demanded that the peo-
> ple had to live "one thousand years in one lifetime," from loincloth
> to the three-piece suit and computer knowledge in a simple step.[40]

While the first "barrier" to the "transplanting" is articulated with Māori words (iwi, reo[41]), Rawiri supports the popular perception of "one thousand years in one lifetime," which is (especially with the use of words like *loincloth*) derived from the same set of assumptions as his Nanny's "cannibals."[42] Later in the chapter, however, Porourangi writes to Rawiri and describes the contemporary changes to the Māori communities in Aotearoa:

> [Porourangi] had gone with Koro Apirana to Raukawa country and had been very impressed with the way in which Raukawa was organising its youth resources to be in a position to help the people in the century beginning with the year 2000. "Will *we* be ready?" he asked. "Will we have prepared the people to cope with the new challenges and the new technology? And will they still be Maori?"[43]

Porourangi's questions about "technology" echo the claims about "steps" taken by the Indigenous peoples in Papua New Guinea. The pairing of these two conversations about technology and preparedness for certain kinds of futures suggests a closer relationship between Papua New Guinea and Māori than Nanny Flowers's stereotyping would initially admit.

After including himself in the colonizing "we" who attempt to "tame" the "countryside," then recognizing the local "iwi" and "reo," Rawiri finally considers the relationship between Papua New Guinea and Aotearoa, recognizing some of the key differences but also suggesting the articulations of the two "communities":

> In many respects the parallels with the Maori in New Zealand were very close, except that we didn't have to advance as many years in one lifetime. However, our journey was possibly more difficult because it had been undertaken within Pakeha terms of acceptability. We were a minority and much of our progress was dependent on Pakeha goodwill. And there was no doubt that in New Zealand, just as in Papua New Guinea, our nationalism was also galvanising the people to become one Maori nation.[44]

As he recognizes similarities between Aotearoa and Papua New Guinea, Rawiri becomes newly conscious of the situation at home. The differences between the two places ("except that we didn't have to"; "however, our journey was possibly more difficult") also sharpened his awareness of the situation in Aotearoa. Finally, Rawiri realizes the local possibilities of Pacific regionalism:

> So it was in Australia and Papua New Guinea that I grew into an understanding of myself as a Maori and, I guess, was being prepared for my date with destiny.[45]

Significantly, Rawiri does not lose his sense of being Māori when he begins to identify with Papua New Guinea, but these connections enhance his "understanding of [him]self as a Maori."

Unsurprisingly, Rawiri's enhanced identification with the Indigenous people of Papua New Guinea does not bode well for his relationship with Jeff or his family. After a year and a half, Jeff and Rawiri have a conversation about Rawiri's position there:

> "You're getting homesick, aren't you Rawiri?" he said . . .
> "A little," I replied. Many things were coming to a head for me on the plantation, and I wanted to avoid a collision. Jeff and I were getting along okay but his parents were pushing him ever so gently in the right direction, to consort with his own kind in the clubs and all the parties of the aggressively expatriate. On my part, this had thrown me more into the company of the "natives," like Bernard, who had more degrees than Clara had chins, and Joshua, who both worked on the farm. In doing so I had broken a cardinal rule and my punishment was ostracism.[46]

Rawiri's connection with "the natives" in Papua New Guinea is longer general but is quite specific; he names individual Indigenous people and has a sense of their lives and histories. The humorous juxtaposition between Bernard's multiple degrees and Clara's multiple chins points out the irony of claims that the "natives" are lazy and that Europeans are industrious. Rawiri's friendship with Jeff is complicated by the actions of Jeff's family ("family is family" indeed), and as Rawiri starts to change the pronouns by which he describes himself (throughout the section, "we" is a very unstable term as Rawiri claims membership in multiple groups with shifting parameters), Jeff is more closely aligned "with *his own kind* in the clubs and all the parties of the aggressively expatriate." Rawiri's in-betweenness ("Although . . . I was a Maori . . . I was still too dark") had posed a risk to the social structure in

Papua New Guinea since he arrived at the airport, and his ostracism from the "expatriate" scene has "thrown [him] more into the company of the 'natives,'" which "[breaks] a cardinal rule" of the colonial structure. Jeff and Rawiri hold their conversation beside the water, and Rawiri continues to narrate the scene:

> I had picked up a shining silver shell from the reef. I had taken it back to the beach and was listening to the sea whispering to me from the shells' silver whorls. . . . I placed the shell back to my ear. *Hoki mai, hoki mai ki te wa kainga*, the sea whispered.[47]

Interestingly, for this Pacific reading of the novella, at the end of this episode with Jeff, it is not Jeff's acceptance of his departure ("if you have to go, I'll understand") that speaks most deeply to Rawiri but rather the sea. Furthermore, the sea now speaks Māori.

The imminent "collision" is one of three events that convince Rawiri that he "should be homeward bound."[48] Rawiri attends a wedding reception for a "young expatriate couple," and although Clara assumed he wouldn't attend, "Jeff said I was 'one of the family' and insisted that I accompany them."[49] At the reception, Rawiri overhears Clara:

> "He's a friend of Jeff's. You know our Jeff, always bringing home dogs and strays. But at least he's not a native."
> Her laugh glittered like knives.[50]

This comment confirms that Rawiri is neither one of them ("dogs and strays") nor "a native," an in-between position from which he is forced to make a choice on the way home that evening when the "collision" he has feared turns out to be literal:

> We . . . were driving home to the plantation. Jeff was at the wheel. We were all of us in a merry mood. The road was silver with moonlight. Suddenly, in front of us, I saw a man walking along the verge. I thought Jeff had seen him too and would move over to the middle of the road to pass him. But Jeff kept the station wagon pointed straight ahead.[51]

Rawiri is one of the occupants of the vehicle, shuttered from the outside environment and protected by the encasement of the car, and yet he also has a special view of the surroundings. Perhaps an allegorical reading is possible here, in which Jeff's family keeps "pointed straight ahead" toward the "plantation" despite the literal presence of the Indigenous body. Rawiri's view of the "countryside" is no longer from the position of the "we" it had been a moment earlier, and he realizes that his view is fundamentally different to Jeff's. The "collision" has disastrous circumstances for the "man walking along the verge":

> The man turned. His arms came up, as if he was trying to defend himself. The front bumper crunched into his thighs and legs and he was catapulted into the windscreen which smashed into a thousand fragments. Jeff braked. The glass was suddenly splashed with blood. I saw a body being thrown ten metres to smash on the road. In the headlights and steam, the body moved.[52]

To follow our allegorical reading, after the body is struck by the car, it obstructs the view of the occupants; significantly, the glass is not only "splashed with blood" but also breaks "into a thousand fragments," one perhaps for each year of so-called progress brought about by colonialism. (Of course, one would not want to follow the "collision" too closely as an allegory, given that this episode would suggest the impossibility of modernity—indeed, a fatal impact—for the "iwi" of Papua New Guinea.)

Finally, Rawiri is forced to reckon with the impossibility of continually occupying a middle space within the sharply binarized hierarchy of Papua New Guinea's colonial context—he must stay in the blood-splattered car, or he must get out:

> Clara screamed. Tom said, "Oh my God."
> I went to get out. Clara screamed again, "Oh no. No. His tribe could be on us in any second. Payback, it could be payback for us. It's only a native."
> I pushed her away. Tom yelled, "For God's sake, Rawiri, try to understand. You've heard the stories—"
> I couldn't comprehend their fear. I looked at Jeff but he was just sitting there, stunned, staring at that broken body moving fitfully in

the headlights. Then, suddenly Jeff began to whimper. He started
the motor.

    "Let me out," I hissed. "Let me *out*. That's no native out there.
That's *Bernard*." A cous is a cous.[53]

Rawiri recognizes the rhetoric justifying the maintenance of the position
inside the car ("payback," "you've heard the stories"), and he also realizes that he finds Jeff's paralysis ("he was just sitting there, stunned") and
weakness incomprehensible: "I couldn't understand their fear." When Jeff
"start[s] the motor" of the car, in effect agreeing to the racist, exploitative,
and literally violent terms—as well as the "fear"—by which he will go on to
inherit the legacy of the plantation ("The station wagon careered past me.
I will never forget Jeff's white face, so pallid, so fearful"), Rawiri takes his
departure. The colonial system in Papua New Guinea operates to protect
the hierarchies in place, and the inquest decides:

    It was an accident, of course. A native walking carelessly on the
    side of the road. A cloud covering the moon for a moment. The
    native shouldn't have been there anyway.[54]

The decision relies on a deliberate distortion of facts in which it is the
"native" (not a named "native"; "natives" are infinitely substitutable) who
is "careless," and the moon is covered by a cloud "for a moment" despite
the clear descriptions of the light in the area, both from the moon and the
car, and Rawiri's own clear view of Bernard before and after the "collision."
Later, Rawiri confirms that that moment signaled Jeff's inextricability from
the colonial structure ("I don't blame you. . . . You can't help being who you
are"[55]), and he admits his own "sadness that a friend I thought I had would
so automatically react to the assumptions of his culture."[56]
    It is important, for the sake of the claims I am making in this chapter,
that Rawiri's reason for getting out of the car is twofold:

    "Let me out," I hissed. "Let me *out*. That's no native out there.
    That's *Bernard*." A cous is a cous.[57]

First, he does not see a "native" but instead his friend Bernard, and the
tragedy that the specific man they have struck is his friend who had been

highly educated in the Western system is not lost on Rawiri, who ponders later,

> All I could think of was the waste of a young man who had come one thousand years to his death on a moonlit road, the manner in which the earth must be mourning for one of its hopes and its sons in the new world[.][58]

However, Rawiri asserts not just a *familiar* but a *familial* connection: "a cous was a cous," exactly the same words he used in Sydney to explain his connection to relatives in King's Cross. This familial claim articulates an Aotearoa-inclusive Pacific, privileging and mobilizing whakapapa relationships to recognize and subvert the context of colonialism. Having arrived in Papua New Guinea using the language of "tribalism" and viewing work on the plantation as "hard work" and "getting down to business," Rawiri becomes aware of the racist and violent hierarchies that underpin the situation there. He connects with the "iwi" in Papua New Guinea in a completely opposite way to that which sees them as "natives"—"a cous was a cous"—and this leads him to a realization that despite his own claim of difference on arrival (*"although* Jeff had told her I was a Maori") and despite the in-between status he had precariously occupied during his time there ("at least he's not a native"), his "[being] a Maori" makes him a "cous" indeed:

> *And would I be next?* There was nothing further to keep me here.[59]

Rawiri realizes that his connection with the "iwi" in Papua New Guinea makes him "a native" and therefore interchangeable with any other "native," and having made this connection with the Pacific, he heads home.

Kanohi ki te Kanohi: Hinewirangi

Hinewirangi's collection *Kanohi ki te Kanohi* was written in the 1980s and published in 1990, the 150th anniversary of the signing of the Treaty of Waitangi and fifteen years after the Land March and the establishment of the Waitangi Tribunal. A precocious collection, exploring the possibilities of articulating connection with other Indigenous peoples when most Aotearoa-based Māori writers were still writing exclusively about the Māori community in terms of connection with Pākehā, *Kanohi ki te Kanohi* is structurally divided into four parts: the Great Turtle, Hawai'i noa, Aotearoa, and Asia. Roughly covering four geographical areas, Hinewirangi explains the order of the four sections in her introductory comments:

> So many questions of when [sic] the Maori came from. It has always been my belief that we left Egypt, then to the Americas, on the islands of the Pacific and finally here to Aotearoa.[60]

Her section on the Pacific—"Hawaii noa"—contains eleven poems and moves through a series of points of connection. In her introduction, she explains her sense of connection with the people and place of Hawai'i:

> I first went to Hawaii, romantic and lonely, found the native Hawaiian people, and was soon lost to their struggle for one of their sacred islands.
>
> The feeling of having been to this island before was very strong. I recognized places, met with kuia who see her people in my colouring, in my body. The tikanga was so strikingly similar, and I knew that my geneologies led me here.[61]

Hinewirangi's language shifts while she describes her time in Hawai'i, from a borrowed outsider perspective near the beginning ("Hawaii, romantic and lonely") to an incorporation of Māori language ("kuia," "tikanga"[62]) and a focus on points of connection unique to Māori and Hawaiians near the end. The final sentence relies on the reader knowing the meaning of *tikanga*, which redistributes the power so the insider reader is privileged, and she finally suggests that her travel to Hawai'i is the result of a previously unrecognized genealogical imperative.

The structure of "Hawaii noa" echoes the structure of Hinewirangi's introductory comments about that section. The section opens with "Firekeeper," which describes an interaction with "native Hawaiian people." In the narrative of this poem, the poet describes a series of speakers whose conversations are not marked clearly in the text:

> Sky woman, you are sky woman.
> Yes I have waited so long
> for you to come
> I am from the island of Kaua'i

the firekeeper, the secrets
the healing fire, food fires
warmth fire, the secrets
but today
Sky woman
I have travelled
a long way to find you,
you, old you, belong to me
my genealogies.
His eyes shone sparkling . . .

At first frustrating to read because it relies on the distinctions between "I,"
"you," and "he," which do not enable one to distinguish the various voices
of the poem—is the "I" who has waited the same as the "I" from Kaua'i and
the "I" who has traveled?—it is productive to move beyond fixing the voices
to detect a single narrative. Perhaps the difficulty of distinguishing between
the various speakers echoes the idea of "genealogies" in which identifying
the boundaries between one individual and the next is less important than
recognizing continuities and matrices of connection. Near the end of the
poem, a gift is given: "his gift is mine / I know only an elder will / understand / his words on a modern tape." The speaker realizes that "only an
elder" will have the appropriate skills to comprehend the language (which
has been identified earlier: "he speaks / he is Hawaiian"), and it is possible
that it would take an "elder" to "understand" the conceptual complexity or
narrative contained in "his words" or, indeed, that a Māori "elder" would
have the linguistic proficiency to understand the Hawaiian language because
of the close links between Māori and Hawaiian, affirming the cultural and
linguistic links between Aotearoa and Hawai'i. To some degree, the claim
of situational illiteracy is ironized—or perhaps just differently contextualized—by the fact of the speaker's ability to capture the words even without
"understanding" (on "this modern tape"), by the poet's voice speaking in
the poem, and by the writing of the poem itself on the page.

Following "Firekeeper," a series of poems about "struggle for one of
their sacred islands" describes the poet's time on Kahoolawe, an island
rich in spiritual meaning and an important site for religious observations
that the U.S. Navy alienated and used for target and weapons practice from
1941 (after the events at Pearl Harbor) until the navy officially returned the

island to the state of Hawai'i in 2003 (despite the navy's promised cleanup being incomplete) as a result of Hawaiian insistence and activism, including constant Hawaiian pressure since 1976. Without exception, each of the poems in this series provides an opportunity to relate to Aotearoa. "Kaho o lawe," for example, describes excitement about going to the island and acknowledges that the speaker of the poem is in the company of people from many nations "come to protest," and yet the poem moves not to a reflection on similar protest in Aotearoa but to a sense of being "home." The next part of the poem echoes Patuawa-Nathan's "Omamari," recounting how the poet came to be from Aotearoa in the first place:

> my oldness remembers
> this journey
> waka, canoes
> races
> ancestors lost in the storm
> am I home
> did I not just leave
> Uenuku
> drove us from these islands
> Takitimu
> Kupe
> Toi
> Whatonga
> Maru iwi
> I have been here
> Maui

Moving back ("my oldness remembers") through an atavistic memory of an ocean journey ("waka, canoes / race / ancestors lost in the storm"), the poet names specific histories (as alluded to by "Uenuku") and specific navigators ("Kupe / Toi / Whatonga") until she arrives at the name that has the unique ability to fix her in place and no-place, time and no-time: "Maui."

In Hawai'i, of course, there is a unique slippage between the name of an island (Māui) and the name of an originary ancestor (Māui). The poet describes the specific time and place of her present visit to Hawai'i ("I have been here / Maui") and yet also uses this utterance of Māui's name to reflect on Māui the pan-Polynesian ancestor and fisher of islands. Later in the poem, this pun on Māui (Māui as person, Māui as island) is mobilized more explicitly:

> reaching the shore
> when the sun begins its journey
> facing Maui
> Hale a ka la
> Mountain
> house of the rising sun
> I saw Maui
> climbing the mountain
> with nets
> to stop the sun
> from revolving fast

The repetition of "Maui" draws an important connection with Hawai'i on the basis of similarity (sharing Māui) and at the same time acknowledges the unique relationship Hawai'i has with Māui (the sun that Māui famously slowed down rose from Hale a ka lā on the island of Māui). While the second "Maui" here ("I saw Maui / climbing the mountain" clearly refers to the ancestor, the previous Maui could refer to the man or the mountain. Hawai'i thereby provides the poet with an opportunity to "[see] Maui": to acknowledge the place on its own terms as distinct from Aotearoa (the island named Māui) and to see the connection between the two places on the basis of shared—in Hinewirangi's own introductory words—"tikanga" and "genealogies." The poem ends with an articulation of connection to Hawai'i: "I knew this was the / place / where the stories of old / happened / yes, I belong here too." Significantly, the space for an Aotearoa-inclusive Pacific that has been opened up through kanohi ki te kanohi connection with Hawai'i enables the poet to include Rarotonga as well. The remainder of the section oscillates between Hawai'i, Aotearoa, and Rarotonga, teasing out points of familial (shared "genealogies" and culture) and also familiar (colonial experience) connections.

Aotearoa-Based Māori Writers

Like the narrators in their texts, Ihimaera and Hinewirangi write from an experience of being mobile, and through their creative work, these writers provide an opportunity for their readers to experience the realm of tapa too. Ihimaera and Hinewirangi—and Dunsford, Taylor, and Tuwhare—have traveled around the Pacific; their creative work stems from their direct experience in the region, suggesting that Aotearoa-based Māori writing about the Pacific region depends on physical mobility and lived relationship. Indeed, the difference in mobility of the writers in this chapter and those in the previous chapter may be one of degree rather than of kind. Maybe the realm of tapa is most available—or perhaps most visible—to those who travel around it. But does this mean that Aotearoa-rooted Māori writers have limited capacity to imagine connections with and around the Pacific? (If connecting with the Pacific region depends on mobility around that region, the realm of tapa is going to be shaped by class and physical ability as much as by any cultural or political impulse.)

These texts, and the others named early in the chapter, represent and produce a reciprocal relationship between engaging more deeply with the Pacific and engaging more deeply with what it is to be Māori. While each text articulates specific moments of recognition in which Māori respond to aspects of the Pacific which they perceive to have cultural, experiential, familial, physical, or philosophical similarities, they take the opportunity to reflect on the ways in which connecting with the Pacific brings about new perspectives on Aotearoa. In "Kaho o lawe," Hinewirangi acknowledges her position as a Māori person in the Pacific (specifically in Hawai'i) on the basis of shared political aspirations, then recollects earlier connections that ultimately suggest the possibility of relationship on the basis of simultaneous continuity and discontinuity–similarity and specificity—and finally ends up in the position to speak. In *The Whale Rider*, the explicit racism of Jeff's family and identification with the Indigenous people in Papua New Guinea prompts Rawiri to reorient his own allegiances and identifications away from his friendship with a white Australian and toward a renewed sense of his own location within the Pacific and also within the enduring colonial system. As in the previous chapter, however, Pacific identification does not dilute Māori identification, and his connection with other "natives" and anticolonial orientation eventually catalyze Rawiri's physical return home to Whāngārā. Significantly, unlike most of the texts treated in this book, Rawiri's travel to Melanesian Papua New Guinea in *The Whale Rider* moves beyond Māori connections with Polynesia on the basis of linguistic and genealogical links and affirms the possibility of Māori connection with the whole Pacific.

Very few new Māori poets have come into publication over the past ten years, but one writer who has made a great contribution is poet–songwriter–singer Hinemoana Baker. Baker's second collection, *Koiwi Koiwi,* includes the poem "what the destination has to offer," which is about, among other things, the migratory pattern of eels. Although the eels are at home in the Horowhenua, where Baker has tribal connections, their life cycle involves a massive trip to Sāmoa and back to the same river. The migratory cycle of eels suggestively shadows the process by which these Aotearoa-based Māori writers articulate their connection with the Pacific—the question of which end of the trip is "home" and which is "away" depends on the place from which you're looking:

> Salt, fresh, salt, he says.
> The opposite of salmon.[63]

The Realm of Tapa

CHANTAL SPITZ'S *L'Ile Des Reves Ecrases* was the first novel published by an Indigenous writer from Polynesie Francais (French Polynesia), and sixteen years later, in 2007, the Māori publishing company Huia launched Jean Anderson's translation of the novel as *Island of Shattered Dreams*.[1] Of the several characters in the novel, Tetiare is the most creative and least easily shaped by the colonial institutions of schooling, militarism, and patriotism. She drifts for some time before going overseas, and the narrative of her return to Tahiti is worth quoting at length:

> Tetiare has finally come home, after years of wandering round the Pacific, in a vain attempt to heal the wound in her soul. She has met the cousins who came with them long ago in their big canoes, born of the same dream of freedom, but who stopped where the wind had blown them on tiny hopeful islands, over the centuries forgetting the ones who journeyed further. She has found them again, so similar in body and soul, yet made different by the various foreign governments that have been squatting on their land. She has discovered them, peoples of the first people, attempting through little disorganised movements to shake off the Foreigner and immerse themselves again in their origins, to be themselves, the lost children of this huge family in search of one another.[2]

Tetiare "wander[s] round the Pacific" to grapple with violence and loss; individually, she is "attempt[ing] to heal the wound in her soul," and yet her travels fit into broader contexts of movement in the region, including the historical migrations ("long ago in their big canoes," stopping on "tiny hopeful islands") as well as more recent attempts to reconnect.

Indeed, Tetiare meets many "cousins" who are themselves engaged in reciprocal projects of reconnection. Given the "forgetting" that has occurred "over the centuries" in the various specific locations of the Pacific, however, how does one remember someone whom one has already forgotten? For Tetiare, recognition is multilayered: there are shared physical and cultural characteristics ("so similar in body and soul"), shared political positions ("peoples of the first people"), shared political predicaments ("attempting . . . to shake off the Foreigner"), and shared kaupapa[3] and aspirations ("to be themselves," "in search of one another"). Importantly, while the "cousins" may all be "members of this huge family," they are deeply inflected by their various and specific experiences of colonialism: "made different by the various foreign governments that have been squatting on their land." Perhaps one of the more difficult dimensions of articulating a regional consciousness is that privileging a genealogical or migratory basis for regionalism can risk either demanding refusal of real difference or paying attention to difference to the extent that it obstructs meaningful (or indeed any) engagement.

If we once were Pacific, then as well as seeing Tongans in Tonga and Niueans in Niue, one might look at Aotearoa New Zealand and see Māori, look at Guam and see Chamorros, and look at Hawai'i and see Hawaiians, reversing the Western gaze that sees these places in terms of their occupying nation-states. Certainly Māori need not be included in every single Pacific thing; Pacific places other than Aotearoa and Hawai'i (and perhaps Guam) have similarities and shared issues that pertain only to them and their social, political, cultural, ecological, and environmental conditions. Conversely, Niue, Tonga, Sāmoa, Vanuatu, the Solomon Islands, and Tokelau have things in common that they don't share with Aotearoa. Many Pacific people go to New Zealand (or Hawai'i, or perhaps Guam) because it is a first world metropole, and from this perspective, Auckland is more similar to Los Angeles than it is to Nuku'alofa. Aside from Aotearoa's physical location farther south than any other Pacific people, Māori have been "made different by the . . . foreign government[ ] that ha[s] been squatting on their land." And yet how do we account for the idea that when people move to Auckland (or Aukilani or Okalani[4]), they also move to Tamaki-makau-rau?[5] The remedy is to be vigilant: to explicitly clarify whether and how particular groups are included in each configuration of the Pacific.

Perhaps the main way in which Māori currently practice Pacific regionalism is by connecting with Hawai'i. We need to note, for example, that in this part of Once Were Pacific, Māori identifications and networks with Hawaiians predominate; consider that Te Rangihiroa, the Polynesian Cultural Centre,

Wineera, Sullivan, and Hinewirangi all write from or about Hawai'i. Writing reciprocally from a Hawaiian perspective, Ty Kāwika Tengan confirms a history of Māori and Hawaiians gravitating toward each other:

> [Hawaiian and Māori] histories are similar to each other but different from the colonial projects carried out in other parts of Oceania, where cultural imperialism seems to have been far less complete and oppressive. Since the 1980s, Hawaiian and Māori groups have actively engaged one another and other peoples involved in the transnational indigenous movement. Common experiences of marginalization in English-speaking settler societies have helped them reconnect through their shared Polynesian genealogies to exchange strategies of cultural revitalization and self-determination in ways they have not pursued with other Pacific Islanders.[6]

Tengan's explanation is, of course, a logical and productive account of the present situation. Certainly it would be *un*-productive to expect Māori and Hawaiians to ignore their "similar" realities, and the relationships between Tangata Māori and Kanaka Maoli have been, and continue to be, dynamic and effective. Yet it can feel almost ironic that when Māori and Hawaiians, who are at the farthest points of the Polynesian triangle—as far apart as it is possible to be in the Pacific—articulate the basis of our mutual connection, we mobilize genealogical and cultural connections that, presumably, are shared just as much, if not more so, with the "other Pacific Islanders" over whose heads we fly when traveling between Auckland and Honolulu to connect with our relatives.

Spitz plainly states that the "cousins" have been "made different by the various foreign governments that have been squatting on their land," and when we refuse to recognize this difference or discuss how we ourselves might be shaped by it, we risk undermining our own attempts to articulate a Pacific region. Although Spitz does not romanticize the connections between the "cousins" by ignoring the deep impacts of colonialism, she also does not allow that the "cousins" have been "made different" beyond recognition and does not allow that some have been "made different" (or made *more* different), while others have not. Simply acknowledging the source of these differences is not the end point, though, and once Tetiare returns to Tahiti, she starts to write about specific and regional histories as a way of imagining alternative possible narratives for her people. Ultimately, the "cousins" are framed by another, deeper discourse: despite, and yet not apart from, these differences, they remain members of "this huge family in search of one another." This combination of genealogical and experiential connections is central to the realm of tapa and will echo also throughout the realm of koura.

Manu Aute: Māori Diasporas

One of the major interventions staged by this focus on the realm of tapa is the treatment of writing from Māori outside Aotearoa. These writers and texts are included in the present discussion because they articulate connection with the Pacific, but there is scope for much wider and thorough treatment of Māori diasporas beyond this project.[7] None of the writers of *Mahanga, Opening Doors,* or *The Whale Rider*—foundational texts for imagining an Aotearoa-inclusive Pacific—was resident in New Zealand at the time of writing. Neither Vernice Wineera nor Evelyn Patuawa-Nathan has been included in dominant discussions of Māori writing in English, and both have also been left out of almost all discussions and collections of Pacific writing; their impressive offerings, *Mahanga* and *Opening Doors,* are themselves a pair of books behind closed doors.[8] *The Whale Rider,* though published in New Zealand, was written while Ihimaera lived in New York as a diplomat. (This is why this book is not treated in the chapter on Pacific-based Māori writers.) Immediately under the closing words "Hui e, haumi e, taiki e" of the New Zealand edition of *The Whale Rider,* the authorial endnote reads, "New York, 14 August, 1986." Indeed, in the introduction to their 1988 *Penguin Book of Contemporary New Zealand Short Stories,* Davis and Haley cite Ihimaera as occupying an important border zone of New Zealand literature because although his commitment and literary focus were, and are, very firmly New Zealand, he was living in the United States at the time of the anthology's publication.[9]

In *The Whale Rider,* Rawiri's first stop on his trip overseas is Sydney, Australia, where he is—like, perhaps, some readers of the novella—surprised to find so many Māori away from Aotearoa:[10]

Wherever you went, the pubs, the shows, the clubs, the restaurants, the movies, the theatres, you could always count on bumping into a cousin. In some hotels, above the noise and buzz of the patrons, you were bound to hear somebody shouting to somebody else, "Kia Ora, cous!"[11]

For Rawiri, Sydney is peopled by relatives.[12] I have already suggested that Rawiri's trip to Australia to (re)establish ties with the non-Aotearoa-based Māori is an essential step before moving on to Papua New Guinea and recognizing the links between Māori and other Pacific people through whakapapa and historical relationships. The politically crucial focus on fixed Indigeneity in the treaty-defined context of Aotearoa New Zealand can obscure the mobility that Rawiri observes and, indeed, that Ihimaera manifests in the final endnote to the New Zealand edition of the novella. Once our focus on the Pacific enables us to notice the place of Māori writers based outside Aotearoa, we can take another step and extend our view to all Māori writing from outside New Zealand, such as Jean Riki's story "Te Wa Kainga: Home," included in the Australian collection *Waiting in Space*, and U.S.–U.K.-based Paula Morris's writing, some of which is published in New Zealand and some elsewhere.[13]

Significantly, taking for granted that Māori writing in English includes a diasporic dimension enables us to notice different texts and to read the same texts differently, but it also points to the nonsense of the idea that Māori literature is merely a subset of New Zealand literature. Craig Womack has famously argued that the relationship between American Indian literatures and American literature is wrongly inverted by those who believe American literature to be the trunk of the tree and American Indian literature but one of its branches;[14] similarly, I would argue that though Māori writing has a relationship with New Zealand, this is only part of its scope. In the realm of tapa, then, Māori—including Wineera and Patuawa-Nathan, but also Te Rangihiroa, Barney Christie, Sullivan, Ihimaera, and Hinewirangi—literally, imaginatively, politically, and critically *exceed* the borders of occupying nation-states.

How can we imagine a form of Indigenous diaspora that neither limits the claims Māori can make about connection to specific place nor limits the capacity of Māori to be understood as mobile? One potential metaphor to help us think through the complexity of Māori diasporas is the manu aute, the distinctive kite that echoes the design of kites made all around Polynesia and that uses tapa in its covering, bearing testimony to the circulation of physical and agricultural knowledges around the Pacific. The "aute" in "manu aute"—literally, "birds made of aute"—is decorative and mnemonic, sure, but it is used because of its durability, physical lightness, and strength. The aute itself is a rich metaphor for diaspora because, like the aute, culture and social structures need to be flexible to be taken over vast distances, and when replanted in the new soil, they provide the ability to adapt to a new landscape and also to remember previous homes. Furthermore, the difference between a kite and any object that just flies away with the wind is the string that is held at the ground, a string that works best when it is taut. Diasporas are communities that retain a link—even if only an emotional link—with home but do not imagine returning there permanently. When thinking about Māori diasporas as manu aute, we have the opportunity to ask, of what material is the string made? Who holds the string? What winds take kites away in the first place? What perspective or resources does a kite contribute to the at-home community? What happens if the holder of the kite lets go?

A Realm of Tapa

For Tetiare in Spitz's *Island of Shattered Dreams,* the experience of "wandering round the Pacific" ultimately fuels a regional–political consciousness and a creative sensibility. On her return, she finally settles into her position as a writer. Perhaps it is not a coincidence that the highly mobile Tetiare—the one who left Tahiti and who didn't gravitate toward the usual outside destination of metropolitan France—becomes the writer. Perhaps writers ultimately bear the pleasure and responsibility of "healing the wound" not only in their own "soul" but in all of ours, and perhaps writers seek "healing" beyond the usual spheres of connection and identification on behalf of all of us. The "wound" Tetiare seeks to "heal" is intimately tied to memory. The "cousins [of the] big canoes" have been separated over time and space, and this separation is tied closely to forgetting and recollection. Just like the two layers of migration, there are two layers of forgetting: historical amnesias about "the ones who journeyed further" but also more contemporary disconnection from cultural memory that is implied by the resistance to the "Foreigner" that involves "immers[ing] themselves in their origins." Because the historical migrations and contemporary movements across the Pacific region are paired in this way, we might explore the relationship between the original reason for migration—"the same dream of freedom"—and the motivation behind the mobility in Tetiare's time. Despite the "cousins" being deeply inflected by the colonial process, they are ultimately compelled by the same desires. The "forgetting" that took place earlier—the "forgetting" of a regional perspective—was incomplete because otherwise, the deep familial pull ("this huge family in search of one another") would surely be less strong. Indeed, the ability of the "peoples of the first people" to "shake off the Foreigner" in any one context is linked to a deeper compulsion to "be themselves" by reconnecting to their immediately previous configurations and to "their origins" in terms of "long ago" regional migrations and genealogical networks. Re-remembering "the same dream of freedom" is crucial to the contemporary project of decolonization but also, more specifically, to the project of writing in which Tetiare and so many other writers from Te Moananui a Kiwa—the realm of tapa—are passionately engaged.

This is the realm of tapa. Like the aute plant in Aotearoa, this realm is marked by impressive historical continuations and significant recent amnesias. The reasons for the aute plant becoming extinct are remembered differently by different people. Although Te Rangihiroa, citing Colenso, blames European farming for the demise of the remnant aute plants, some commentators prefer a narrative in which Māori deliberately discarded the aute once European fabrics of cotton and linen started to arrive, speculating that there was no longer a need for the difficult work of maintaining a tropical plant in Aotearoa's climate.[15] It feels logical to argue that Māori simply let the aute die out once they could make clothing from European fabrics, until we recall that this was not what aute was used for in the first place. The aute plant never grew big or plentifully enough in Aotearoa to make sheets of cloth; it was used for decorative, small, and—in the case of manu aute—specific items for which cotton and linen would not have been a useful substitute anyway. The narrative feels comfortable for those who take European superiority for granted, but it fails to notice the complexity of Māori material culture on the ground and to imagine that there might be aspects of Māori culture for which Europeans have no equivalent. Most likely, it was a combination of factors that led to the demise of the aute. Neither strictly cattle nor solely cotton but a combination of these, and more besides. Ultimately, what matters is that tapa was produced in Aotearoa to remind us of who we were and the wider Pacific context from which we came, and it still has the capacity to do that for us today.

· II ·

Koura: The Pacific in Aotearoa

We've got a lot in common. . . . You have a malae, I have a marae. You say *malamalama,* I say *maramatanga.*

Apirana Taylor, "Pa Mai," *He Reo Aroha*

TE PAPA, New Zealand's national museum, opened its new exhibition Tangata o le Moana: The Story of the Pacific People in New Zealand in October 2007. Such a major permanent exhibition requires compelling, clear, and "Pacific" branding, and a photograph titled "Double Afro" taken by Glenn Jowitt outside Hillary College in Ōtara during the Māori and Pacific secondary schools dance festival in 1981 seemed to lend itself to the task. A young Polynesian man, with an afro and early-eighties-era clothes, looks straight at the camera with a shy smile and wears a sweatshirt that reads "London Paris New York Rome Otara." The meanings of the photograph are densely layered. In general terms, it is a rare example of a positive and seemingly candid representation of a young Polynesian man. More specifically, the sweatshirt subversively juxtaposes the very local place name "Otara" with major northern hemisphere urban centers, humorously suggesting that despite its apparently peripheral and invisible location from the point of view of the usual centers, New Zealand—and specifically Ōtara—might be a center for some. Another layer is that for a knowing New Zealand audience, Ōtara is not just any local suburb mischievously masquerading as a metropolitan space but a very specific low-income neighborhood marked in mainstream popular discourse by a particular chain of signifiers: large Māori and Pasifika communities, government housing, factory and other manual labor, poverty, crime, gangs, violence, dysfunction. A further layer is that Ōtara derives its name from Tara, who is memorialized in the names of several other features of the landscape around the area. Like the name of the young man wearing the sweatshirt in the photo, Ōtara is simultaneously knowable, known, and unknown.

In a September 2007 newspaper item, communications manager Jane Keig enthused, "It will be really lovely to find out who he is—he's the star of our exhibition."[1] On the strength of their excitement, Te Papa sought information about the man depicted in the photo, and after the *Manukau Courier* (the free local newspaper distributed in the broader area that includes Ōtara) ran a piece about the search, Te Papa was put in touch with Daniel Maaka. Born and raised in Ōtara and now working as a telephone counselor, Maaka was as enthusiastic as Te Papa about the use of the image: not for his own sake but for that of his beloved Ōtara. The *Manukau Courier* coverage of Maaka's serendipitous identification reports that he was pleased that it "gives a positive outlook on [his] home town." Maaka continues, "I'll always be proud of where I'm from. I want people to see good things come out of this place,"[2] extending the Ōtara-centric claim of the sweatshirt he wore back in 1981; he is still invested in challenging and countering the negative press Ōtara usually receives. One might imagine that Daniel Maaka would reinforce the spirit of the exhibition Tangata o le Moana. Indeed, Keig responded to the revelation that Maaka had been located by saying that Te Papa was "really looking forward to meeting him. . . . It'll be great to put a face to the name and hopefully have him join in our celebrations."[3] The plot thickened, however, because on tracking down the real Daniel Maaka, they found that, as TV3 put it (and as some might guess was a possibility from his last name), "the face of the Pacific is actually Maori."[4]

Immediately there was a problem. A Pacific exhibition in New Zealand could not be advertised by an image of a young Māori man. Whereas the Polynesian Cultural Centre in Hawai'i regularly uses the image of an identifiably Māori man as a symbol of the Pacific region, Te Papa apparently cannot.[5] Cherokee writer Thomas King describes some people responding to his appearance and activities by claiming he's "not the Indian [they] had in mind," and perhaps in this case, Maaka was not the "Tangata" Te Papa had in mind. Maaka is not the right kind of Pacific person either because Māori people aren't Pacific people or because, in New Zealand at least, Māori people aren't Pacific people in the same way that non-Māori Pacific people are Pacific people. A spokesperson for Te Papa, Paul Brewer, attempted to clarify the situation:

> No one here is disputing the fact that Maori are not [*sic*] Pacific Island in origin but clearly the exhibition is about more contemporary arrivals (and) having a Maori as a hero image is probably not as appropriate as having someone who is Pacific Island.[6]

Putting aside questions of why a marketing campaign for a museum is busy-ing itself with the task of providing "hero images" and how such a "hero image" might relate to "actual" representation, Brewer's comments point to the problem of timing. While Māori are certainly Tangata o le Moana (people of the ocean) historically ("in origin"), the focus of the exhibition is on recent ("more contemporary") migration. At a spatial level, Māori may fit the migration history from tropical Pacific islands farther north that is signaled by the exhibition ("o le moana"), but they do not satisfy a chronological requirement. This difference in chronology is both represented and slipped over by the distinction Brewer makes between "Pacific Island in origin" (i.e., Māori) and "someone who is Pacific Island"[7] (i.e., someone from the Pacific who is not Māori). Despite the name of the exhibition, the difference isn't one of people (tangata) or place (moana) but history: Māori are indeed "tangata o le moana," but not within the historical scope of the New Zealand nation-state and its activities.

None of this would have mattered if Maaka had not been located. Indeed, Daniel Maaka was more use to Te Papa when he was unknown, when his Māori body was able to stand in for the Pacific just as the Māori name of his home suburb did. It might seem strange that the fact of being Māori overrides any other readings of his Polynesian body. He is still the same man as the one depicted in the photo: in 1981, he was young, Polynesian, Ōtara-centric, with an afro, in a specific urban space. More broadly, the joke on his sweatshirt is still funny, and the photo still suggests the complex relationships between modernity, capital, race, gender, migration, place, and colonialism. And yet once the real Maaka was outed, his body could no longer be productively illegible: his Polynesian body was forever and irrevocably marked by the more specific detail of his being Māori. The problem for Te Papa wasn't putting, as Keig had put it in her media statement, "a face to the name." The problem was putting a name to the face.

Intriguingly, although Te Papa decided that using a Māori body to advertise a Pacific exhibition was too problematic, the concept of Jowitt's image was not scrapped in favor of another representation of Tangata o le Moana. Instead, Te Papa decided to reproduce the photo with a newly illegible (but guaranteed properly "Pacific Island") body: a young Pacific man around the same age as Maaka had been in 1981 and who also wears an afro, wears a replica sweatshirt, and poses for a 2007 version of the image. The new photo does not update the previous image: alongside the blatantly reproduced sweatshirt, details such as the light blue shirt poking over the edge of the collar and an identical pose suggest this is a case of deliberate mimicry. It is worth noting that Te Papa is in Wellington and Ōtara in Auckland. Whereas the sweatshirt in the spontaneous 1981 photograph is Ōtara based and worn by a young man from Ōtara, Te Papa (and, presumably, the reprinting of the sweatshirt and posing of the new photo) is in Wellington. Where a familiar visual image is copied (the *Mona Lisa* or a Gauguin painting, for example), the prominence of the original means that the reproduction is clearly marked, and so meanings can be derived from the simultaneous similitude and difference between the original and the reproduction. In this case, however, the new image reproduces a largely unknown visual image that is sidestepped because the specificities of a particular back story—the whakapapa of Daniel Maaka—threaten to contaminate the representation of a true Pacific, even if that back story remains virtually unknown. At what point, we might feel compelled to ask, does this kind of mimicry become forgery: forgery undertaken not in the name of deceit but in the name of so-called truth? Although Maaka cannot be "Pacific Island" because of the truth that has been uncovered, the exhibition's "hero image" is not simply an image of another (and Te Papa approved) truth but is instead a simulacrum: a copy of a Pacific moment that never existed.

The press coverage of the story about a single photo staged by Te Papa in emulation of an earlier photo snapped at an event in the 1980s prompts a series of questions. What is the effect on the branding of a Pacific exhibition when the real person in the original photo is Māori? Would Pacific Island communities mind the man in the photo being Māori? Would Māori communities mind the man in the photo being Māori? If an exhibition about the people of the Pacific was staged elsewhere in the Pacific, could Māori stand in for Pacific, and if so, then why is it different when the question is asked in New Zealand? Ultimately, when in New Zealand, are Māori people Pacific? Part I of this book treated an Aotearoa-inclusive Pacific in which Aotearoa is part of a geographic region and Māori are part of ancestral and ongoing stories of cross-oceanic navigation. Here in part II, we focus on the national context, the here and now—certainly the here, and for the reasons of temporality mentioned earlier, also the now.

Part II is the realm of the koura: the Aotearoa-based Pacific, the Pacific that is found within the borders of Aotearoa. In exchange for tapa, the Māori man in Tupaia's painting extends a koura. A photograph used in Te Papa exhibition publicity materials may be explained away as an isolated incident with very few potential effects on the way real life plays out in Aotearoa New Zealand or the broader Pacific. This incident may be representative of very few similar moments (it may stand in only for itself), or it may be one of many such examples. My interest in the photo used for the Te Papa exhibition Tangata o le Moana is not to decide whether the right decision was made but to ask *how* and *why* Te Papa might have felt compelled to make a decision at all. Although the Te Papa photo might be a coincidental constellation of specific people and factors on one level, on another level, it foregrounds a range of cultural and social categories and so, in turn, draws our attention to the intersection of a number of strands: representational, historical, political, national. Te Papa is "Our Place," the national museum of New Zealand, after all, and this emphasizes the national context within which Māori articulate a connection with the Pacific.

Part II focuses on the koura in the outstretched hand of the Māori figure in Tupaia's painting. In the realm of koura, things are local and specific: discourse, trade items, Māori. In the realm of tapa, though, Māori are part of a larger Pacific region; here Māori have a special position, and other Pacific communities relate to Māori on these terms. Although the regional Pacific might provide the metaphor of tapa, this perspective is balanced by a focus on the space within which Māori are tangata whenua. In popular usage, the phrase *tangata whenua* is often literally translated as "the people of the land" to suggest a singular meaning of the phrase that is contemporarily and popularly translated as Indigenous. In New Zealand, and to the nation-state, Māori certainly are Indigenous, and this translation can indeed provide the English speaker access to a useful dimension of the phrase. Another meaning, however, that is not completely separable from but also not overtly suggested by the idea of Indigeneity is the dimension of hospitality. Māori are tangata whenua, hosts, in Aotearoa, and one natural extension of this is that everyone else is manuhiri, guests. Part II, then, explores the relationship between tangata whenua and manuhiri, host Pacific people and guest Pacific people, Māori and Pasifika.

As the frame changes from region to nation, so does the language. In the context of New Zealand, a new entity emerges: Pasifika, those communities who are not Indigenous to the North or South islands of New Zealand but for whom New Zealand is now (a) home. The legal and political (and perhaps affective) basis of most Pasifika migration to New Zealand—and Pasifika migration has been happening for generations—is through relationship with the settler nation-state. For non-Māori Pacific people, New Zealand is the entity that grants visas and checks passports at the door.[8] In theory, at least, Pasifika communities are legally guests, and then citizens, of New Zealand (rather than Aotearoa) and so are either compelled by—or at least complicit with—the attitudes to the position of tāngata whenua that serve the needs of that settler nation-state. Importantly, though, Māori and Pasifika communities have at least two avenues by which connection can be both articulated and practiced: one is the legacy of connection treated in part I of this book, including the cultural, linguistic, and whakapapa links that preexist the arrival of Europeans to the region, and the other is the shared experience and often physical proximity of Māori and Pasifika communities, which often come about as a result of both communities suffering at the hands of the racist colonial settler nation-state. This twinning of shared cultural backgrounds and shared social predicaments appears over and over in articulations of the connections between Māori and Pasifika communities in Aotearoa New Zealand.

Certainly the historical precedents for Pasifika connections with Māori communities in Aotearoa are numerous and deserve their own historical treatment. Just as Pacific people arrived in Aotearoa and became Māori over a period of time here, so, too, Pasifika is a localized and accumulated identity. In this book, *Pasifika* is used as a term that transliterates *Pacific* to uniquely express a diverse and dynamic experience that is additional to, rather than a replacement for, home island identification. When used carefully, *Pasifika* is not simply a homogenizing umbrella term under which particular Pacific identifications and preoccupations huddle but is a particular constellation: migrant, with connection to New Zealand; diasporic; manuhiri, guests. Importantly, although the representation of Pasifika communities by mainstream media has tended to be narrowing and stereotypical, there is a vast array of diversity within the Pasifika community, dependent on originary home, present location, and various cultural and historical specificities. Although it is helpful to attribute the presence of large Pasifika communities in New Zealand at present to the labor migrations of the 1950s, 1960s, and 1970s (and perhaps the more recent short-term worker visas targeted at Pacific migrant labor will produce a further iteration), small numbers of Pacific people migrated to New Zealand before this period, especially for military and educational reasons.

One of the early and recently re-remembered episodes in the history of Māori–Pasifika connections is the inclusion of Pasifika soldiers in the celebrated Twenty-eighth Māori Battalion in World War II. Louise Mataia, whose master of arts thesis is titled "Odd Men from the Pacific,"[9] has been at the forefront of this research, and Te Papa's Tangata o le Moana exhibition includes a display of all Pacific soldiers who participated in New Zealand's armed forces, including with the battalion. Indeed, the Pacific men were usually placed in D Company, which is the company in which my own relatives (including my grandfather and great-uncle) were located. Alistair Te Ariki Campbell's brother Stuart enlisted with the battalion and was killed overseas; I consider Campbell's poetry about the battalion in chapter 4.[10] In some ways, this part of the discussion belongs in the first part of this book, which retains a regional focus, because most of the Pacific men were not resident in New Zealand at the time. However, the men enlisted in New Zealand's national armed forces, and so the story belongs here; otherwise, we risk failing to recall that Sāmoa, Niue, Tokelau, and the Cook Islands were part of New Zealand's territory at the time, and so from the point of view of the men (and, to some extent, the military), they were in the national space at the same time. Elaborating Pacific connections in the military did not stop after World War II; many such interactions, between Māori and Pasifika as well as between Māori and Pacific people, have taken place in New Zealand's armed forces since then.[11]

Boarding school is another site in which Pacific and Māori connections were historically established in New Zealand. Actually, the schools are not entirely disconnected from the military spaces mentioned earlier: several of the solders on whom Louise Mataia's research focuses had spent time studying at a Māori boarding school. The historic Māori boarding schools provided a particularly rich space for emergent Māori–Pasifika connections: boys from around the Pacific—Sāmoa and the Cooks but also the Solomon Islands—attended Te Aute. For example, in 1968, a Solomon Islands student at Te Aute, Gina Tekulu, contributed a piece of writing to the Māori magazine *Te Ao Hou*.[12] In *Vainetini Kuki Airani Cook Islands Women Pioneers: Early Experiences in Aotearoa New Zealand,* several of the women refer in their interviews to girls from the Cook Islands who attended the Roman Catholic Māori girls' school Hukarere. Mama Aere Cuthers's sister Tutai went on scholarship to Hukarere in 1925 and became close friends with the Reids, "a Maori family who lived in Taupo;"[13] ten years later, Mama Alice Ani Maka Beritane attended Hukarere before boarding with a Samoan family in Auckland. During World War II, Komera Trubovich recalls meeting her "Aunty Metu" and spending time with her and "Boy Tomoana's father and his wife":

Then they would invite us to come and visit them. From then on
they started to raise funds for the war effort. They asked me to help
them with fundraising and this meant dancing in front of people.[14]

In a slightly different school space, we might turn our attention to Māori and
Pacific students attending the Latter-day Saints boarding school, which was
known as Maori Agricultural College before it became Church College.[15] All
these Māori religious schools attended by Pacific students have contributed
to relationships between individuals, families, and communities. In his
novels *Ola* and *The Mango's Kiss,* Albert Wendt places Māori and Pacific
children side by side in boarding situations, echoing his own experience at
New Plymouth Boys and gesturing toward boarding schools as important
spaces in which friendships between Māori and Pacific children had the
potential to produce attitudes and sensitivities that would stay with people
through adulthood.

There are so many spaces in which Māori–Pasifika connections have been
established: workplaces, sports teams, activist organizations, educational
institutions. Mama Cuthers attributes the many people who worked as
farmhands in Porangahau "and other Hawke's Bay locations"[16] to the work
of Tuku Tukutamaki; Komera Trubovich got work with Sonny Edwards's
shearing gang, where a Cook Island woman was the head cook. (Members
of the shearing gang put in money so she could go on a trip to Rarotonga,
and Komera brought back fruit for the people who had contributed.) Mere
Tepaeru Tereora took seriously the links between Cook Island Māori and
New Zealand Māori destinies and joined the Māori Women's Welfare League,
was involved in the establishment of the immersion language early childhood education movement Te Kohanga Reo (and went on to be a major
feature of the Cook Island equivalent, Te Punanga o te Reo Kuki Airani o
Aotearoa), and was involved in the Aotearoa Moananui-a-Kiwa Weavers
group. In terms of sports, the whole area of Pasifika participation in Māori
sports teams is fascinating, as is the negotiation of Māori national teams
to play alongside Pacific teams in regional competitions for rugby league
and other sports.[17]

Part I focused solely on Māori writers, but here, in the spirit of connection
and reciprocity, we consider Pasifika texts alongside Māori texts. Part II
opens with chapter 4, "Māori–Pasifika Collaborations," which explores

specific moments in which Māori and Pasifika people have deliberately collaborated by mobilizing whakapapa connections and/or social predicaments to achieve specific ends. Following the treatment of explicitly collaborative work, chapter 5, "'It's Like That with Us Maoris': Māori Write Connections," considers Māori writers who represent connections between Māori and Pasifika communities in New Zealand, and chapter 6, "Manuhiri, Fānau: Pasifika Write Connections," pays attention to Pasifika treatments of the same. Finally, chapter 7, "When Romeo Met Tusi: Disconnections," foregrounds three texts that mobilize Shakespeare's *Romeo and Juliet* as a structuring mechanism for exploring the disconnections between Māori and Pasifika people and, in doing so, treats perhaps the most difficult aspect of this entire project. Disconnection between Māori and Pasifika communities is rarely treated in published texts, and given the plentiful anecdotal and lived evidence of these layers of disconnection, I wonder if this has more to do with who gets to publish their texts than with whether articulations of those connections are urgent or important. While a Pacific-region-focused analysis might expect the communities represented in these texts to connect on the basis of their shared common heritage of navigating through the Pacific by the stars, Māori–Pasifika couples in these texts produced and set in the nation-state are more likely to be presented as tragically star-crossed lovers.

Several articles in the publication *Te Ao Hou* report on the arrival of people from around the Pacific and their welcome not only to New Zealand by the state but also to Aotearoa by local Māori people. In 1967, for example, a group from Tokelau was taken to Maketū for a marae welcome and was also met along the way by students from a Māori boarding school and by various Māori community leaders and workers. At Maketū,

> both the Maoris and the Tokelauans presented musical items
> during the ceremony, and after the evening meal the visitors were
> entertained at a concert, again reciprocating with many of their
> own traditional items.[18]

The group was then taken to Rotoehu, where they were welcomed not only by the local iwi but also by Tokelauan and Fijian workers already resident in the area. The entangling of Tokelauan and Fijian histories in the context of Pacific histories in New Zealand deserves treatment, but that is not the only relationship that was being forged in those moments. During the evening in Maketū, the cultural performances that were exchanged echoed, albeit softly, the exchanges between Tupaia and the Māori people with whom he interacted two centuries earlier. Although these Māori–Pasifika connections were not universally experienced, and though dominant ways of recalling Pacific migration to New Zealand have been through a narrative of labor provision for the settler state, these moments of encounter and the relationships they produced are an important dimension of the realm of the koura.

CHAPTER 4

Māori–Pasifika Collaborations

THIS CHAPTER FOCUSES ON three specific collaborations in which a single text has been produced by a group made up of Māori and Pasifika people. Before focusing on more recent texts, it is worth considering a slightly earlier creative alliance. A single archived program for the Takapuna Free Kindergarten's 1943 fund-raiser provides a quite different view of Auckland-based Pacific performance than that presented by the Pasifika Festival (which is treated in the conclusion of part II) fifty years later. A wartime fund-raiser held at His Majesty's Theatre in December, the event is billed as a "South Sea Festival," and the first page of the program provides further detail:

> By various groups of Islanders now in Auckland, including Samoan, Tongans, Niue Islanders and Hawaiians, supervised by Mrs Eric Sharp; also members of the Ao-te-roa [sic] Maori Club and the Rotorua Concert and Entertainment Party.[1]

The event takes place in a very different New Zealand. In 1943, although there has been a great deal of Indigenous Pacific mobility,[2] the lineup of the Pacific does not yet reflect the range of communities who are yet to arrive and to become nationally visible. New Zealand's explicit colonial ties with Sāmoa and Niue are represented, as is the close connection with Tonga, but the inclusion of Hawai'i feels inexplicable. Perhaps there are Hawaiian members of the Auckland community by that time, and perhaps, too, we can take into account the huge rhetorical impact of Pearl Harbor and the Pacific War, which deeply affected New Zealand through the departure of local soldiers and the arrival of American armed forces. The link between the "Islanders" and Māori is, although implied by Māori inclusion in a "South Sea Island Festival," not clearly articulated. Indeed, the language of "Pacific" or "Polynesia" is completely absent from the program altogether. Instead, the organizing concept is "South Sea Island" and "Islanders"; individual performances and performers are assigned their more specific identifications.

The show is in two parts, and the position of the Māori performances does not demonstrate the acknowledgment of difference that has been suggested by the earlier distinction between "Islanders" and Māori performance groups. The use of the appropriate vernacular, rather than complete translation, to describe the various performances seems significant. Part I opens with a "Samoa Sila Sila (Welcome Song)" and "The Kava Ceremony," which is "descri[bed] by our Speaker, Mr C L McFarland," and these are followed by "Fa'a fia fia," which includes Samoan and Tongan dances as well as a hula. This is followed by "Fifteen Minutes with Members of the Ao-tea-roa Maori Club" and then another song and more hula. After the interval, a similar lineup continues, although it also includes a bracket titled "Moments of Mirth with Alan McElwain" and finishes with the farewell triplicate of the popular Māori, Samoan, and English songs "Haere Ra," "Tofa Mai Feleni," and "God Save the King."

Fund-raising is the major reason for the event, and advertisements are included in the program: Takapuna Beauty Salon, Clendon's Fruit Store, JL Yarnton, Stuart's Milk Bar, SH Crowe & Co General Store, and Strand Shoe Store. All these businesses are based in Takapuna. BOVO sandwich spread is also advertised, for which patrons are directed to their local grocer. Finally, alongside these other advertisements is one for a Grey Lynn business: "For Parties, Dances, etc, see Bertie Mann for his Melodious String Band." Bertie Mann is a performer in the show itself: "Daisy and Bertie Mann" perform a "Pese (Song)" in the first half, and Bertie is a soloist in the group who plays "Guitars, Ukuleles, etc" to accompany a "Siva" as well. Two other Manns also perform: Nola presents a hula (with Daisy), and Louisa performs a "Siva." That Bertie Mann (and "his Melodious String Band") advertises the availability of his group for performances at private functions is an additional layer of "South Sea Island" performance at the time. We can assume that for Mann, as well as for the Takapuna Free Kindergarten, Pacific performance had a strong economic imperative.

Exactly thirty years later in the same city, the demographics and culture of Auckland had shifted immensely, and a one-off newspaper called *Rongo* was published that responded to the political and social position of Māori and Pasifika communities at the time. The newspaper was coproduced in 1973 by two activist–educational organizations, Nga Tamatoa and the Polynesian Panthers, and the contributors came from a range of Māori and Pasifika backgrounds. Nesian Mystik is a hip-hop group based in Auckland with wide national recognition that produces chart-topping single tracks and has released three albums; the group is made up of Māori, Cook Islander, Samoan, and Tongan members, and in this chapter, I will focus on their track "Lost Visionz." Finally, Polynation is a performance poetry collaboration that has been featured at poetry festivals in west Auckland and Brisbane. Polynation, like Nesian Mystik, is predominantly Pasifika and includes Māori, Tongan, Samoan, and Fijian performers; this discussion will focus on the DVD *Polynation,* which records their performance at the Queensland Poetry Festival 2008. To some extent, these are all liminal texts: their circulation depends on particular kinds of distribution, they are produced by people who are not widely recognized as writers,[3] and the texts themselves are not widely recognized as literary. While *Rongo* is an explicitly activist text and treats very specific contexts and moments, and Nesian Mystik and Polynation produce explicitly creative texts, all the collaborations take for granted that creative and political–critical–cultural work belongs together, and indeed, each affirms that creative work can be critical and vice versa.

Although collaborative work can be immensely stimulating creatively and socially, Hau'ofa reminds us that it can be at the service of resistance and, ultimately, sovereignty when he describes the potential of alliances between Māori and Islanders in Aotearoa in his essay "Our Sea of Islands":

> Alliances are already being forged by an increasing number of Islanders with the *tangata whenua* (indigenous people) of Aotearoa and will inevitably be forged with the Native Hawaiians. It is not inconceivable that if Polynesians ever get together, their two largest homelands will be reclaimed in one form or another.[4]

This chapter turns its attention to specific instances of collaboration—of "alliances," of "get[ting] together." Each of these collaborations—*Rongo,* Nesian Mystik, Polynation, and perhaps even the South Sea Festival—relies on, articulates, and nurtures the alliances to which Hau'ofa refers.

Certainly this chapter is a mere starting point for sketching out the limits and shape of Māori–Pasifika alliances over time. To take just one example, after the police raids on a Māori settlement (and several individual houses around the country) on October 15, 2007, a number of Pasifika people contributed their creative work to accompany work by Māori (and Pākehā and African American) people in the multigenre compilation *Burn This CD*.[5] Responding to the same event, the musician Tigilau Ness, who was a contributor to *Rongo* in 1973 and who was also involved in supporting the Bastion Point occupation described by Reeder in "Lost Visionz," traveled to Rūātoki with his band Unity Pacific shortly after the events to provide support and entertainment for that community, which had suffered at the hands of the New Zealand police:

> Help and support poured in from around the country including an offer from two Auckland based bands [Unity Pacific and Three Houses Down] to play a free concert at Te Wharekura a Ruatoki. For Unity Pacific's Tigilau Ness, the raids rained upon Ruatoki are reminiscent of the dawn raids of the 1970's executed against the Pacifika community and a period that cemented his friendship with Tame Iti, as respective members of Maori and Pacific rights movements, Nga Tamatoa and Polynesian Panthers.[6]

Artistic alliances have also been far more plentiful than those named here. For example, Niue writer John Pule was among the lineup of writers at an event called "Maori Writers Read," organized by Roma Potiki in 1983. The event was a fund-raiser to support the Spiral Collective's printing of Keri Hulme's *the bone people,* a book that no publisher would touch and that remains the only New Zealand novel to date to have won the Man Booker literary prize.[7] This small moment, in which a Pasifika writer lends his talents to support a Māori writer by participating in a reading by other Māori writers, is a quiet but significant form of creative collaboration. Māori and Pasifika practitioners of musical, dance, visual, theatrical, and literary arts have worked together in multiple ways, and the dance company *Black Grace* headed by Neil Ieremia, the band Herbs, the Niue–Māori hip-hop practitioner Che Fu, and Ngapaki Emery's performance in Fijian playwright Nina Nawalowalo's *Vula* are further examples. More broadly, "getting together" also takes institutional forms such as the decision of Māori publishing company Huia to publish Pacific writers, the inclusion of Pacific programming on Māori TV (documentaries; feature films; the series *The Market,* discussed in chapter 7 of this book; the magazine-style show *Tagata Pasifika*[8]), the former Department of Māori and Island Affairs, ministers of Pacific Island Affairs who are ethnically Māori, Māori–Pasifika research and student support units at universities, and so on. As more scholars engage with Māori and Pasifika cultural production, and with Māori histories (beyond Māori–Māori and Māori–Pākehā histories), these fascinating and complex stories will surely be researched and written about as thoroughly as they deserve.

Rongo

In 1973 a newspaper called *Rongo* was collectively produced by a number of organizations, including Te Huinga Rangatahi o Aotearoa (the renamed New Zealand Federation of Maori Students), the Polynesian Panthers, Nga Tamatoa, and Nga Kuri a Wharei.[9] More specifically, the bibliographic detail at the beginning of the newspaper reads, "Rongo is produced by members of Te Huinga Rangatahi O Aotearoa and published by Brian McDonald, Ngahuia Volkerling, and John Miller."[10] The Polynesian Panthers was made up predominantly but not exclusively of people from Pasifika communities and drew its name and inspiration from the Black Panthers and other socially minded activist groups in the United States. Nga Tamatoa, a Māori organization that is often remembered by dominant discourses as a radical activist group of the 1970s, was deeply engaged in issues around the 1970s crisis of the Māori language.[11] To put the newspaper into an historical context for the Māori and Pasifika communities, *Rongo* came out just prior to the 1975 Hīkoi[12] and the Dawn Raids, which started in 1974. Despite its rather auspicious timing and production team, *Rongo* has not yet received scholarly treatment.[13] I found a copy of *Rongo* at the bottom of an uncataloged archive box of Witi Ihimaera's papers in the special collections of my home institution's library. The copy had been cut up (presumably, given the file in which it was found, so Ihimaera could keep track of the poetry for a later anthology), but a pristine version of the newspaper is held at the National Library. The catalog information at the National Library reads,

> Subject: Maori (New Zealand people)—periodicals
> Polynesians—New Zealand—periodicals
> Note: Title from cover "Rongo is produced by members of the Huinga Rangatahi o Aotearoa"—t.p. verso
> Language note: In English, Maori, Samoan, and Tongan.

This catalog description is bare and simple, and the limited details mean that researchers would be hard-pressed to recognize the nature of the document described. The topics treated in the twenty-four-page newspaper are wide ranging in theme and short ranging in time: the focus is very much the present, and where the past is recalled, it is for the purpose of explaining or contextualizing a present-day predicament. In its opening pages, *Rongo* goes to some length to acknowledge the various contexts and concepts from which it emerges, and it proceeds to treat the topics of culture and language, housing, the work of Nga Tamatoa and the Polynesian Panther Party, prisons (including practical advice about legal assistance available through Nga Tamatoa and prison visiting hours), parliamentary politics, racism, protest and activism, education, arts, and media. Alongside these articles are artworks, photographs, poems, and letters to the editor. Although it is tempting to conduct an article-by-article analysis of *Rongo*, this present discussion focuses on those aspects that pertain most clearly to the collaboration between Māori and Pasifika people both through structural and editorial choices and through the content of specific articles in the newspaper.

"Rongo" is the name of a Polynesian deity with responsibility for kūmara and also for peace. Kūmara is known to be a staple food for Māori, which suggests that the newspaper will be nourishing and central, but kūmara is also used in many areas as a metaphor for knowledge. Furthermore, because kūmara was acquired during early Polynesian exploratory travel to South America, the title *Rongo*, echoing human as well as vegetative distribution around the region, turns our attention to the relationship between migration and Indigeneity. In the first page of text in the newspaper, an explanation "He whakamarama mo te ingoa 'Rongo'" appears in Te Reo and emphasizes that this is an ideal name for the publication because Rongo is recognized in "nga moutere katoa o Te Moananui-a-Kiwa"[14] as a deity that explicitly foregrounds Polynesian unity, a theme to which the newspaper returns both in content and structure. Finally, although the whakamārama, or "explanation," does not explicitly reference this additional meaning, the title of *Rongo* is a pun that ties the cultural and political context to the function of the newspaper: *rongo* in Te Reo also means "to hear," "fame," "hearing," "information," or "news."

Rongo is aware of its textual genealogy as an example of Māori engagement with print media, as an extension of existing journalistic forms, and as a challenge to others. In the first page of text, an article titled "A History of Maori Newspapers" is written in Te Reo and is accompanied by an image of a front page of *Te Paki o Matariki*, a Māori-language newspaper from the Waikato region established in 1892. In this article, the genesis of Māori newspapers is traced not only through the importation of the printing press, which is described as "te Pakeha taonga," but also through the older Māori practice of collaboratively sharing and disseminating information for public debate. The article lists several Māori newspapers of the nineteenth and early twentieth centuries and, after placing *Rongo* in this genealogy, explains,

Ehara tenei pepa a *Rongo* hei tango mai i te mana o nga pepa Maori e whakawhiti ana i nga rongo ki nga hunga e marara ana i runga i te mata o te whenua.[15]

Rongo self-consciously attends to the historical context of its production and elaborates its role as an addition to the existing range of spaces in which to kōrero[16] rather than as a critique of those spaces that already exist. At the same time, *Rongo* pays attention to the political and journalistic context that contributed to its appearance. Directly underneath the story about the Māori-language newspapers, a piece titled "Why the Need for Rongo?" outlines the limits of mainstream media and the desire of the editors to provide a newspaper that is "produced solely to cater for the needs of the Maori and other Polynesian people." The other item on this first page of text is the explanation of the newspaper's name, and these three genealogies—the historical, the political, and the cultural—both compel and underpin this unique and significant, even if only one-off, publication. Indeed, these three geneaologies underpin not only this specific newspaper but the relationships between Māori and Pasifika communities more broadly.

The textual genealogy of *Rongo* is explored not only across time but also across space. Connection with other Indigenous newspapers is demonstrated by the inclusion of a story titled "Why Wounded Knee in 1973?" excerpted from a section of *Akwesasne Notes* that is itself, according to the information provided alongside, excerpted from *The Seventh Fire*, the newspaper produced by the Minnesota chapter of the American Indian Movement (AIM). The article responds to "White America ask[ing] 'Why Wounded Knee in 1973?'"[17] The page on which this article appears includes a number of pieces about the context of ignorance and prejudice within which Indigenous people continue to live, including snippets from various New Zealand newspapers that demonstrate the bias of the press and a Rowley Habib poem titled "Go Home Maori" that gently explores the gradual impact of racial prejudice on a single individual. Next to the Wounded Knee story, an explanation of

Akwesasne Notes appears alongside information about how to subscribe to that publication. The note opens as follows:

> Read of the American Indian Peoples [*sic*] struggle for Survival and Freedom in THEIR Land of America. Their problems and aspirations closely parallel ours. They publish eight times a year.[18]

The "close parallels" between the Polynesian Panthers, Nga Tamatoa, and AIM and the producers of *Akwesasne Notes* are articulated contextually ("their problems and aspirations") but also organizationally in a small note encouraging *Rongo* readers to contribute to postage costs: "The Notes People are probably as rich as we are (!) so to help out with postage . . ." Furthermore, these "parallels" are not merely gestured toward in theory but form the basis of relationships between key members of the organizations. This reference to other Indigenous newspapers reinforces the layering of collaboration and relationship and broadens the connections already inherent to the newspaper itself.

One of the most obvious features of *Rongo* is that the various articles appear in Māori, Tongan, Samoan, and Niuean as well as English. (Although the National Library catalog notes Māori, Tongan, Samoan, and English, it does not mention—or perhaps recognize—the pieces in Niuean contributed by Tigilau Ness.)[19] *Rongo*'s commitments to highlighting and addressing the politics of language are demonstrated by the multilingual publication, a feature even more ahead of its time because of the editorial decision to not provide translations of the content that does not appear in English. Along with the formal decision to publish texts in various languages, there are also articles and poetry in *Rongo* that directly address the politics of language. The inaugural Māori Language Day (now an annual government-sponsored Māori Language Week) was brought about as a result of the activities of Nga Tamatoa, and the newspaper includes articles by several members either reporting on how the day was celebrated around the country or outlining the context and possibilities of Māori-language revitalization. Some of these articles are printed in Te Reo and some in English, and a short selection of writing in Te Reo by school students is published alongside articles about the place of Māori language in schools and homes. Interestingly, although some of the articles that appear in Te Reo are written by fluent and highly accomplished writers of the Māori language, some appear to have been produced by writers whose level of proficiency was not so high. Their decision to write in a language with which they were less comfortable and yet to which they desired to express a deep commitment further underscores their understanding of the politics of language.[20] Reading all the pieces in Te Reo side by side, therefore, one acquires a sense of the range of capacity in Te Reo at the time and the great significance of choosing to publish the languages untranslated.[21]

Another aspect of language use in *Rongo* is the struggle to make English work as flexibly as possible to appropriately describe the people by whom and about whom *Rongo* was produced. An editorial note reads,

> In keeping with the sentiments expressed in the above article ['Ilolahia's "We Are All Polynesians"], the term "Polynesian" (Po-ronihiana) will be used in Rongo to cover all of the Maori and Island peoples in New Zealand. Although we would encourage wider use of the application of the term "Polynesian," we think it neces-sary that a more suitable word or phrase be introduced—adapted perhaps from elements of vocabulary common to all Polynesian languages. If anyone has any ideas on this please let us know.[22]

The problem, of course, is one that applies also to *Once Were Pacific*: we are asking English—and Polynesian languages—to do something they never had to do, and the terms themselves are unable to be pried away from the very historical, social, and political contexts that make them problematic. The awkwardness of the terms only reflects the awkwardness of the power relations between the communities they attempt to describe, and the search for "a more suitable word or phrase" is both crucial and foreclosed in the political climate of the 1970s and today. Significantly, the editorial note refuses simply to claim the power to assert or produce a new term to which others must agree but moves to enter into a negotiated engagement ("if anyone has any ideas on this please let us know") that is perhaps the only way in which meaningful language change of this kind can occur. Indeed, perhaps with an eternally absent and yet necessary "more suitable" term such as the editors are seeking, the thrill—the possibility of change—is in the chase.

Rongo affirms the place of creative work by publishing individual poems and drawings, profiling Māori artists, reporting on a hui for Māori writers and artists, and including reviews of two novels. In terms of layout, the creative work is published alongside relevant critical, informative, and visual texts, and this enables creative work to participate in the political and editorial work of the newspaper rather than being sequestered into a separate "creative" section. For example, Rowley Habib's "A Photograph from Home," which celebrates the diversity and vitality of the Māori community as evidenced in a photograph of Māori children, is placed on a page about the need for Māori language to be taught in schools, and Henare Dewes's strikingly tender poem "Whakarongo," which mourns the loss to the individual but also to his community while he is in jail, is printed alongside an article about problems at the notorious Paremoremo Prison and information about legal rights when placed under arrest or in prison. Indeed, recognizing this role of the arts in politics is a feature not only of the early 1970s but also of Pacific political traditions, in which song, performance, clowning, visual arts, and so on, are crucial to social organization and communal memory. On one of the last pages of the newspaper, two book reviews appear side by side: one of Albert Wendt's *Sons for the Return Home* and one of Witi Ihimaera's *Tangi*. Both are first novels for their writers, and both are also the first from their respective communities. Significantly, although the novels were published around the same time, they are usually discussed alongside other texts. Ihimaera's novel is most often placed within a context of New Zealand literature, and Wendt's work is understood as a Pacific text. Reviewed together, the connections between the novels and the significance of their proximate publication are explicit. In this way, *Rongo* manages to achieve in the literary sphere a version of its broader mission to assert that "we are all Polynesians" and reflect on how this orientation affects the things we take for granted.

The significance of *Rongo* is enhanced rather than diminished by its loss from the memory of the 1970s: it is not just a record of a particular time but also a record of the things we choose to remember about that time. Why did *Rongo* manage to find its way off the historical record, except for in a scattering of brief references? For me, *Rongo* was a serendipitous find. Like Alice Walker, who wrote that she "became aware of [her] need for Zora Neale Hurston before [she] heard of her," for me, the existence of this one-off newspaper was both unexpected and intuited. *Rongo* demands the careful treatment of a larger project, and as the 1970s in New Zealand are beginning to fall into the view of historians and other rememberers, I hope that it will receive the attention it is due. The significance of its loss from cultural memory is poignantly demonstrated in Melani Anae's recent book *Polynesian Panthers,* in which Panther Nigel Bhana recalls a publication that can only be *Rongo* but whose title has been published as *Ronald*:

Ronald was first printed between Nga Tamatoa, Polynesian
Panthers and the People's Union. As far as I know, it was the first
political Polynesian-Maori magazine that came out. . . . *Ronald*
was the first that gave awareness to a lot of young Maori and other
Polynesians; my generation. And it united them.[23]

Presumably this is an honest mistake, an accidental oversight. Typos happen
all the time, and specific terms in transcripts have an unlucky tendency to
be autocorrected by word-processing programs. Unfortunately, though, it
means that as the book about the Panthers circulates, the memory of *Rongo*
will not travel with it. When *Rongo* becomes *Ronald,* the aspirational layers
of meaning behind the name are left aside, as are the politics of unapologeti-
cally publishing a newspaper in multiple Polynesian languages. In terms of
the ongoing struggle for justice, the shifting of *Rongo* to *Ronald* is in many
ways inconsequential. Yet this instance of mis-hearing, mis-recognizing,
or not knowing about a publication that itself attended so closely to the
politics of visibility, history, specificity, and language feels, to me, important.
When we miss the opportunity to remember *Rongo,* we miss the opportunity to recall the extent and modes of Māori–Pasifika collaboration at
the time.

"Nesians Are You with Me?": New Zealand
Hip-hop Articulates a Nesian Style

The neologism *Nesian* was popularized in New Zealand by Nesian Mystik,
a band with Māori, Samoan, Cook Islander, and Tongan members, in their
2002 debut album *Polysaturated.* As I have already suggested, very few
prominent Māori-authored texts or narratives in conventional literary genres
come from the mixed Nesian neighborhoods of Auckland, Wellington,
and Christchurch, and hip-hop artists from these neighborhoods are at
the forefront of articulating the complex relationships between Indigenous
Māori and diasporic Pasifika urban communities.[24] *Polysaturated* advocates
a "Nesian style" within the discourses of Pacific genealogical and navigation
histories as well as the experience of marginalization and racism in New
Zealand. The appearance of the term *Nesian* is one way of reckoning with
being at the limits of language. Because *Nesian* is both a familiar and a new
term, Nesian Mystik has the opportunity to define what it means:

New Zealand hip hop flowing with that hint of Nesian style
Represent straight where you're from cause everyone knows it's a must
Cause this Nesian style mooli is this style we bust.[25]

Reconfiguring Pacific communities as *Nesian* extricates the "island" (-nesian) root from the Western-imposed cartographic and anthropological prefixes (poly-, micro-, and mela-), echoing Hau'ofa's reframing of the (colonially imagined) Pacific as the (Indigenously imagined) Oceania. *Nesian* thereby challenges existing dominant constructions of the relationship between Indigenous and diasporic Pacific communities in New Zealand. Although Nesian Mystik rejects the term *Polynesian* ("Polynesian aint even a label we made up / We were given names by the civilised discovers"[26]), then, their conscious use of terminology that enables Māori–Pasifika connections to congeal echoes 'Ilolahia's claim that "we're all Polynesians" in *Rongo*. Similarly, the neologism *polysaturated,* which the group uses for their album title, is productively ambivalent, at once celebrating and critiquing the "saturation" of Polynesia. This idea of saturation is an appropriate watery metaphor but also speaks to unlawful or unexpected mobility across permeable borders. Nesian people are situated within the boundaries of one nation-state or city or neighborhood, yes, but they participate in the complexity, border crossing, linguistic differences, political positionings, and cultural nuances of the wider Pacific region.

"Lost Visionz," the final track on *Polysaturated,* traces the migration histories and diasporic backgrounds of the group members. Donald opens the track with a spoken section pertaining to his feelings of dislocation, and this is followed by a series of histories: Feleti's family foregrounds a Samoan experience (this section is spoken by Feleti's father, the Reverend Mua Strickson-Pua), Awa speaks about Māori struggle, and finally, Sabre delivers several stanzas of historical commentary. Before Sabre's contribution to the track begins, then, three of the group members offer perspectives on Aotearoa-based Pacific identities and identifications: their own "visionz," "lost" or otherwise. Donald asks specifically about the implications of growing up feeling dislocated from his "cultural history":

Are you educated in your cultural history? To be honest, I'm not. And all I want to know is why.
      Even though I live in another country, I still acknowledge my Tongan ancestry. And even though I don't know it a lot, or as much

as I should know about my culture, just like many other people;
but why?

Donald ties his sense of cultural displacement to his physical distance from
a certain geographic space ("although I live in another country"), which
speaks to many Māori as well as Pasifika narratives. These discourses of
authentic identity ("or as much as I *should* know") exclude lived realities ("to
be honest, I'm not"). The majority of Māori hip-hop artists are urban,[27] the
majority of Pasifika hip-hop artists are New Zealand born or at least New
Zealand raised, and in the face of these removals, an Aoteoroa-based Pacific
gains utility. Donald then asks whether whakapapa and cultural affiliation
have the capacity to trump knowledge or experience:

> I'm proud to be Polynesian, and I take pride in being Tongan. But
> because I don't know much about my culture, does that make me
> any less of a Polynesian, or a Tongan, than I am?

Donald's narrative is reminiscent of the introduction to Wineera's collection,
introducing a relationship between Tongan(ness) and Polynesian(ness) that
seems less of a slippage (in which Polynesian is Tongan, and vice versa) and
more like a concentric relationship. Donald's perspective is represented as
unsure and exploratory, and this section is structured as a set of questions
(the last of which may or may not be rhetorical). Furthermore, on the track
itself, the English-language narrative is overlaid with a woman's voice speaking Tongan that demonstrates both the ongoing survival and frustrating
proximity of the Tongan language. The translation of Donald's experience
from English *into* Tongan signals that although he expresses his experience
in the English language, it is not rendered irrelevant or hopelessly removed
from Tonganness after all. As well as asking whether "not knowing about
[his] culture" makes him "less of . . . a Tongan," he asks whether this "not
knowing" makes him less "of a Polynesian,"[28] implying that Polynesianness
requires knowledge of *specific* culture, in his case, Tongan.

After Donald's piece, Mua Strickson-Pua (who is a poet in his own right
and a member of Polynation, the poetry group discussed later in this chapter,
and who is the father of one of the members of Nesian Mystik) describes
his family's migration from Sāmoa to New Zealand. He consistently refers to
New Zealand as Aotearoa, emphasizing a conscious decision to see New Zealand from the perspective of manuhiri but also making a claim of belonging

in the national space by using the name of the new home as it occurs in the local Pacific language. His speech begins with the statement "Sāmoana" and ends, after considering their time in Aotearoa, with the statement "Fa'afetai e le Atua—Aotearoa—Sāmoana." Aotearoa is thus sandwiched into the concept of Samoanness and, in particular, Sāmoana-ness. From the perspective of a Samoan family, surrounded by a wider church community in Grey Lynn, this spoken section focuses on an Auckland-based family and community and yet also makes reference to the Samoan oral tradition that fuses Christian and Indigenous understandings: "Sāmoana. Sāmoa's founded on God by Tū herself from Malaelā." He narrates his family's migration to New Zealand[29] and the survival of the stories and histories intertwined with their bodily presence. Strickson-Pua underscores the continued prominence of those traditions when he acknowledges his parents, who "paid the price of love and sacrifice / keeping alive our lifeline between Sāmoa and Aotearoa," and he projects this continuation as essential to the survival of the "nation":

> Today, we celebrate the fruits of victory. Our family—our story— our history—lives on. . . . Next generation, you are the hopes of our nations now.

Again, Strickson-Pua maintains a staunchly genealogical approach to diasporic Samoan experience, and rather than lamenting the distance between New Zealand–born Samoan people and their forebears in Sāmoa or in the early years of migration, he passes the responsibility to the "new generation" and describes them as a "hope" for "nations," which, in the plural, suggestively seems to mean New Zealand *and* Sāmoa.

Finally, Awa (Te Awanui Pine Reeder) adds a sung sequence that contextualizes the previous and following discussions on the track in terms of the specifically Māori struggles. The background sound shifts in Awa's section of the track to incorporate the songs of native New Zealand birds, which marks this part of the track as a specifically Aotearoa-based section. Just as the other members of the band name moments, places, individuals, and identifications in their representation of personal and community histories, Awa references several significant events in Māori history:

> Here's an insight to a time
> You've got to step back to before the Springbok tours

Social circumstance conditioned minds had to adapt to survive
Our people at the frontlines . . .

He begins by pushing his listeners to contextualize his own (and their own) personal history with events prior to the controversial 1981 tour of the South African rugby team, an event that has been described as the closest New Zealand has come to a civil war (since, presumably, the nineteenth century). The reference to "people at the frontlines" is ambiguous: it could refer to participation in the "frontlines" of protest and struggle but also to the "frontlines" of war, recalling perhaps the purpose of Māori involvement in World War I, World War II, Korea, Vietnam, Malaya, and so on, as an expression of and payment for citizenship. "Our people" have occupied, and continue to occupy, both positions—citizen and critic—and both are attempts at "survival" in response to "social circumstance." Because "at the frontlines" could mean either of these, both are valid and even interdependent.

Awa's challenge to "step back to before" to understand the contemporary situation ("always historicize," as some would put it) is both enacted and modeled in a sung bridge in the track:

> We do remember Bastion Point
> We do remember Parihaka
> We do remember Waitangi

Awa names three specific events from the most recent to the most historical, following his own call to "step back" and ultimately reciting history as a genealogy rather than a chronology. Briefly, Bastion Point is a specific piece of land around which Auckland has arranged itself and which the local iwi Ngāti Whatua occupied for 507 days in 1977–78 to retain their land base. Although this event was a specifically Indigenous struggle, many Pasifika people assisted and supported the protestors, including members of the Polynesian Panthers, and it became the basis of many activist and community networks. Parihaka is the settlement in Taranaki that, after bitter fighting in Taranaki from the 1860s and the total confiscation of all land in the region, was led by the prophets Te Whiti and Tohu, who advocated passive resistance. In November 1881, government and local militia stormed Parihaka, arresting men and taking them south and looting and razing the homes and other buildings. The story of Parihaka was suppressed for many years and has become known as a particularly shameful moment in

New Zealand's history. Finally, Waitangi is a reference to the place where the infamously and unfortunately mistranslated Treaty of Waitangi, the document by which the British Crown extended its sovereignty over New Zealand, was signed in 1840.

Most obviously, the repeated claim "we do remember" confirms that "we" indeed remember and asserts that this history is not forgotten. The repeated pronoun "we" could speak on behalf of Māori as opposed to non-Māori, although it is also possible to understand the "we" as Pacific inclusive. After all, not just Awa but all of Nesian Mystik produced the track, and so perhaps all of them "remember." Repeating the phrase "we do remember" both describes and enacts an act of memory: it is at once a statement of confirmation addressed to those involved in the specific struggles, a challenge to the colonizing power that the memory lives on, and a mnemonic device in and of itself that encourages and enables the re-memory of these events. Being Pacific in Aotearoa is thus tied to "remembering" Māori struggles, potentially even those that happened before the arrival of one's own family. When Awa is singing "we" on behalf of his relatives, he asserts a specific Indigenous memory of national history, and when it is on behalf of Nesian Mystik (and, in turn, their respective communities), he articulates a model for Pasifika recognition of recent and historic Māori struggle and the formal treaty-derived bicultural basis of this country of which they are a part. This again echoes Hau'ofa's vision for Hawai'i and New Zealand about "alliances [between] an increasing number of Islanders with the *tangata whenua* (indigenous people) of Aotearoa."

"We Are Polynation"

A group of Māori and Pasifika writers and musicians came together as a group called Polynation for two shows in 2008: the West Auckland Poetry Festival and the Queensland Poetry Festival. Directed by Tusiata Avia, who also performed as a poet, Polynation's performance in Brisbane was recorded and produced as a DVD by another group member, Doug Poole.[30] A still camera records the performance, which takes place on a simple stage with three fixed microphones. The performers walk into and out of the light over the course of the show, the bright lights of the space from which pieces are read becoming a dually visible and vulnerable space. In his written reflection of his experience, Poole relates his own fears about walking into the lit space—"Three sentinel microphone stands await on a flying carpet . . ."[31]—and compares the darkened space to the Samoan conceptual space of darkness in which both he and the contents of his poem "Cautionary Tale" also "await": "I have waited in Pouliuli, they have waited, the beatings, abuse, death. My blood coursing backward, I walk toward the microphone."[32] Having opened with the first lines of Selina Tusitala Marsh's "Fast Talking PI," and deriving a sense of structure from her occasional return to the stage to contribute more lines of the poem, the show moves toward a final piece—"We Are Polynation"—in which all the performers are on stage.

The individual contributions from the members of Polynation are varied in form and theme. Several relate to the question of representation and stereotyping, including the public release of the infamous Clydesdale report, in which a Massey University economist branded Pasifika communities a "drain on the economy."[33] Several of the Pasifika performers reference aspects of Aotearoa. Selina Tusitala Marsh's long poem includes the lines "I'm a fale PI, a marae PI," and "a Matariki PI," and this incorporates Māori (and mixed Māori–Pasifika) PIs into the realm of Pasifika experience in New Zealand. In Karlo Mila's poem for Luamanuvao Winnie Laban, the Samoan woman MP, she compares her white hair to the kotuku, a heron not only native to Aotearoa but also symbolic of special status; this reference quietly demonstrates Mila's familiarity with Māori concepts. In "O/E," Tusiata Avia imagines traveling in Russia and bumping into atua Māori (Māui, Hinenui te Pō, Rangi, Tangaroa) who are engaged in exceedingly everyday activities. Having long been involved in a range of collaborations with Māori communities and political causes, Mua Strickson-Pua (who speaks in Nesian Mystik's "Lost Visionz") includes Aotearoa in his naming of "islands" from which Polynation comes, and in another poem, he describes his relationship with his grandchild through the use of a Māori rather than Samoan word: "Cheden and I / mokopuna, Papa." The only poem entirely in a language other than English, Daren Kamali's "Viti" is in Fijian but includes the word "Aotearoa."

The Māori member of Polynation is Kath Hayward-Nathan, and unlike the rest of the performers, she wears overtly traditional items—a large carved comb in her hair and a feather cloak—throughout her performance. Poole recalls,

As Kath walks onto the stage, the iridescent light of her Korowai, Moko, Pounamu Taonga, and Heru, pushes aside the darkness.[34]

Though the Pasifika women wear large flowers behind their ears, they are all clearly plastic and so, while they are traditional in terms of function perhaps, they are also engaged with contemporary representation, kitsch, and the possibilities of its ironic fold back. This visual differentiation cannot help but distinguish between Pasifika as engaged with modernity and Māori as timeless. Although it would be absolutely incorrect to suggest that heru or korowai are necessarily timeless in and of themselves, or indeed that heru and korowai cannot themselves contain subversive or ironic claims, the visual impact of the korowai made of natural materials compared to the bright clothing of the Pasifika women is rather stark. Interestingly, the male performers are dressed in T-shirts and blue jeans, with the exception of Strickson-Pua, who wears a tie and shirt and, in the final piece, "We Are Polynation," a tie with a large Māori graphic design.

"We Are Polynation" merits longer discussion in part because it is the title piece of the show but also because it is a collaborative single work. Each of the members of the group walks onto stage and states "we are Polynation" and then contributes her own perspective on how this might be configured, the next performer coming on stage in time to join the person in her final claim, "We are Polynation." In this way, "we are Polynation" becomes the first and last thing uttered by each performer, and all the members on stage join in for that single line. The performers stay on stage after they have spoken, which means the effect of repeating "we are Polynation" is both connective and cumulative: like a chant, these words are repeated and become the customary way by which individuals are woven into the group. Like call and response, it is spoken by the whole group and then echoed back by the newly included member as a sign of his own joining to the whole. As the members of Polynation gather in the light—out of the Pouliuli, to use Poole's words—their claim is declarative and demonstrative. In an inversion of Nesian Mystik's strategy of reframing the suffix -nesian of Polynesian, Polynation makes use of the prefix poly-, for "many." This is a declaration and demonstration of multiplicity at the same time as the prefix poly- in the New Zealand context is always inflected by the hegemony of Polynesian. It is worth mentioning that like any continually chanted phrase, the words themselves lose the immediacy of connection with precise meaning and slip into producing meaning through their sound and rhythm as much as their definitions. At some point, "we are Polynation" starts to sound like "we are Polynesian," a slippage that is exclusive (especially with the presence of a Fijian member in the group) but that also provides a mechanism by which the Aotearoa-based Pacific and Aotearoa-inclusive Pacific find their connection. Being Polynesian grants Māori access to Polynation in ways that being PI or Pasifika does not. It is also worth putting some pressure on the "we" here: is this an articulation of the group itself, the poly- (perhaps Pacific, perhaps multiple) dimensions of the New Zealand community, or a multiculturalist vision of the entire New Zealand nation?

At the same time as they declare Polynation into existence by insisting on repeating the line "we are Polynation,"[35] the members demonstrate the multiplicity and parameters of what this means by their physical presence and through their own verbal contributions. Daren Kamali offers the connective tissue provided by their shared kaupapa: "Pacific poets from different island nations / Brought together to form a perfect combination." The Aotearoa context of this "polynation" is alluded to in Mila's articulation of "fingering the long white cloud," but Strickson-Pua explicitly focuses on the place of tāngata whenua in his understanding of himself as one who is (as he states in one of his individually performed poems) "becoming Samoan." Wearing a Māori tie, he recites Māori words that provide an opportunity to connect: both for himself and his aiga to Aotearoa but also for the group Polynation:

> Atua, Tupuna, Matua,
> Whanau, Aiga, Mokopuna
> Samoa Aotearoa China
> Whakarongo Kaupapa
> Whakapapa
> Aloha Alofa Aroha
> Aue aue hī.[36]

Strickson-Pua brings Sāmoa (and China and Hawai'i) into the poem, and yet the Māori words provide not only thematic structure but also conceptual and aural shape.

Finally, Kath returns to the stage—the last of the Polynation members to join the group—and after joining in with the phrase "we are Polynation" recited by the others, she sings her contribution, which is a Christian blessing in the Māori language. In this way, her participation in the "polynation" the members have produced through uttering its name takes the same form as the Pasifika members but is also distinctive: she does not wear the same style of clothing as the others and does not contribute an articulation of "polynation" in the same way, either in terms of type or language. In some ways, perhaps, this is an appropriate position: the Māori member is simultaneously poly- in terms of Polynesian but tāngata whenua in terms of the -nation. Conversely, it would be interesting to imagine what other possibilities there might be for Māori inclusion in a "combination" (as Kamali puts it) such as this. Perhaps the inclusion of more than one Māori member would relieve Kath—her literary contribution and her body—of some of the burden of representation. After Kath sings, the entire group ends the show with another chant from a much older series of migrations. Poole writes,

> Our last calls bless the audience, our words, our journey. We reach to heaven, pulling down the wairua of our ancestors, drawing them deep within ourselves, we take our last breathe [sic], exhaling. . . . *Taiiki* [sic] *E!*[37]

The closing of the chant—"haumi e, hui e, taiki e"—is a ritualized Māori articulation of journey and migration, and this acknowledges the particular place of Māori in the poly- nation. The final physical gesture, a staged pūkana in which the performers strike an iconic Māori pose, which Poole describes as a "final act of defiance," underscores this Māori dimension to the configuration of Polynation. Yet, although the performance is extremely well directed and presented overall, I admit that the members of Polynation appear to strike this final pose a little awkwardly. The least assured or confident part of the performance, perhaps this moment gestures toward a space somewhere between anxiety and confidence.[38] I do not offer this as a criticism as such but instead as an acknowledgment that the vulnerable moment in which this group attempts to match its own (literal) performance with its aspirations offers a rich parallel to the broader national (and regional) projects of collaboration: alliances and combinations. Perhaps, to echo Strickson-Pua's words, the group—and maybe any group—is at its most productive when it is in a process of "becoming" Polynation.

Māori–Pasifika Collaborations

Through collaborative work, Māori and Pasifika people in the national space have produced activist and creative work that not only articulates Māori connections with the Pacific but also embodies and recalls those connections through lived relationships and shared artistic vision. Each of these collaborations has taken shape in Auckland, and this confirms the centrality of the urban space in the negotiation of connections in the national context. Work on Māori experiences of the city should take account of these kinds of connections, and work on Māori–Pasifika connections cannot help but engage with the urban space. Additionally, all of these connections have consciously selected terminology that joins the members through Polynesianness—Rongo the Polynesian deity, the neologism *Nesian*, and *poly-* the prefix—and yet, in each collaboration, the specific position of Māori on the basis of Indigeneity is marked. The collaborative work of *Rongo,* Nesian Mystik, and Polynation produces a unique, historicized, specific articulation of Māori–Pasifika connections, but it also produces a record of the relationship to which we can look back to remember those connections should we risk forgetting them.

In its book review section, *Rongo* proposes the connections between texts authored by Māori and Pasifika writers when it reviews *Tangi* and *Sons for the Return Home* side by side. Certainly there are striking similarities between these books, which are the first novels by a Māori and Samoan writer, respectively. At the heart of both novels is a young man who attempts to reconcile himself to his place in his family and community; both narrate the process of moving from a rural or island origin to Wellington city and back again, and in both novels, a Pākehā girlfriend is used as a representative and catalyst for further introspection. Finally, the young male protagonists in both novels are understood by their families to have had exceptional opportunities in Wellington, and yet both seek to connect with an element of home, which, in both cases, is done through the process of finding a way to grieve appropriately for an older male relative. However, the novels offer two very different visions of 1970s New Zealand (and, indeed, 1970s Wellington). Whereas Māori are frequently mentioned in *Sons,* and the plot is partly propelled by the process by which the young Samoan man realizes that his belittling view of Māori is inappropriate because of physical but also cultural proximity, there is no Pasifika presence in *Tangi.* The next two chapters consider the representation of Māori–Pasifika connections by Māori and Pasifika writers, respectively. Although these texts are all individually authored, it is worth bearing in mind the initial urge of *Rongo* to read such texts alongside each other. Within the texts, and in the broader conversations (or perhaps vā, or space between, according to Wendt's own formulation) between them, when looking at them in a certain way, alongside one another, they all participate in a larger collaborative process: the production of a genuinely Pacific (Māori *and* Pasifika) literary history in New Zealand.

CHAPTER 5

"It's Like That with Us Maoris": Māori Write Connections

W HEN WITI IHIMAERA'S *Tangi* was reviewed alongside Albert Wendt's *Sons for the Return Home* in *Rongo*, there was a striking difference between the presence of Māori in the Pasifika text and the absence of Pasifika in the Māori novel. It is unproductive, uncurious, and intellectually bossy to admonish texts for not being what one hopes them to be, and certainly *Tangi* made a significant contribution not only to the world of Māori literature but also to New Zealand literature. At the same time, it does feel unfortunate that Māori creative production still tends toward representing experiences that are solely Māori or Māori–Pākehā rather than Māori–Pasifika. Because most Māori live in urban areas and a sizeable proportion of Māori children are of mixed Māori–Pasifika descent, we can assume that many members of Māori and Pasifika communities interact regularly and in close proximity. In spaces like schools, sports teams, workplaces, and church organizations as well as in the rather more intimate space of family life, Māori and Pasifika individuals and families develop and elaborate long-standing relationships. So it is, to be frank, astounding that there are so few treatments of Māori–Pasifika connections in the corpus of published Māori writing in English. This section foregrounds texts by Māori writers who engage in representing the relationship between Māori and Pasifika communities in New Zealand. In this context, these texts by Taylor, Grace, and Grace-Smith are particularly significant because they take for granted that the relationship between Māori and Pasifika people is a part of the Aotearoa they represent.

"Ua malamalama": Apirana Taylor

Apirana Taylor's 1986 multigenre literary collection *He Rau Aroha: A Hundred Leaves of Love* contains the short story "Pa Mai."[1] To place the collection in context, *He Rau Aroha* appeared around the same time as three major works of Māori fiction: Hulme's *the bone people* (1984), Grace's *Potiki* (1986), and Ihimaera's *The Matriarch* (1986). While these texts gained wide and ongoing acclaim, they offered three very different ways of apprehending the ongoing impacts of Māori encounters with colonialism and put forward three particularly 1980s visions of rural-focused decolonization. Whereas a novel both suggests and requires structural wholeness, Taylor's multigenre collection of poetry and short fiction implies a diversity of experience—including apprehension of colonialism in its many forms, decolonization, and Māori centrism—without needing to produce the continuities between these various experiences or between each experience and a broader national history. This is not to suggest that *He Rau Aroha* shies away from speaking to the national context; rather, it is a collection of short fiction and poetry that contains various strands and narratives and leaves room for the reader to determine how these different elements might connect. The broader intervention made by the collection and, indeed, by Taylor's work more generally, especially given the wide distribution of his now iconic earlier poem "Sad Joke on a Marae,"[2] is that he foregrounds and nuances urban Māori experiences. "Pa mai" introduces perhaps the first developed Pasifika character in a fiction text by a New Zealand–based Māori writer.

Written entirely in dialogue, the humorous story recounts a casual, fast-paced conversation between two men drinking in a pub: one is Māori and one is Samoan. Because the story is not told from the perspective of a narrator, the reader participates by figuring out details as they are revealed through dialogue. The men are already familiar: they know each other by name ("You imagine things, Harris"; "Sione mate"[3]) and refer to previous experiences they have shared together ("And there's us sittin' in the lounge"[4]), and these details confirm that this is not a moment of "first encounter" between them. In this way, Taylor represents a Māori–Pasifika friendship that extends beyond the present temporal frame of the immediate narrative. Over the course of the story, which is a mere three pages in length, the men articulate a series of differences between Māori and Samoan communities, reflect on their shared experiences of racism and colonialism, and conclude with a discussion about their collective cultural and linguistic heritage.

The opening lines of the story are uttered by Harris ("here's me, a Maori"[5]), who immediately foregrounds the distinctions as well as continuities between Māori and Samoan treatment in the racist context of New Zealand by talking about the service he receives at the bar. Harris is both knowledgeable and naive about racism. On one hand, he can recognize and read the treatment aimed at someone on the basis of his appearance ("that Pakeha bar girl slops my beer all over the place and just about throws the change in my face"), but on the other hand, he acknowledges that "[he has] noticed something [he] never noticed before." He suggests that he is receiving the treatment "'cause she thinks I'm Samoan," which points to the layers of racialization that take place in the story. Although the conversation between Sione and Harris focuses on their own experiences and thereby, over the course of the story, elaborates a picture of their respective families and communities, from the point of view of the bartender, their proximity renders them indistinguishable from one another ("she thinks I'm Samoan"). At this point in the story, the two men are careful to describe each other as "you": "here's me, a Maori, drinkin' in the bar with you Samoans"; "all you Samoans"; "you Maoris"; and so on.

After acknowledging the experience of racism in the context of the bar, Harris extends his observation to the national sphere:

> I notice she treats all you Samoans like that. Imagine that, eh? You come all the way from Samoa to New Zealand and spend the rest of your life gettin' the beer chucked in ya face.[6]

Harris's reference to Samoan migration to New Zealand provides Sione with an opportunity to make a comparison between Māori and Samoan mobility: he does this by cracking the oldest joke in the book, which reappears in countless television shows, books, and verbal conversations:[7]

> You Maoris came over here on your canoes. Then came the Palagi on their canoes, but we Samoans got smart. We waited for two hundred years and then flew over on Air New Zealand.

Sione includes Pākehā in his version of the joke but calls them "Palagi" in this conversation with a Māori man in the mid-1980s, which speaks to his ability to assume that Harris is familiar with the term. Also, although Palagi in the cliché usually arrive in ships, here they arrive "on their canoes," which connects them to "Maoris . . . on your canoes" and produces "we Samoans" as the distinctive group. Also, when Sione names the specific airline Air New Zealand, the national carrier and therefore a symbol of the relation between the New Zealand state and Samoan migration, and also a reminder of the close connection between nation (New Zealand) and business (Air New

Zealand), Sione highlights the link between Samoan migration to New Zealand and the labor needs of private companies.

Harris and Sione banter about recent migrants from Sāmoa, including Sione's Uncle Fauma, who has recently arrived in New Zealand. The story focuses on Uncle Fauma's unfamiliarity with English and establishes language as a line of humor—and connection—that will continue throughout the story. Harris responds to this first anecdote by linking it back to the theme of racism with which the story opened:

> It's stuff like that, Sione, what gets you fellas a bad name. Makes people call Samoans ignorant.[8]

The word *ignorant* is countered by Sione's response—"It's not ignorance really. It's innocence"[9]—and the men relay stories about their families, and later themselves, adjusting to new situations. They start with Sione's mother and her naivety about marijuana—"I know you been drinking the Marijuana"—and then discusses her naivety about the English language: "I know you been smoking the pots and the pans."[10] This memory prompts early memories about language, and at this point, the experiences of the Māori and Samoan characters start to align more closely.

After laughing about Uncle Fauma's, Sione's, and Sione's mother's use of English, Sione relates his own experience at school:

> I came out from Samoa when I was ten and apart from a few words, I couldn't speak English. Samoan is my mother tongue. I had to learn English at school.[11]

Sione continues to outline his own experience not long after this admission, but before he continues, Harris interrupts:

> That's a bit like what happened to us Maoris. I remember one of my uncles telling me about how it was when he was a little boy.[12]

The distinction is retained between the two communities ("us Maoris"), but a clear link is made between their similar experiences of school when it came to the English language. Harris implies that although his own generation has not interacted with English for the first time at school, he is able to point to a parallel to Sione's experience in the generation before him.

This articulation of shared experience ("that's a bit like what happened to us Maoris") is the first direct comparison in the story. Up until this point, Harris's and Sione's connections were based on proximity ("a Maori, drinkin' in the bar with you Samoans"; "and there's us sittin' in the lounge"), but Harris had merely observed the Samoan experience rather than connecting it with the experience of him or his own family: "I notice she treats all you Samoans like that." Now Harris recognizes a point of connection, and even if the generational distinction between Māori and Samoan experiences of compulsory English-language classrooms means that connection is not derived from his own lived experience ("one of my uncles [told] me about how it was when he was a little boy"), it has become a communal memory that provides a basis of connection for himself ("us Maoris") as well.

Sione and Harris swap funny stories about children (Sione himself and Harris's uncle) misunderstanding or misusing English at school, which extends the scope and form of the bartender's racism into the school space, while it also quietly confirms the presence of another language in both families. A discussion about Māori and Samoan experiences of racism and marginalization transitions into the connections between the languages both young boys (Harris's uncle and Sione) spoke when they went to school. At this point, Sione tells a story about Sāmoa that steps away from the language question for a bit, focusing instead on the matter of practice or tikanga. He tells a funny story about another uncle's first wife who died and would come back to harass his second wife. After describing his uncle's successful remedy, and the punishment he suffered for carrying out his plan to interfere with his first wife's bones, he concludes,

> The funny thing about it is the local church Minister found out
> about what my uncle had done and told my uncle off. And later the
> police came round and beat up my uncle for rearranging the bones.
> So that's the conflict. The old *wha* Samoa versus the new law.[13]

On one level, this conclusion to the story pertains to the connection that has already been explored earlier: the negotiation of cultural change in the specific context of colonial institutions (school, church, police) that insist on introducing "new law." Sione rightly describes this negotiation as a "conflict," and we can reflect on the multiple ways in which negotiating new circumstances has been an important aspect of all the anecdotes shared.

However, a further level of this comment from Sione is found in the phrase "the old *wha* Samoa," a phrase that refers to fa'asāmoa[14] but that is written in Māori (i.e., *wh* instead of *f* and no glottal stop) on the page. In this way, Taylor produces a rich contradiction: "*wha* Samoa" and "fa'asāmoa" sound identical to the ear and yet are transcribed differently because of the different styles of orthography preferred by the missionaries who worked with each language. (This is only an aural resonance; as far as meaning goes, the Māori cognate for the prefix *fa'a-* is *whaka-*, not *wha-*.) Indeed, as a result of orthographic specificities in various places, some sounds are pronounced more differently now across Polynesian languages than they were before they were written down. Perhaps this gestures toward orthographies not only of language but of the nation. Echoing Spitz's formulation of Pacific people having been "made different," aspects which were previously more similar may now be more deeply differentiable as a result of differing national orthographies. When the concept of fa'asāmoa appears as "*wha* Samoa" on the page, although Sione is speaking, it is the Māori orthography that is preferred. This is the realm of koura after all.

This reference to "*wha* Samoa"—and the nonverbal particularity of the slippage between *fa'a* and *wha*—provides the opportunity for Harris and Sione to reflect on the linguistic connections between Māori and Samoans *apart from* the shared experience of English at school. Harris is explicit about the "Polynesian" basis of their connection:

> It's like that with us Maoris quite a lot. We've got a lot in common. We're Polynesian. You say *paepae*, I say *paepae*. You have a *malae*, I have a *marae*. You say *malamalama*, I say *maramatanga*. *Ua malamalama*.[15]

This discussion of language brings Harris to introduce the collective "we" for the first time since the men recalled spending time together on a previous evening. This "we" is more inclusive than just the two individuals, though: after telling all their stories, Harris and Sione have rhetorically populated their time together with various family members. We might also note that the linguistic and cultural connection is described in much stronger terms ("it's like that with us Maoris quite a lot") than the experiential connections mentioned earlier ("that's a bit like what happened to us Maoris"). Harris goes through several key conceptual words and phrases with identical or very similar pronunciations in the Māori and Samoan languages. He then finishes his comparison with a phrase that appears only in Samoan: "Ua malamalama." Significantly, Harris makes this comment about understanding or comprehension in Samoan rather than in Māori (or English). As they recite shared concepts and closely related words that speak of regional historic connection ("we're Polynesian"), they also demonstrate more recent and ongoing connections between the communities as exemplified by their mutual knowledge of Samoan words and their cognates in Māori.

Finally, the two aspects of experience and language come together in a single phrase. Unlike the previous words, which pertained to symbolic structures and knowledges, the final phrase is practical and links with the everyday of the men:

> Last night when we were on the grog, Saina says to me, "E Harris, pa ma le awhi." I laughed 'cause I knew what he said. We say pa mai te ahi, which means: Have you got a light. Cheers mate.[16]

Harris's reference to another friend, Saina, confirms the broader network of Māori–Pasifika friendships in which the men are involved. In this anecdote, as in the comment about "wha Samoa," a Samoan phrase is written down according to Māori spelling conventions. "Pa mai le awhi" would usually be spelled "pa mai le afi" in Samoan; awhi has another meaning in Māori altogether. Unlike when Harris's uncle, Sione's uncle, Sione's mother, and Sione encountered English and found themselves belittled and marginalized by the experience of the new language, Harris and Sione find great pleasure and richness in their experience with each other's languages, and they experiment with each other's phrases. The story ends with the men trying out this new pairing on each other:

> E Harris, pa mai te ahi.
> Pa mai le awhi, Sione.[17]

Again, a Samoan word is spelled according to Māori orthography ("awhi"), and this time, each man speaks each other's language. Indeed, because awhi means "to embrace" in Māori, the men simultaneously ask for a lighter and for recognition of their close connection. Furthermore, their sentences themselves perform an awhi of sorts when Sione uses the Māori definite article te with the Māori word ahi, while Harris uses the Samoan definite article le with the Samoan word afi, which Taylor has spelled "awhi." Although the story opened with the generalized "me, a Maori" and "you Samoans," by the end of the conversation, the men use each other's personal names and languages. This both specifies and humanizes them: the contexts of racism (treatment at the pub) and colonialism (treatment at school) are sidelined by their own excitement that they have "got a lot in common."

"Everybody Danced": Patricia Grace

Patricia Grace's second children's book, *Watercress Tuna and the Children of Champion Street*,[18] is located firmly in Cannon's Creek, a neighborhood of Porirua, a predominantly Polynesian suburb of Wellington that enjoys similarly narrow and negative representation in mainstream discourse as does Ōtara of the Te Papa photo discussed earlier. The premise of Grace's book is that a magic tuna,[19] who dwells in the nearby creek, visits children in houses on Champion Street and invites them to pull things out of his magical throat. The children extract various musical and cultural items specific to their own ethnic groups and end up leading their communities in a dance on Champion Street "all day and all night." Grace's writing and Robyn Kahukiwa's illustrations work in combination in *Watercress Tuna*, one of the first books to represent the children and physical environments of New Zealand's large brown neighborhoods.[20] Not only does the book highlight invisibilized ethnic groups, it also centers the urban working class (there are Pākehā children on Champion Street as well). Although my reading focuses on the ethnic dimension of the text, colonialism, racism, and class are inextricably linked.

Watercress Tuna starts with Tuna leaving Cannon's Creek (the stream after which the neighborhood gets its name[21]) and journeying through a series of familiar landmarks, each of which bears the (European) name of the creek:

over Cannon's Creek tavern,
over Cannon's Creek shopping centre,
over Cannon's Creek primary school
and on to Champion Street.[22]

Each of these landmarks is a marker of a local landscape, but each also speaks to the impact of colonialism: alcohol and dependency on capitalistic acquisition of goods and schooling, respectively. The second part of the book recounts Tuna's interactions with different children from different Pacific backgrounds who live on Champion Street. These interactions are described in a parallel structure, and on the first page of each interaction, the child reaches into Tuna's throat and retrieves an item:

> Tuna bounced into [names of child]'s house and opened his mouth wide.
>   [Name of child] reached in and took out [an item].[23]

On the second page of the interaction, the child uses the item "and [begins] to dance." Several children, material items, and backgrounds are introduced: Kelehia takes out a kie, Karen takes out "buckled shoes," Hirini takes out a piupiu, Tuaine takes out a pate, Roimata takes out a poi, Kava takes out a hau, Nga takes out a pareu, Losa takes out an ula, Jason takes out a paper streamer, and Fa'afetai takes out an ailao afi. The names of the children are from their languages of origin, which reinforces their location within their respective communities but doesn't perhaps reflect the use of English-language names in many Aotearoa-based Pacific communities; there are no Māori kids called "Natasha" or Samoan kids called "Faith" in this configuration.[24] The third section of the story brings the children from the family-centric–origin-centric space of the private house out into the public space of Champion Street. Along with Tuna, they "danced and danced. Everybody danced." Each child retains her own style and yet joins with others in a common space for a shared purpose. This section of the book privileges a shared public space, the illustrations depicting a dancing crowd with a diversity of generations, cultural groups, and genders. On the final page, the children are all sleeping in their own beds, with the treasures they extracted from Tuna's mouth at the ends of their blankets. Far from depicting a beige-inducing melting pot, then, the shared action of dancing in the shared space of the street is both enabled by and supports the maintenance of cultural distinctiveness in the family space.

Although one possible reading of *Watercress Tuna* would focus on its multicultural politics, I argue that the place of the Tuna in the structure as well as the narrative of the story compels another, perhaps additional, reading. Whereas the children "dance" with the material culture and style of movement relevant to their own family backgrounds, their continued connection relies on a meaningful relationship with a Māori structuring—perhaps spiritual, perhaps governmental—presence. While the two Māori children (Hirini and Roimata) are a part of the crowd and have the same overt interaction with Tuna as the other children, the central role of Tuna compellingly suggests that the lingering and vibrant Indigeneity of local Māori is a source of, and mechanism for, the dance in which the children and their communities participate. This vision resists the version of multiculturalism that empties out Indigenous difference and gestures instead toward a treaty-derived relationship between tāngata whenua and manuhiri, providing room for Pasifika as well as Pākehā acknowledgment of Māori in Aotearoa.

The illustrations in *Watercress Tuna* are typical of artist Robyn Kahukiwa's style: vivid, with an emphasis on color and action. The demeanor of the children is confident and active, which challenges the widely distributed image of urban Pacific youth and children as lazy, violent, oppressed, nihilistic, disadvantaged, and so on. Throughout the text, the children exhibit confidence in their own cultural backgrounds, and the environments in which they are raised—as made most visible perhaps by the homescapes in which each child is visited by Tuna—further support the experiences and cultural orientations of their families. So houses are decorated with a woven fan on the wall, a shelf with old bowls on it, poutama-design wallpaper and a bookshelf with a carved gourd, island-style fabric at the windows for curtains, a framed picture of an ancestress and a wakahuia, island-design cushion covers, a small wooden carving on a shelf and a wooden ceremonial object on the floor, a woven mat pattern on one wall, a cabinet with a clock and animal ornaments, and tapa.[25] The maintenance of culture despite location within an urban environment directly challenges the mythology of urban areas,[26] and the material culture standing in for cultural values and mores has extra significance because the houses themselves are all so-called state houses.[27] Perhaps the personalization of each house to reflect the background of its residents suggests how Aotearoa-based Pacific identities might operate within the national (or nation-sponsored or nation-subsidized) space.[28]

"Hibiscus-Coloured Shirts Instead of Black": Briar Grace-Smith

Briar Grace-Smith's short story "Te Manawa" appeared in the 2006 compilation *The Six Pack,* produced by the organizers of New Zealand Book Month.[29] The visually distinctive book contains writing by six New Zealanders, five of whom were selected by a team of celebrity judges and one of whom was chosen by public vote on the Book Month Web site. *The Six Pack* was widely available in New Zealand for a price of six dollars (in New Zealand, a standard fiction paperback usually costs between thirty and fifty dollars), and its publication was designed to get the public excited about books. One of the most interesting things about the Six Pack competition, which ran three times (producing *Six Pack 2* and *Six Pack 3* as well), is that the selection was blind (authors' names were removed for judging) and most of the judges were well-known people in areas other than the literary arts. In 2006, the judges were John Campbell, current affairs television presenter; Maggie Barry, gardening expert; Sarah-Kate Lynch, ex-editor of the *New Zealand Women's Weekly* who has turned her hand to popular fiction; Tom Beran, bookseller; and David Kirk, ex-captain of the All Blacks national rugby team and medical doctor. These "inexpert" judges, the people's vote, and the blind judging meant that the competition offered a chance for novice writers to win literary kudos. There can be quiet suspicion of literary prizes and awards, especially in a place as small as New Zealand, and this competition offered a democratic chance for all. Unsurprisingly, perhaps, in all three years of the competition, the winners were a mixture of published and new writers. In the first Six Pack book, one of those writers was Māori playwright, fiction writer, and screenplay writer Briar Grace-Smith.

"Te Manawa" tells the story of a Māori woman who undergoes a heart transplant after illness and receives a heart from Mele, a Samoan female donor who has been killed in an accident. The story is about hearts of all kinds—literal hearts, figurative hearts, emotions—and this is made all the more complicated by the cross-cultural bodily transaction. Each of the three male characters struggles with the depth of love he has for one of the female characters, a wife or sister, and by the end of the story, each finds a way to make peace with the intensity of his feelings and the difficulty of letting go. The recipient of the heart, who is unnamed throughout the story, finds that Mele's heart propels her like "a giant horseshoe magnet"[30] out of her own house and along to Mele's previous home, where she would "peer in at the man called Spencer and his children, sleeping."[31] Spencer suffers from horrific nightmares as a result of losing his wife, and she hears him struggling in his sleep while she walks around the house, both Mele ("tak[ing] the spare key from its hiding place"[32]) and not Mele ("the man," "his children"). Meanwhile, the recipient's husband, Eru, realizes that she is sneaking out each night and is convinced that she is having an affair but cannot bring himself to confront her directly: "as Eru draped a blanket over her he prayed that she had at least included him in her dreams."[33] Finally, her brother Tem visits after her recovery from the operation, before which he had gone hunting in desperation for his sister's needed heart and had returned to the hospital with an impossibly still-pumping pig's heart, which the doctor had ridiculed and which Tem planted under a young kauri tree, only to witness the buried heart miraculously pump soil to the surface every day.

"Te Manawa" examines the strong link between bodies and memory. Rather than gradually losing its memory of being in a Samoan body, the recipient's heart recalls being a part of Mele more strongly as time goes on. Eru notices small changes—"hibiscus-coloured shirts instead of black"[34]— and she begins to cook Samoan food ("sapasui"[35]) and to speak Samoan. Meanwhile, her visits to Mele's previous home become more invasive, and she indulges her senses there through smelling, touching, hearing, looking, and—a giveaway for Spencer, who knows Mele's favorite food is apricots, which he leaves out and finds nibbled each morning—tasting. The recipient's body inherits Mele's bodily memories and desires, but these do not override its prior nature, and it records its own memories of the recipient's nighttime sojourns, which she then discovers when she wakes up back in her own home, dirty and sore-footed from walking on the streets with no shoes and with hives from her allergy to apricots. Her use of Mele's language increases, and simultaneously, her recollections of her pretransplant life fade until Tem visits her one day and she violently rejects his customary horseplay and only speaks in Samoan to him, a doubly unfamiliar situation to which he responds by leaving, "feeling hurt and confused."[36] Tem sails to the South Island, reflecting on his interaction with his sister and quietly "rub[bing] the scar that ran in a thick and raised cord from his knee to his ankle,"[37] which he had acquired from the boar whose heart he had seized in his failed attempt to provide for his sister. Eru, too, suffers bodily transformation as a result of the circumstances, although unlike his wife, whose body inherits the memory of its new heart, and Tem, whose body bears the mark of a past event, at the point of deciding to leave his wife, Eru suffers an imaginative physical distortion in which he pictures himself turned inside out as a desperate outward sign of the agony he feels inside.

Finally, the recipient is in the kitchen at Mele's house one evening, having found herself incapable of consciously resisting "the beat of this strange new heart which now smacked inside her chest,"[38] and for the first time, Spencer wakes while she is there. She puts on Mele's clothes and, through her body, recalls more of Mele's memories: "The wrap she had bought at the Ōtara Market when she had visited her sister in South Auckland for Christmas. Feeling the cool wash of its cotton against her skin she remembered the last time she had worn it."[39] The narrator refers to the recipient as "Mele" when she ties the lavalava in a familiar way, and she finds the bowl of apricots Spencer has left for her. Spencer confronts Mele, who talks about her experience of death and bids him a loving farewell, giving last instructions before she leaves the recipient's body. Immediately, Spencer is freed from his mourning and is able to let Mele go, and at the same time, the recipient gets her own body back, including consciousness of its familiar responses: "The first thing she felt was an unpleasant sting. Raising a finger to her face she felt the hard sting of hives."[40] The recipient realizes that "she is in a house that [is]n't hers"[41] and with a man she does not know. This transition is not an exorcism: a tinge of Mele's memory is left in her body ("she knew without doubt he had a raised mole on the back of his neck"[42]) but she is free to leave and returns home.

Does it matter that Mele is Samoan and that the recipient is Māori? It might not. Yet the story would not work as well if the recipient were not Māori because the physical links between the recipient and Mele are secured in their mutual Polynesianness. While Spencer recognizes his dead wife's behaviors in the bites taken from her favorite fruit, he also recognizes her by the "thick strands of glossy black hair"[43] found on the couch, strands that could be a sign of Samoan presence but could equally be Māori. In this way, he both recognizes and misrecognizes the recipient as Mele, and the reader has no way to know whether the hair is a remnant of Mele's former presence before the accident or recently left there by the recipient. Did the new heart need to come from a Samoan donor? Perhaps not—although arguably, the cultural markers of a Pākehā donor would perhaps be less stark in a Māori family that cannot help but bear the marks of two centuries of colonialism: the recipient and Eru speak English to one another, and any attempt to render clothing or even food distinctively Pākehā could have been difficult without creeping toward caricature. Indeed, the story manages to trade on the convenience of Māori and Samoan phenotypic similarity, which is paired with cultural distinctiveness.

Conversely, subtle aspects of the story work particularly well because of the established and ongoing relationship between Māori and Pasifika communities. Although many Māori families have adopted sapasui as one of their own foods, this family is apparently not one of them, and so it becomes a familiar marker—for Eru, but also for the reader—of difference: "Eru, who had a lisp and hated saying sapasui, hated it even more." Like Harris's knowledge of "Palagi," Eru knows sapasui well enough to call it "sapasui" (rather than its Anglicized derivation, "chop suey"), and to know that he struggles to pronounce or even eat it. Furthermore, Eru's fear of his wife's lover takes particular expression when he notices these changes about her, which seem to betray Pasifika contact, and he imagines his rival along quite stereotypical lines:

> A smooth and handsome man from the islands perhaps. A law-yer or a dancer with a body with skin that clung to his muscles like bronze gladwrap. Maybe even a white-coated doctor who'd injected the woman with his language and given her hives just from looking at him.[44]

Of course, the reader realizes that the hives come as a result of her interaction with a Pasifika heart that is far more intimate than that of a lover. The story is not about being Samoan or even about being Māori. It is about a heart—"te manawa"—and *whose* heart is unspecified in the story: it could be the failed heart of the recipient, the homesick heart of Mele, the broken heart of Eru, the grieving heart of Spencer, the worried heart of Tem, or even the ever-pulsing heart of the boar. Three hearts literally end up outside of their original bodies—the recipient's, Mele's, and the boar's—and the three other hearts are figuratively broken and healed again. In the end, Mele being Samoan and the recipient being Māori are devices for the story, but they are also central to it. In terms of the connections between Māori and Pasifika communities, the story demonstrates familiarity as well as difference and takes for granted that Māori and Pasifika live and, yes, die in close proximity.

Māori Write Connections

Taylor, Grace, and Grace-Smith are not the only Māori writers who write about the connections between Māori and Pasifika communities, and yet their contributions are significant because they are rare. Indeed, each of these three writers is highly productive, and most of their other work does not engage with Pasifika either.[45] Although it is unproductive to bemoan writing that is not published, and thereby to imply dissatisfaction with what is, it is important to ask questions about why certain experiences are left off the page. (Certainly these are not the only experiences that are yet to find wide and varied expression in published Māori writing in English.) Explanations for this small number of Māori texts engaging the Māori–Pasifika "interface," as McIntosh would call it, could rest with the writers or with the nature of publication. We can be sure that Māori people are engaging in relationship with Pasifika people: the evidence for this is plentiful. We can also assume that any community will have writers, and this is confirmed by the archives as well as bookshelves of Māori writing. This leaves us with publishing and distribution; perhaps publishers are not interested in material that treats these relationships; perhaps publishers do not believe there would be a market for this material; perhaps this material is not being produced in genres with which usual publishing and distribution mechanisms work; perhaps this writing is not making it to the front door of publishers.

Ultimately, if you were to rely on Māori writing in English to get a full picture of Māori experiences, you would be unlikely to realize the multiple long-standing relationships we have with Pasifika individuals and communities in particular spaces. At the same time, however, many Pasifika writers are actively talking about their relationships with Māori. This means that some of the most engaged representations of particular Māori experiences are in fact produced by Pasifika writers, and so at this point, *Once Were Pacific* hands the mic to them.

CHAPTER 6

Manuhiri, Fānau:
Pasifika Write Connections

PASIFIKA COMMUNITIES are in two places at once: in New Zealand, as citizens and residents of a settler nation, and in Aotearoa, as manuhiri in a group of islands in the Pacific populated by relatives. The corpus of published Pasifika writing is uneven but weighty, and like many areas of Pasifika creative production in New Zealand, the literature has enough practitioners to allow us to trace generations of writers. Pasifika writers produce across the spectrum of forms and genres, although it is worth noting that contemporarily in published and produced work, performance arts have been dominated by men, and poetry has been dominated by women. Although the focus of much Pasifika creative and critical work is on the Pasifika relationship with New Zealand, the entity represented by the name "Somes," this chapter proposes at least two ways in which Pasifika writers articulate a sense of connection with Māori that correspond to the two narratives about my island called "Matiu." The word *manuhiri* in the title of this chapter is from the Māori language and so demonstrates cultural familiarity with Māori drawn from previous encounters and interactions. *Fānau* relates to Māori linguistically and culturally but is sourced, as identified by its spelling with the letter *f*, from outside Aotearoa.

Talking about Pasifika communities as "manuhiri" acknowledges Indigeneity as represented by the story of Matiu Island in relation to a fish and a navigator. Using the term in this context is explicitly derived from a section in the Tongan poet Karlo Mila's *Dream Fish Floating*,[1] for which she won the New Zealand Book Awards prize for best first book of poetry in 2005. Mila pays focused attention to Māori as tāngata whenua in specific poems, and she more broadly pays attention to Māori through the terminology by which she structures two of the six sections of the book (tuakana and wero). In a Māori cultural context, manuhiri are visitors defined by their relationship to tāngata whenua. During the encounter ritual of pōwhiri, in particular, tāngata whenua engage in very specific ways with manuhiri, recounting and establishing preexisting connections to constitute the manuhiri in relation to the host group. While manuhiri are visitors, there is always, ritually, the possibility of welcoming and absorbing manuhiri into the ranks of tāngata whenua. Being manuhiri in Aotearoa is not the same as citizenship: it cannot account for or replace Pasifika relationships with New Zealand and instead is an additional, differently configured, relationship.

Another approach to Māori–Pasifika connection, "fānau," recognizes the deep connections between Māori and Pasifika since the migrations to Aotearoa, during which, at one point, Matiu was named "Kupe." This term is drawn here from Albert Wendt's treatment of Pasifika connections with Māori in his only published play, *The Songmaker's Chair*,[2] which centers on the Peseola family and articulates Samoan connections to Aotearoa and New Zealand through the narrative and makeup of the family. In New Zealand, the lives of the Peseola family are inextricably tied to Māori, and thereby to Aotearoa, in literally intimate ways through the mixed couple Nofo (Samoan) and Hone (Māori) and their two children, Mata and Tapu. Nofo is the second of the two Peseola children born in Sāmoa (the remaining children are New Zealand born), and her name emphasizes her relationship to place.[3] Nofo and Hone do not enjoy an easy partnership, and Nofo's wider family is aware of the rockiness in their marriage. Just as fa'asāmoa and afi appear on the page as "*wha* Samoa" and "awhi" in Taylor's story "Pa Mai," Mata describes her Māori relatives as "our fanau up north."[4] A cross-linguistic homonym, *whānau*/*fānau* are used in Māori and Samoan to designate family (although *aiga* is more likely in Samoan), and yet, because this is a play script, the proximity of *fānau* to *whānau* would be lost on the live audience. Because Mata is referring to her Māori relations (as denoted by "up north"), the spoken word would be understood as "whānau," and yet, in the pages of the published text, the word appears as "fanau." This slippage is intriguing: it simultaneously points to the potential for misrecognition (audience members could misrecognize it as a Māori word) and cross-linguistic understanding (audience members could understand the meaning of the Samoan word even without realizing it was Samoan) in the contemporary context and to the deep linguistic (and cultural) connections between Aotearoa and Sāmoa.

Many Pasifika writers have treated this relationship in their work, and in this discussion, we will focus on Alistair Te Ariki Campbell from the first generation of Pasifika writers and Karlo Mila as a writer from a later generation. Although both also engage with their specifically Cook Islander and

Tongan backgrounds, respectively, our focus here is on their articulation of their "fānau" and "manuhiri" relationships with Māori. Pasifika writing demands and deserves much wider and lengthier consideration than what this chapter can cover, and there are many other key writers whose work should really be included here too. The elephant in the room is Albert Wendt, whose deep and ongoing creative, teaching, editing, and critical commitment to elaborating the relationship between Pasifika and Māori communities is unsurpassed and probably unsurpassable.[5] It is worth noting that although in a following chapter, we will look more carefully at articulations of *dis*connection, which are a significant feature of the relationship between Māori and Pasifika communities, in this chapter, we will focus on connection.

Dear Arita: Alistair Te Ariki Campbell

Alistair Te Ariki Campbell is a kaumātua of the Pasifika writing scene in Aotearoa: he has been publishing his poetry since the 1950s and has produced a huge corpus of poetic and fictional texts since then. His father, Jock Campbell, was a Pākehā New Zealander from Dunedin, and his mother, Teu Bosini, was from Tongareva. Campbell was born in Rarotonga, but after he and his siblings were orphaned as children, he moved to New Zealand, where he was raised in orphanages. The autobiography he wrote in 1984, *Island to Island,* opens with the phone call by which he became reconnected with his relatives from the Cook Islands.[6] Although his connection to his own family was disrupted by his distance from them for many years, he remained an active part of the Māori writing scene while it became established. He spent time with Māori writers, wrote about Māori topics, and was the only writer who is not (New Zealand) Māori to be included in Ihimaera and Long's 1982 anthology *Into the World of Light.*[7] In his 2006 master of arts thesis "Savaiki Regained: Alistair Te Ariki Campbell's Poetics,"[8] Māori poet Robert Sullivan argues that treatments of Campbell's poetry have often tended toward Eurocentrism and have failed to acknowledge or explore the Polynesian dimension of his writing.

As well as writing about his Cook Island background, Campbell's collections have ranged over a number of Māori topics, including a long sequence on Te Rauparaha and, in 2001, a collection titled *Maori Battalion: A Poetic Sequence.*[9] The book is structured around the four main campaigns of the famous World War II Twenty-eighth Māori Battalion—Greece, Crete, North Africa, and Italy. Each section includes poems written from a range of perspectives: some from the view of specific individuals, some narrating events, and some outlining the emotional landscape of war. Māori deities and ideas, such as Tū, Reinga, and Māui, are named in the poems, and because these figures and ideas appear elsewhere in the Pacific, these references could be an articulation of a particular Māori-centric space but could also be an articulation of Pacific connection. *Maori Battalion* is a memorial as well as poetic project and opens with a black-and-white photograph of a young man in military uniform and the caption "Stuart Alexander Maireriki Campbell." Two pages later is a dedication:

> To the Memory of my Brother
> Private 446853
> Stuart Alexander Maireriki Campbell
> 28 (Maori) Battalion
> Killed in Action
> 11 April 1945[10]

The dedication is a marker of very specific grief but is also an important intervention into the dominant ways of memorializing the Māori battalion as a Māori-only (and I mean New Zealand Māori here) organization, whereas in reality, a number of Pacific soldiers fought in that battalion, most often as members of D Company. Unlike the Pacific soldiers in the Twenty-eighth who signed up while living outside of Aotearoa or while at boarding school in New Zealand, Stuart signed up as a young man based in New Zealand.

Each poem in the book is numbered, and poem 68, in the "Italy" section, is titled "Letter from Stuart Maireriki."[11] The poem is written as a letter from Stuart to Alistair himself after Stuart has been killed. It opens by naming the writer and recipient of the letter and disorienting (or affirming) the reader by using their Cook Island names: "Dear Arita—Tuati here" (when transliterated, "Arita" is rendered "Alistair," and "Tuati" is "Stuart"). Naming and language matter for Campbell, who writes about his own acquisition of English once he arrives in New Zealand: "the price was high—the loss of my mother tongue, Penrhyn Maori, which I've since come to regret."[12] In death, then, Tuati returns to his originary home, including his originary linguistic home, and thereby reverses the process of loss not only for himself but also for Alistair. In this letter from the grave, Stuart regains his Cook Island name "Tuati," and from the perspective of his brother, who has gone to be with his relatives on the other side, Alistair has the opportunity to experience himself as a Pacific man by being named as one: "Arita." Furthermore, both men recall being known by their Māori names in childhood, when they lived with their mother's family, and so Stuart's death imaginatively enables Campbell to move back in time but also to reverse the process of migration to New Zealand. Later in the poem, this return home takes another step:

> Dear Grandfather Bosini
> he wept and called for me, his Maireriki ,
> his "Little Flower," when he heard that I had been
> killed in Italy.

Having renamed himself from "Stuart," the legal name under which he was listed in the army and therefore the name under which he died, "Tuati" (and with him, "Arita," ever the writer and reader of the letter) reaches back a generation beyond their mother to their "Grandfather Bosini," who names him a third name: "Maireriki." This third name, which is one of Stuart's middle names, is not a transliteration but a name from within the cultural context of the island. Alistair does not receive a parallel name of this kind in this poem. The layering of names "Alistair–Stuart," "Arita–Tuati," and finally "Maireriki" suggests a series of cultural contexts in which, if "Maireriki" is a name associated with originary family and place, and "Alistair" and "Stuart" are associated with public lives, "Tuati" and "Arita" are in between these two. These are linguistically in-between names because they are transliterations, but they are also cultural in-betweens because they are neither the names "Grandfather Bosini" uses nor the names the army would recognize.

In this opening of the poem, the two names—the two brothers—stand side by side and are connected on the page by a single dash that both joins and separates them. Throughout the poem, the connection between the two is negotiated, and even though the poem is ostensibly about the experiences of "Tuati," the voice of the poem keeps directly addressing the recipient, "Arita": "As you know," "as you know," "don't ask me," "would you believe it," "I thought you'd like to know," "you once told," "can you imagine," "did you know," "to my family, to you," "your girl," "I knew you." For the reader, this repeated direct address emphasizes the sense of reading over some-one's shoulder—the poem doesn't mean *me* when it says "you"—and yet because the implied "you" of the poem ("Arita") is also the writer of the poem, Campbell becomes the ever-present writer–recipient of the letter. Indeed, Campbell's place in the poem is complicated. This is a somewhat biographical poem of his brother whose life story he offers through the conceit of a poetic autobiography through the further formal conceit of a letter. Yet to some extent, this is autobiographical: Campbell is writing to himself ("Dear Arita"), and yet not exactly to himself but to himself as his brother might have seen him and also—particularly given the use of the name "Arita"—as his mother's relatives would know him. This is a poem written by Alistair to and about Arita: ultimately, Campbell addresses his Cook Islander self from which he was distanced by his migration to Aotearoa. However, he is able to address his Cook Islander self because he is looking through the eyes of his dead brother, who is, at least on one level, writing about the Māori Battalion in a book about the Māori Battalion.

Near the middle of the poem, far from his own greeting to Arita at one end and the farewell given to him by Grandfather Bosini at the other, Tuati recalls his position in the Twenty-eighth:

> D company
> was my whanau. They called me Sam, and
> accepted me, although I was an Islander.

This short reference to the place of Pacific soldiers in the Māori Battalion is primarily about connection, but this is neither homogenizing nor complete. Tuati expresses his sense of connection with his peers in Māori terms—"whanau"—and recognizes the ways in which this connection was reciprocated. First, because names have such significance in this poem (and Polynesian cultures), it seems important that the men from his company "called [him] Sam." This is the only English name in the whole poem, and the tone of the phrase does not indicate whether this name was detested, tolerated, or enjoyed. Was he misnamed because they did not know his name? Does this misnaming show an inability to really know him because he is "an Islander"? Or, if in each relationship and each space in his life, he acquires a different and appropriate name, does "Sam," as his name in that particular space, emphasize his subjectivity as a soldier and, specifically, as part of the whānau of D Company? The relationship does not end with a name, however, but also includes "acceptance." Of course, this "acceptance" is conditional—"although I was an Islander"—and yet an earlier comment that he "did win . . . some good-natured ribbing" from his "mates" leaves open whether this was understood by Tuati as a derogatory or a humorous exchange.

In his 2007 collection *Just Poetry,* Campbell returns to imagined corre-
spondence from his brother, and "Tuati" writes to "Arita" from the grave at
the "Faenza Military Cemetery"[13] once more. The poem again begins "Dear
Arita," but the name "Tuati" does not appear until the very end of the letter–poem. The names of the two brothers are separated this time by the body
of the poem, and before the final sign-off, Tuati makes a more final farewell
to his brother: "My dear poetic brother, goodbye. / *Tuati.*" As if Tuati had
continued to mature while buried at Faenza, his voice in this poem is older
and more reflective. The earlier poem is more focused on Tuati's experiences
in the Battalion and his immediate environment, whereas this later poem
runs through a series of memories about, as the poem's title suggests, "A
Childhood in the Islands." The poem recites names and places and narrates
specific memories of events and relationships both boys experienced while
growing up. The speaker of the poem doesn't address the reader–recipient
as often as the previous poem, until "Tuati" directly comments to "Arita"
near the middle of the poem,

> You were the bad apple—no, that's too
> strong. You were naughty, into every
> bit of mischief going. I suppose there
> has to be a touch of wickedness in any
> family of kids to balance an excess
> of goodness . . .

After this, Tuati coerces Arita in his act of memory by starting a series of
memories with the word "remember," a word that both prompts a memory
(do you remember?) and commands it (remember this). Although the latter
poem ostensibly deals with different subject matter, the effect is the same in
that both men (poet–recipient and brother–imagined writer) are returned
through memory to Penrhyn (Tongareva) and to relationships with their
mother and grandfather. Not only is the effect of the war reversed but so,
too, is the period of time spent in the orphanage and growing up in New
Zealand. Of course, one outcome of this imagined return to Penrhyn and
implied departure from New Zealand is that Campbell's engagement with
Aotearoa is also diminished. Perhaps this is the result of Campbell's own
journey into deeper understanding of his Cook Islander side, but perhaps
it is also a result of his understanding of (New Zealand) Māori ideas of
returning to Hawaiki on death. Campbell passed away in 2009, a significant

star not only in the constellations of Pacific and Cook Islands writing but also in the writing of Aotearoa.

te ariki

Alice Te Punga Somerville

go now, e te ariki,
to your mates, your beloved, your blood

let those hands which held all those pens
magicked a thousand thousand words
lie still and empty at last

spend no more nights dreaming of an infancy in the sun
go back home
with no return ticket this time
your mother has been waiting for you

go the way your friends have gone;
the tracks may still be warm from hone's recent journey:
you've been one of us on these rugged frozen isles
since arriving with a luggage tag on your small boy's jacket
all those years ago;
you and your brother fighting alongside us
since before we can remember,
one in the 28th, the other on pages;
the least we can do is loan you a pathway home

no longer perch on the edge of these cliffs with an eye on the tide:
follow sand to water,
leave us behind,
go

alistair te ariki campbell:
firsts and firsts
accomplishments
and now you've breathed your last

"Not Exotic Anymore": Karlo Mila

We have read Mila's first collection *Dream Fish Floating* in Victoria University of Wellington's introductory New Zealand Literature and Theatre course since it was published in 2005. Students love the text: it is a pleasure to prove wrong the students who think they hate poetry, and Mila's gentle, forceful language and images broach issues of politics, love, families, the body, and culture in ways in which first-year students—no matter what their age—are invested as they start to navigate their way around university. The theme of the course is "cultural encounters," and in a settler nation-state like Aotearoa New Zealand, most of the encounters explored both in the course and in the texts of the course include Pākehā as one of the encounterers. However, in the section "Wero," the colonial context of New Zealand, and the Palangi (Pākehā) community, are held in a different relationship with Pasifika and Māori elements of the poetry.

Māori have many places in *Dream Fish Floating.* The first section, "Tuakana," takes the Māori form of a pan-Polynesian word that denotes an older sibling of the same gender as the speaker. The "Tuakana" section comprises four poems dedicated to four writers, and in this way, Mila begins her first book with the elaboration of a literary genealogy. None of these writers is Māori—the poems (in order) are written for Sia Figiel, Albert Wendt, John Pule, and Alice Walker—and yet Mila uses a Māori term to conceptualize their position as elder siblings. Mila's knowledge of a specific tribal saying from the Waikato region is demonstrated and extended in the poem "He piko he taniwha." In perhaps her most well known poem, "Eating Dark Chocolate While Watching Paul Holmes' Apology," Mila reflects on the use of the word Holmes used to describe Kofi Annan—"Darkie"—in her own childhood, adolescence, and adulthood.[14] She replies to Holmes's apology by pointing out a compromised coming of age, and while recollecting the shape of New Zealand–based racism at age six, she remembers being relieved that "no one called me manu off playschool or darkie": a Māori-named doll on a daytime kid's show "manu" is turned into racist mocking on the school playground. The slippage is between racist slurs: to be "manu" in this school was to be "darkie."[15]

In "Wero," rather than being the topic of the poetry, the Māori material provides the frame. In this section, Mila adds a further tuakana: Papa Sean, a teacher in Palmerston North for whom she names two poems. Although wero is most often translated as "challenge," which may appear from an outside perspective to be negative, the wero is an important part of Māori protocol by which the encounter between tāngata whenua and manuhiri is moderated. The whole process is geared to articulating connection and intentions to ultimately establish and negotiate relationships between the two groups. At the point of the wero, the manuhiri have two options: continue, and thereby follow further processes by which the relationship can be negotiated and by which, although maintaining distinctiveness, manuhiri are incorporated into the home community, or refuse the challenge and thereby set themselves in opposition to the tāngata whenua and, ultimately, maintain separation. Significantly, the section is not clear about whether it is the wero itself or the response to a wero (or series of wero) issued elsewhere. Is Mila challenging the reader? Is Mila challenging herself? Is Mila describing a challenge issued by tāngata whenua? Is the wero directed toward Mila alone, or Mila and the reader, or only the reader? Mila refuses to unambiguously "answer" the wero within the space of the section: in this way, "Wero" is an open and productive challenge in and of itself rather than a description of a choice or, indeed, a resolution of that choice.

All of the poems in "Wero" describe Mila's connection with Māori, which she has explained as an outcome of being raised in the small provincial city of Palmerston North; if she had been raised in Auckland, perhaps she would have a stronger sense of being Tongan but a less strong sense of being manuhiri. Indeed, the first poem of the section foregrounds not only her position but others in relation to tāngata whenua. Three poems about the pine tree on the top of Maungakiekie (One Tree Hill) in Auckland— "Manuhiri," "On One Tree Hill Falling," and "Poroporoaki"—supply an opportunity to reflect on her own complicity with colonialism as well as the multiple structures of resistance one can identify once one pays attention to complexity rather than oversimplification. Other poems in the section explore unexpected as well as taken-for-granted connections between Mila and tāngata whenua in terms of physical objects, personal relationships, and specific spaces. For the purpose of this discussion, we will focus on "Manuhiri," the first of what I call the "Maungakiekie poems."

"Manuhiri" logically responds to—makes visible, acknowledges, depends on—tāngata whenua that have necessarily come first (or else they wouldn't be manuhiri), and this acknowledges another realm of precedent—even if unwritten—to set beside Mila's literary "tuakana." Who exactly "manuhiri" refers to is ambiguous; it could be everyone in the Manawatū other than Rangitāne (acknowledged tāngata whenua), Pākehā, tauiwi,[16] the New

Zealand state, the reader, or Mila herself. Any of these is possible, and each of these produces a new way of reading the remainder of the poem:

> in the Manawatu
> pine needles stitch together
> a patchwork of green pastures

The first imagery of the poem slips between the natural environment ("pine needles") and domestic handiwork ("needles stitch together / a patchwork"). The trees are named as "pines," which are an introduced species and become a metaphor for manuhiri over the course of the three poems. In this poem, Mila takes advantage of the pun on "pine needles" to balance the metaphor for settler agricultural colonialism ("pine") with reference to settler domestic space. This produces a sense of complete domination: women and men, inside and outside, are teamed in the same task. The industriousness valued by the machinery of colonialism (and its attendant Protestant work ethic) manages to exert architectural control over the landscape: on one level, the flat pastoral fields of the Manawatū are nicely captured in the metaphor of a green patchwork quilt; on another, a quilt might remind one of covering, concealing, hiding, and perhaps warming. Comparing the process of pastoralization to a patchwork quilt ironically links the sense of colonial accomplishment to a sense of comfort and warmth.

An additional reading of the quilt is also possible: the patchwork has been a dominant form of craft for colonial and working-class women (and, memorably, enslaved women) because it enables the patchworker to make aesthetic and practical use of fabric offcuts and ends. Additionally, the work of creating a patchwork has often been a collective exercise at which the social exchange has been as important as the product. The Manawatū is a space made up of multiple pieces: literally, the fields surrounding Palmerston North are put to a number of uses and so appear to be patchworked, but conceptually, the Manawatū could be understood as a conglomeration of various offcuts: remnant and small communities, working together in a deliberate pattern to produce something of value. To extend this metaphor, often a patchwork is perceived to be made up of small pieces of cloth, each of which brings memories of previously worn garments and the times and places in which they were worn. This creates a metaphor of functional multiplicity that is not undermined but cherished and perhaps sentimentalized by the previous lives and contexts of its members: a vision of multiculturalism indeed. To read this metaphor back onto the title, the manuhiri is allowed space to elaborate itself as multiple, and being in relationship with tāngata whenua does not require other pasts or identifications to be discarded. In this moment, I argue, we find something other than multiculturalism: as in Grace's *Watercress Tuna*, we find that which Kai Tahu media scholar Jo Smith has described as "aspirational biculturalism."[17] This vision of multiple, nuanced manuhiri produced both by and in relationship with tāngata whenua explicitly counters the mythology touted by monoculturalists who attempt to disband the possibilities of biculturalism by claiming that it does not allow for multiculturalism.

The major features of the poem are established at this point, including the pine to which this poem and the other two Maungakiekie texts will return and which stands in for a range of things, including a commodity (New Zealand's forestry and its invisible labor force, including a large number of Māori and Pasifika workers), a symbol of introduced species, a simultaneous symbol of the destruction of native ecosystems and land erosion, and at the same time a symbol of a positive sense of growth and regeneration. The poem continues:

> oh those pines
> they're everywhere you go

The descriptive and deeply metaphoric tone shifts with the "oh" into something that sounds like a flippant comment or indulgent aside. That "those pines" are "everywhere you go" extends the poem beyond the Manawatū that the "pines" themselves border. Possibly this refers to the coverage of the pines around the Manawatū, but perhaps the more productive reading is that this is but one example of a widely spread phenomenon. The uniqueness of the Manawatū is undermined by the "pines" being "everywhere."

This is all followed by two lines of defensive replies by a clearly demarcated "they":

> We're not exotic anymore they argue
> We have roots here too they say

The "they" of this poem could well be the trees: the trees are not exotic because they have passed a temporal line in the sand between "exotic" and "having roots." Indeed, this is an inversion of the logic by which Te Papa argued that Daniel Maaka was not "Pacific Island" because Māori had passed a temporal distinction between "Pacific Island" and "Pacific Island in origin." Here the remedy for being coded "exotic" is to point to the existence of "roots": a botanical metaphor already used colloquially to express a sense of belonging to a place. Whether the response is indignant at being described as manuhiri or as "being everywhere" is ambiguous. If "they" are arguing against being manuhiri (in relationship with tāngata whenua), then claiming roots could be a defense against Māori claims of Indigeneity (which always trump those who feel "not exotic anymore"). Conversely, if "they" are speaking back to the idea of being "everywhere," the roots provide a basis for specific identification in the face of a perceived homogeneity of white settlers "everywhere." Furthermore, Mila's humor in the final lines of "On One Tree Hill Falling" ("the 'dying race' you were supposed to commemorate / did the dirty / and lived longer"[18]) leaves room to recognize the pun on the word *roots*, which, in New Zealand at least, is a rather crass term for sex and so enables a genealogical reading as well.

Another reading hinges on a pun on the word *exotic*, which is a botanical term for a plant not originally from the area and, at the same time, a popular description of Pacific people. Indeed, Pacific people have been rendered "exotic" by European travelers and texts, and throughout this book, there are examples of writers responding to this kind of representation. If, indeed, the "we" is "exotic," it is possible that the "we" (or "they") of the poem are specifically Pasifika communities instead. In this reading of the poem, where "we're not exotic anymore they argue" is a Pasifika response, we can imagine a doubled rejection of the term *exotic*: on one hand, refusing to be produced in romantic European stereotypes of the Pacific, and on the other, refusing to be understood as not belonging to the local area (Manawatū) or, indeed, to New Zealand. To read this back on the previous lines "oh those pines / they're everywhere you go," a comment about ubiquity could also be understood as a racist frustration about Pasifika communities being increasingly visible in New Zealand—even in the Manawatū. Furthermore, to then reread the first lines of the poem, it is possible to recognize the place of Pasifika labor ("pastures" and "stitching") in the production of the contemporary settler nation of New Zealand.

The end of the poem ties the Manawatū (and the poem itself) to the pair of poems later in the section that treat Maungakiekie:

Ask that old guy on One Tree Hill
and Tane Mahuta's laughing

This is an abrupt ending and seems to shift the focus away from the Manawatū altogether. The "old guy on One Tree Hill" is the pine about which Mila goes on to write in two other poems, and calling the tree "that old guy" gestures toward her affectionate way of writing about the tree. When we read this poem in our first-year lecture, students are often outraged that the ending of the poem doesn't deliver a solution to what it means to be manuhiri but seems to deflect attention elsewhere. Perhaps, though, this is part of the meaning of the poem itself: just as the "pines" found in the Manawatū are elsewhere ("everywhere you go"), the possible remedies—or at least parallels—to this predicament can also be found outside. Perhaps, too, the situation described in the present poem is eternally linked to a much larger network of relations: national ("One Tree Hill") and spiritual–cosmological ("Tane Mahuta"). The directive at the end of the poem is clearly stated— "ask"—and yet the speaker and intended recipient of this suggestion are unclear. The suggestion that the addressee should "ask that old guy on One Tree Hill" is an invitation to change perspective both spatially (from Manawatū to Auckland) and temporally because the tree on One Tree Hill has a longer history of symbolic contestation than do the trees in the Manawatū. Perhaps the "old guy" offers an example and elaboration of how to think about relationship to place over a longer period of time and is therefore an inspiration for the Manawatū trees: perhaps he is a long-standing model of how to be manuhiri. Conversely, perhaps the "old guy," now that he is more remembered for demise than for position (the single tree on One Tree Hill was destroyed in a symbolic protest), is a cautionary tale for the Manawatū "pines" and stands in for the limits of identification with place when one is a "pine"—when one is manuhiri. Either reading points to the question of memory: the "old guy" is not just planted for the sake of memory but is also now the basis of claims about memory, including memory pertaining to the historical context of planting and to the fate of the tree itself. The irony, after all, is that an appeal to "roots" is coupled with a refusal to engage with history. Like the pieces of patchwork from early in the poem, the "old guy" is sentimentalized and fills a symbolic as well as aesthetic role. Perhaps also like the patchwork and indeed the pines—manuhiri—by which it was made, focusing on memories of the "old guy" produces amnesia about the circumstances around its planting, which means that contemporary protest focusing on the tree (wero from tāngata whenua indeed) seems to come from out of the blue.

Māori and Pasifika Write Connections

Mila and Wendt suggest two ways of imagining connections at the levels of individual relationships and community, and both formulations provide room to acknowledge Māori as tāngata whenua but also to recognize the presence of Pasifika communities in Aotearoa. *Manuhiri* is explicitly derived from a Māori cultural and linguistic context, whereas *fānau* is a provocative slippage between Māori and a Pasifika language. As indicated earlier, this chapter is merely a gesture toward the range of Pasifika voices and cannot account for the range of Pasifika writers who are creatively working through their relationship to Māori and to Aotearoa: Selina Tusitala Marsh, Tusiata Avia, and Serie Barford are three poets whose work is precocious in this regard.

The connections between Māori and Pasifika people have been explored, negotiated, shaped, and extended over many decades and in a range of creative forms. Surprisingly, given the range and vitality of texts treated in this chapter, the links between Māori and Pasifika communities find their way into little critical scholarship about Pacific literatures. This chapter and the preceding have given attention to individual Māori and Pasifika writers who articulate connections between these communities. However, all is not perfect in the relationship between Māori and Pasifika people because there is a third party involved: colonialism. As this discussion about Pasifika representation of Māori enlarges, it should leave space for the highly popular *Brotown*, the cartoon televised on prime time created by a group of male Pasifika creative practitioners. *Brotown* has been described as a Pacific *Southpark*: nothing is sacred, and in theory, the comedy as well as politics of such shows depends on rehashing stereotypes and taking things too far to hold them up to a kind of critique. Yet it is difficult to know whether or how to laugh at the comedic creation of a Māori character, "Jeff da Maori," who has a perpetual running nose, talks in a stereotyped hori way, is not very bright, and lives with his many stepfathers. Is this the perspective of manuhiri, or fānau, or someone else? While we have focused on various forms of connection up to this point, the next chapter pays attention to another side of the story.

CHAPTER 7

When Romeo Met Tusi:
Disconnections

THE RELATIONSHIP BETWEEN Indigenous Pacific (Māori) and migrant Pacific (Pasifika) communities in the neighborhoods of New Zealand's metropolitan centers has been less than smooth. At its most innocuous, this disconnection might be merely implied and reinforced by separation and invisibility. At its most acute, it can take the form of undermining, sabotage, deeply held prejudice, enforcement of social (including sexual) prohibitions, and violent confrontation. We know from the preceding three chapters that Māori–Pasifika relationships have not been singularly competitive and distrustful. Many sites of collaboration and connection are negotiated and work well, in politics and community relationships[1] and in families that include children affectionately known by some as haka hulas, offspring of mixed Māori and Pasifika relationships. However, a project that only focused on *connection* would be a naive approach to a set of relationships that can at times be limiting, violent, and tortured. While the vision of Pacific connection finds real expression in collaborative and connecting projects such as those described in the previous three chapters, these are accompanied by rivalries and competition. Surely a discussion that focuses on Māori–Pacific connections should be shaped as well by the rather embarrassing genealogies of disconnection.

It is worth reflecting on what it means to write about Māori–Pasifika disconnections, including the decision people have made to write and produce the texts under discussion as well as my own decision to write this chapter. Even as this chapter proceeds, there are questions to ask about methodology and voice. Especially in a context in which mainstream New Zealand appears to be unknowledgeable (or only murkily knowledgeable) about Māori–Pasifika disconnections, how does one tell what can feel like family stories in public? What are the ethics of talking about the prejudice that Māori and Pasifika communities have for one another? At what point does writing only about connections become irresponsible? At what point does writing about Māori–Pasifika disconnection because of prejudice become irresponsible? Within the frame of the New Zealand nation-state, might it be productive—or is it even possible—to discuss these as connections between Indigenous and non-Indigenous Pacific communities, as 'Ilolahia might, rather than as between Māori and Pasifika? What would that terminology make possible, and what might it obscure?

In the realm of tapa, Māori once were Pacific. In the national space, Māori are also tāngata whenua. In New Zealand, this results in a tension—at its best and most hopeful, a productive tension—between Māori and Pasifika genealogical and experiential connections, as treated in the previous chapters, and the distinct and often competitive roles of migrant and Indigene. While Pasifika communities may well assert Indigeneity in their originary islands, no one is Indigenous to the entire Pacific region, and Māori are Indigenous here. There is a fine line between appealing to utopic regionalism to address disconnection between the communities, on one hand, and undermining or even foreclosing the ability of Māori to assert tangatawhenuatanga[2] on the other. This fine line is made all the finer by the fact that this negotiation is never fully extricable from the context of the colonial settler state, its own ambitions, and the limits of its capacity to recognize dynamics of relationship outside of itself.

Some people believe that race relations are miraculously worked out between the sheets: that intermarriage or interracial intimacy and its human products necessarily bring about and demonstrate changes in attitude and, eventually, in power relations. Unfortunately, there is little historical evidence to support this miscegenist dream: if anything, interracial sexual connections tend to reveal and even emphasize more inequities than they eradicate. Certainly it is helpful to be a little suspicious of texts that try to make the relationship between two individuals represent relationships for their respective communities, in which their bodies stand in for collectives, even though this has been one way that people have talked about the connections between Māori and Pasifika communities in New Zealand.[3] And yet, the figure of intimate partnership as a *symbol* of much broader dynamics is well developed, and perhaps this dream therefore does bear some weight, not as an actualized and robust solution to racial tensions but as a possible symbolic register in which communities can ask the hard questions. Rather than sexual relations solving problems of Māori–Pasifika disconnection, therefore, perhaps they provide a way to think them through.[4]

While there is a long history of representing Indigenous–non-Indigenous relationships in the context of the colonial state through intimate partnerships, this chapter focuses on three specific texts that center on a story of young innocent love between a Māori teenager and a Pasifika teenager as a way of thematizing, metaphorizing, and talking about Māori–Pasifika relationships. In previous chapters, we briefly considered some texts that foreground the proximity and relationships of those communities in the specific space of families: in Paula Morris's *Hibiscus Coast,* Samoan Siaki and Māori-Chinese Emma are ex-lovers and engage in high-stakes art forgery, and in Albert Wendt's *The Songmaker's Chair,* Māori Hone has become a part of the Peseola family through his marriage to Nofo.[5] The three texts treated in this chapter all explicitly mobilize the Shakespearean story of Romeo and Juliet to explore the broader contours of relationship between the Māori and Pasifika communities. Oscar Kightley, cowriter of the earliest, has commented, "To me Shakespeare is like James Brown: he's someone you sample."[6] Here we will focus on three texts that have sampled this classic story of love despite family: the 1997 play *Romeo and Tusi,* the 2007 play *Once Were Samoans,* and the 2005 TV drama series *The Market.*[7] The important question in the texts, which bravely explore the disconnections between Māori and Pasifika communities by mobilizing *Romeo and Juliet,* is a question of emphasis. Is *Romeo and Juliet* a useful model because it highlights the capacity for love to develop even between individuals who belong to feuding families or because it emphasizes the ridiculousness of family rivalries as exposed when they are overcome by young love? These textual treatments of fraught Māori–Pasifika romantic relationships uniquely acknowledge and interrogate the complicated dynamic of connection and derision that shapes the relationships between Māori and Pasifika communities in Aotearoa New Zealand.

Romeo and Tusi

Oscar Kightley and Erolia Ifopo collaborated on *Romeo and Tusi,* a play developed for performance in 1997 (Christchurch) and rerun as part of the New Zealand Festival (Wellington) in 2000.[8] (Māori) Anaru and (Samoan) Tusi are selected to perform opposite one another in their high school show of *Romeo and Juliet* and, through this device, manage to simultaneously occupy their own roles in the Heke and Aiu families, respectively, as well as in the Montagues and Capulets. The play is humorous and draws heavily from the structure as well as the characters of Shakespeare's play. The use of humor as a theatrical mode and clowning as a form of social commentary in which actors are able to critique authority with full immunity granted by the theatrical space have a long history in the Pacific.[9] In Sāmoa, this clowning theater takes the specific form of fale aitu (literally, "house of spirits"[10]), about which Caroline Sinavaiana-Gabbard writes,

> Scripted clowning, that is, the songs and comedy sketches, provides the only public arena in Samoan society which traditionally allows for overt criticism of figures and institutions of authority.[11]

Although *Romeo and Tusi,* and *Once Were Samoans,* discussed later, are highly entertaining and can feel like a comedy, variety show, or cabaret, the fale aitu overlays not only a theatrical model but also a political weight. The hilarious dialogue and larger-than-life caricatures are underpinned by a highly stylized politics of critique that enables exploration of a serious social issue. Rather than the humor detracting from—or even softening—any "overt criticism of figures and institutions of authority," humor itself can be evidence that such criticism is implicit in the text.

In the opening scene of *Romeo and Tusi,* Tusi Aiu and Anaru Heke meet at Bingo (Housie). Ruby, who is a Puck figure throughout, opens the play with words that echo exactly the opening words of Romeo and Juliet, until the line "be you a human, cat or mousie" is introduced to rhyme with "Housie." The first scene sets up the mutual prejudice between the families but also introduces the main argument of the play: that physical proximity and shared experiences of Māori and Pasifika communities, along with shared whakapapa and cultural background, have the capacity to override or ameliorate disconnections. Despite the dialogue, which reinforces difference, Anaru and Tusi share the lived experience of attending Housie with their mothers at the same venue to participate in the same activity. This contradiction, in which the separation and disconnection suggested by the dialogue is undermined visually and narratively by close proximity and shared experiences and thereby the many connections of the characters, is a device used to great effect throughout the rest of the play.

Anaru and Tusi meet when their mothers win at Housie at the same time. Mrs. Heke and Mrs. Aiu both send their child to check on the numbers, and in the first encounter that follows, the two youth humorously reproduce European stereotypes of the region (historical–romantic and contemporary–derisive) as they describe each other. Anaru mishears Tusi and calls her "Tootsie," claiming, "Tootsie it must mean beautiful Polynesian Princess with frizzy hair," while Tusi replies, "Anaru it must mean Gentle Maori Warrior with big juicy lips." Anaru and Tusi foreground the two major modes of colonial representation of Indigenous people in the Pacific. Anaru refers to the feminized, sexualized Dusky Maiden when he describes a "beautiful Polynesian Princess with frizzy hair," and in turn, Tusi acknowledges the construct of the noble savage: "Gentle Maori Warrior." Their familiarity with these two images emphasizes not only the economy of stereotypes underpinning the play (which the Māori and Samoan mothers will attempt to reinforce) but also the broader context of hegemonic representation within which the play itself circulates. Furthermore, Tusi is familiar with Anaru's name and hears (then pronounces) it correctly the first time, whereas Anaru is less familiar with Tusi's name. This imbalance of familiarity quietly echoes the broader situation in that Pasifika writers engage with the question of Māori–Pasifika connections far more than Māori writers do.

When Anaru and Tusi are assigned their roles in the school production of *Romeo and Juliet,* they describe each other again in these contemporary racist terms, although still humorously reversing their connotations:

ANARU: Look at her hair, it's the finest of wool.
TUSI: Look at his lips they're the thickest of rubber.
ANARU: She's more finer than the juiciest porkbone.
TUSI: He looks even better than a KFC quarter pack.

The humor here relies on two layers of knowledge: whereas the first exchange clearly mobilizes European stereotypes ("hair [of] finest wool," "lips [of] thickest rubber"), the second exchange engages food ("juiciest porkbone," "KFC quarter pack") stereotypically linked to the respective communities. For the humor to work in these moments of the play, the audience needs to possess the appropriate knowledge to get not only the Pākehā but also the Māori–Pasifika jokes. To this end, the racist slurs engaged in the play are simultaneously wrapped up in the broader racist conceptualizations of the settler nation-state ("hair [of] finest wool," "lips [of] thickest rubber") at the same time as they center the experiences of Māori and Pasifika communities ("porkbone," "KFC") and humor.

Romeo and Tusi draws a lot of humor from the protestations of difference despite the relational and spatial proximity played out in the narrative and on stage. The play suggests that parents and children have divergent perspectives on this subject, and generational difference underpins a conversation with his mother in which Anaru brings together the shared experience and shared whakapapa of Māori and Pasifika people:

> MRS. HEKE: Son life is sweet. All you have to do is keep your nose clean, and don't hang out with those stinky islanders, ka pai.
> ANARU: Mum, don't be like that. Some of my mates at school are Islanders.
> MRS. HEKE: Do they go to school? I thought they only went to church for a gossip. Bloody cheeky those Pacific Islanders.
> ANARU: Mum, we're all Pacific Islanders. Aotearoa is an island in the Pacific.
> MRS. HEKE: Yeah it was an island of kumara and kaimoana now it's more like chop suey and taro. I mean look at them, always at Housie, Aue. They virtually live here.
> ANARU: You only know that because we virtually live here too.

This generational difference is in turn tied to specific spaces, and school provides Anaru with the opportunity to spend time with "Islanders" and thereby reject his mother's views on the basis of his lived experience. Mrs. Heke's claims of difference and separation are undermined by her knowledge of Pasifika cultural practice ("church," "chop suey and taro") as well as shared Māori and Pasifika presence in the leisure space of Housie. Furthermore, the close physical proximity of the families at Housie is repeated in their place of residence. The Hekes are aware that the Aius live next door:

> MRS. HEKE: The zoo . . . she wants a blimmin zoo she can check out the Samoans house, now that's a blimmin zoo, she can watch them for free.

Meanwhile, the Aiu family knows their neighbors are the Hekes:

> TUSI: I bet the Hekes next door have heaps of money.
> MRS. AIU: And that Jake Heke is probably spending it all at the pub
> . . .

Despite this close proximity and prior knowledge of each other's families, Anaru and Tusi are meeting each other for the first time because Tusi has been away at boarding school.

After meeting up in the park one day, they realize they both live on the same street (Sorry Avenue) and start to walk home together. As they get closer to home, they discuss their families and recognize that they have similar experiences at home:

> ANARU: My Mum keeps dissing our neighbours.
> TUSI: My Mum keeps dissing our neighbours.
> ANARU: Dad says they keep stealing our clothes off the washing line.
> TUSI: Mum says our neighbours can't even blow their noses properly.
> *They laugh.*

When they approach their houses, they both realize they have fallen in love with someone from the wrong house:

> TUSI AND ANARU: Well this is my house.
> ANARU: That's the Aiu's house.
> TUSI: That's the Heke's house.
> ANARU: Dad would kill me if he caught me talking to you.
> TUSI: Mum would do the same then she'd kill herself.

Continuing the pattern set at Housie, the very things that keep them apart are in fact experienced similarly. Anaru and Tusi repeat the line "my Mum keeps dissing our neighbours" then provide different examples of a similar kind of stereotyping. Significantly, the moment of revelation is shared as well: they announce their respective homes at exactly the same time. The mutuality of the prejudice itself becomes connective, and they decide to keep seeing each other regardless of the expected reactions from home.

Underscoring the point that Māori and Pasifika communities operate according to logics of the racist nation within which they are located, the racist discourse each family reproduces about the family next door reinforces, and is reinforced by, the racist New Zealand state. The mothers in the play react to the news that their children have hooked up at school in the same way: Mrs. Heke calls immigration about the Aiu family having overstayers at their house, and Mrs. Aiu retaliates by calling the police about the Māori family having marijuana in their garden. This moment uses humor to draw attention to the historical and ongoing raiding of Māori and Pasifika homes by actors of the state.[12] Indeed, the very point at which the mothers attempt to protect their families from one kind of incursion (a Māori or Pasifika person) is the moment at which they invite another, much more powerful interruption. This highlights the central role the state plays in Māori and Pasifika competition; although one might imagine, with hope, Māori and Pasifika communities resisting this divide-and-conquer strategy, in this case, the Heke and Aiu families call on the state—both its rhetoric and its enforcement agencies—to maintain the divide between them. At the same time, it is possible to imagine an alternative reading here about Mrs. Aiu and Mrs. Heke exerting their own agency vis-à-vis the state. This reading would notice that the state, in turn, is so captured by its own anxieties about Māori and Pasifika communities that the families—and in particular, these two brown women, who are theoretically the least privileged in New Zealand—are able both to apprehend its own weakness and to manipulate its power for their own purposes.

This struggle between the families lasts until the final scene, when Mrs. Aiu and Mrs. Heke have a showdown, during which the minister asks, "Why are you so prejudiced against each other?" Significantly, the two mothers respond simultaneously: "That's because they smell! They have big families, and they eat too much." The physical act of speaking in unison (an inverted Pentecost of sorts) emphasizes the similarities between the two families despite the dialogue itself focusing on what sets the groups apart. We have returned, then, to the central contradiction of the play: the mutual prejudice between Māori and Pasifika communities and individuals is more marked by its *mutuality* than by its *prejudice*. Tusi recognizes this contradiction and interrupts, "You see how much we have in common, and that's just the bad things. What about the good things?" Mrs. Heke responds, "Like what?" to which Tusi replies, "You know, culture and stuff." In this moment, Tusi repeats the twin connections of experience and whakapapa that provided the basis of Māori–Pasifika connection when Anaru articulated them to his mother back in the first scene ("Mum, we're all Pacific Islanders. Aotearoa is an island in the Pacific . . . we virtually live here [at Housie] too") and beyond, to Apirana Taylor's pairing of the two in "Pa Mai," the pairing of the two in *Rongo,* and so on.

The play's final turn literally engages the audience in the discussion.

Ruby, who plays Puck at the beginning of the play and sets up Anaru and Tusi as Romeo and Tusi, says, "Let's throw it open to the audience." The stage directions then explicitly suggest a "Ricky [sic] Lake–style talk show" in which the audience members actually engage in the discussion. This audience participation is a theater innovation that echoes other Pacific performances that have encouraged interaction and broken through the fourth wall of the performance space.[13] Involving the audience blurs the boundaries between the world of the play and the real world in two ways: it brings members of the real world into the story of the play, but it also requires the audience, through its participation, to recognize that the world of the play is the real world too.

Once Were Samoans

A decade after *Romeo and Tusi*, in 2006 and 2007, an Auckland-based theater company, the Kila Kokonut Krew, performed *Once Were Samoans* in Auckland and Wellington. *Once Were Samoans* echoes and extends *Romeo and Tusi*: again, a Samoan girl (Moa) and Māori boy (Taihape) are the star-crossed lovers. Following the form of the fale aitu, the play engages humor to broker social commentary along with entertainment; is very physical; and includes singing, dance, movement, satire, and burlesque. Moa is the innocent youngest sister in the Tufifi family, which is made up of four sons and two daughters, a single mum, and a grandfather. As in *Romeo and Tusi*, the family—and their so-called racial purity—is headed and guarded by a single woman. Throughout the play, the Tufifi family is preparing for their performance at a family reunion they are attending in Sāmoa, which demonstrates diasporic anxieties of how to perform at home at the same time as it confirms their familiarity with social and cultural expectations in Sāmoa. The play is, after all, called *Once Were Samoans* and so presents itself through the conceit of identity crisis: resonating with Donald's comments from the Nesian Mystik track, the title (and the Tufifi family) implicitly asks, they once were Samoan—but are they still? Additionally, the title echoes (as does the title of this book) Duff's *Once Were Warriors*, gesturing toward the place of Māori in the play and, indeed, in the family.

Taihape Morgan is, like Anaru, a Māori boy who lives next door to the Samoan family. Taihape is mates with the Tufifi brothers and participates in family occasions. However, whereas Taihape can be a friend to the Tufifi boys, going with one of their sisters is not condoned. Interestingly, by 2007, there are new Māori stereotypes: Taihape is a famous golfer, referencing Michael Campbell and Phillip Tataurangi, who had recently brought media attention to Māori success in the primarily white, middle-class sport of golf. His last name, Morgan, quietly references Tukuroirangi Morgan, who earned public notoriety as a politician who misspent public money on luxury personal goods. Despite this success in his career, class and certain forms of success cannot default one out of race, and the brothers continue to ridicule Taihape with the other, more established stereotypes about being Mauli (Samoan for "Māori"). In an interesting reversal—or perhaps extension—of *Romeo and Tusi's* suggestion that these matters may be viewed differently by different generations, the grandfather is the only member of the Tufifi family who agrees to the relationship. However, in the family structure—especially with Mrs. Tufifi, the domineering, larger-than-life Samoan mama—he has little power.

Although the Tufifi family takes seriously the need to protect Moa as a Samoan girl from being contaminated by Taihape and his Mauli blood, it is blood that ultimately undermines the family's objections. Near the end of the play, Mrs. Tufifi reveals that her earlier story about the Pasifika father of the children was a lie. Specifically, in a hilarious sequence, she describes her participation in the early hip-hop scene in Auckland and her relationship with a Māori man! In a dramatic turn, the children realize that they are in fact Māori as well as Samoan, a result that not only explains the heightened anxiety around the purity of Moa's blood on the part of Mrs. Tufifi but also the grandfather's singularly ambivalent attitude to the relationship. On another level, the actor who has played Taihape during the various seasons of the play, Fasitua Amosa, is not himself Māori, and so the audience (or at least the knowing audience) has already consciously racialized a character in one way despite knowledge of blood. In this way, knowing members of the audience are complicit with an act of deliberate amnesia in a way that is not actually all that different to Mrs. Tufifi.[14]

The play ends when the whole Tufifi family is in Sāmoa, performing their item at the reunion. Taihape has accompanied the family and joins in the item as well. In this way, the experience of the Samoan family in New Zealand is inseparable from its experience in Aotearoa. The family cannot separate its performance of New Zealand–based Samoanness from its engagement with tāngata whenua in a number of different, although related, ways. Firstly, the Tufifi family—which, after all, once was Samoan—recognizes that it is connected to Aotearoa through its Mauli blood. Second, like Wendt's *The*

Songmaker's Chair, the play points to the large number of Māori–Pasifika mixed families by foregrounding two Māori and Samoan intimate relationships: Moa and Taihape but also the mother and father of the kids. Third, the play gestures toward a long legacy of Māori and Pasifika connection through shared artistic performance and, perhaps, activism when Mrs. Tufifi reveals her participation in the 1980s hip-hop scene. Fourth, Māori people "once were Samoans" too, according to the histories of navigation in the region, and so Taihape's performance with the family is both immediate reunion (through his relationship with the Tufifi family) and an historical reunion (through his Polynesianness). Finally, echoing the next-door-neighborness of Anaru and Tusi, the Tufifi and Morgan families are connected through shared economic and spatial (and specifically urban) location.

Ultimately, whereas *Romeo and Tusi* elaborated a blood connection between Māori and Pasifika communities in a regional sense ("Aotearoa is an island in the Pacific"), *Once Were Samoans* points to shared blood in a more immediate, recent, and literal sense. Indeed, while the Tufifi family may once have been Samoan, and may have understood itself as engaging in first-encounter connections with Māori through the character of Taihape, the specter of Mauli blood, which turns out to have a more-than-ghostly presence in the family, emphasizes more complex and long-standing connections between Māori and Pasifika than we might take for granted.

The Market

A Romeo and Juliet story hit television in 2005 on TVNZ, although because the state broadcaster buried the show at 10:25 P.M. on Monday nights, it did not achieve a wide audience until it was replayed by Māori TV in 2008.[15] Rene Naufahu, widely known in New Zealand as the Tongan actor who played Sam the ambulance man in the first years of the iconic Kiwi soap *Shortland Street,* and who was therefore already deeply embedded in New Zealand's representational politics, was heavily involved in the publicity around *The Market,* which he cowrote with Brett Ihaka. Certainly this discussion could also sit alongside the Māori–Pasifika collaborations treated in chapter 4 because many prominent and highly skilled Māori and Pasifika actors and crew participated in the project. In this Romeo and Juliet story, two families are not explicitly opposed because of residual and ongoing tensions between the Māori and Pasifika communities but instead because of a very specific incident between two of their family members.

The show is called *The Market* because its central setting is the Ōtara flea market in Auckland, a famous market held every Saturday morning in the predominantly Māori and Pasifika neighborhood named on Daniel Maaka's fated sweatshirt from the Te Papa publicity materials discussed in the introduction to this part of the book. The Ōtara markets (and Avondale markets on Sundays) provide social and cultural space for many Māori and Pasifika families in Auckland, along with the opportunity to buy and sell goods not readily available through the usual shops. For both families in the show, the market is their main source of income: the Limas have a vegetable truck, and the Johnsons sell hangi and watercress. The Johnsons' youngest son, Tipene, who is the Romeo figure, also runs a stand with his best friend, at which they sell T-shirts they design under their label "Brown Brother."[16] In this way, as in *Romeo and Tusi* and *Once Were Samoans,* but also as in "Pa Mai," the relationship between Māori and Pasifika families is tied to physical proximity in specific urban neighborhoods. As well as referencing the flea market, however, the title foregrounds the many markets at play. Over the course of the show, an entangled series of transactions links the characters. Through prostitution, illegal loans, affairs, and illegal fighting rings, the show suggests that anything is up for sale: bodies, friendships and marriages, and communities.

The first episode opens with an extreme close-up of two graffiti artists applying spray-paint to create an initially obscured image on an unidentifiable surface. One, who we later recognize as Tipene, turns to the camera and sprays paint over the viewer's frame of view, as if the screen were part of the surface being painted. The sounds and visuals of the graffiti starkly announce the intervention in which *The Market* is engaged. The perspective of the tagger is marginalized by mainstream television, which prefers to center those audience members who automatically and indignantly align themselves with the suffering of any property owners in the case of tagging incidents. Focusing on graffiti at the moment of production foregrounds the creative, active dimension of the art form, interrupting the representation of tagging as destructive, already-there-when-you-wake-up-in-the-morning, artist-less, and community-less. Centering the tagging, therefore, centers a new audience and new perspectives. The proximity of the camera—and, as the screen is blacked out by paint, the audience—to the tagger, paint, and surface suggests that the show will be up close to people, activities, and forms that are marginalized, ridiculed, resented, and feared by mainstream television audiences. After the opening credits follow the tagging sequence, the Johnsons unveil a memorial picture of their dead son, Ritchie, which may or may not be the artwork produced by spray paint in the opening. This ambivalence about allocating responsibility for the creation of the memorial establishes a pattern of ambiguity about tying specific deeds to specific characters.

Five years before the narrative of the television show begins, Sef Lima (Samoan) and Ritchie Johnson (Māori) were best friends involved in a fight in which Sef killed Ritchie. We learn through various revelations that Sef refused to talk in court about what had happened and mutely accepted his prison term of five years for the murder. The first episode of *The Market* is set on the day that Sef is released from prison, the same day his younger sister Julia arrives back in Auckland after living with their grandmother in Sāmoa for five years. Yes, Julia is indeed the Juliet figure in the series, and like Moa in *Once Were Samoans,* she is characterized by her innocence; unlike Moa, this extends beyond sexual and political innocence to include naivety about her own family. Having been taken to Sāmoa in the aftermath of the events five years earlier, she has no idea about her adored big brother Sef's imprisonment.

After the memorial picture is unveiled, "Māori Elvis," a local man who reappears as a wise yet ridiculous jester (perhaps Puck) figure throughout the series, supports the family by singing a waiata. Significantly, he sings "Ngā Iwi E," which is very well known and gestures toward local Indigenous politics and, specifically, Māori struggle.[17] However, the waiata itself includes the repeated line "Kia kotahi rā te Moananui a Kiwa," a call for unity of the whole Pacific region. The song is an awkward prophecy: in the context of the family feud that is revealed shortly afterward, the kotahitanga of Te Moananui a Kiwa seems a remote possibility. This meaning is only available, of course, to audience members who understand enough of the Māori language to recognize the vision of pan-Pacific unity intoned in its lines. Furthermore, although the composition is strongly identified as a Māori song, the melody is borrowed from the Kanak resistance struggle in New Caledonia and was brought to Aotearoa through Māori and Kanak activist connections.[18] Just as the Tufifi family in *Once Were Pacific* discovers the legacy of previous Māori–Pasifika connections, this waiata subtly commemorates—in the very moment a memorial of a more recent dispute is unveiled—much more long-standing and oceanwide connection.

Ritchie's mother, Ngaire, and younger brother Mike are unable to forgive

Sef for his actions, and both seek revenge in blood. Mike, who idolizes his older brother Ritchie, is a street fighter and participates in illegal fights involving high-stakes betting, looking to meet up with Sef in the same circuit. These fights are partly organized by a relative of the Limas', Uncle Ronnie, and while Mike participates in these events as a fighter, Ngaire conducts a sexual affair with Ronnie in exchange for him fixing the fight so that her son kills Sef.[19] The series leads up to this ultimate fight, and along the way, the Limas continue to function as a family, while the Johnson family slowly implodes. The Limas' moral stamina and the Johnsons' moral decline are paralleled by the Limas' son Sef, who makes his sexual relationship legitimate by asking his regular prostitute to be his girlfriend, while the Johnsons' son Mike is banished from the boxing ring for losing his temper and turns to illegal fighting and street fighting instead. These trajectories of moral regeneration and decline seem paradoxical given that the Johnsons are the family whose son is understood to be an innocent victim and that a Lima has been judged guilty of murder.

As the show works toward the final fight, a relationship develops between Tipene, the youngest of the Johnsons' three sons, and Julia. Their relationship is innocent and yet forbidden. Having met each other in the market the day Julia returns from Sāmoa, without initially recognizing which family the other is from, they conduct their relationship undercover, receiving both help and hindrance from siblings and friends along the way. Like the grandfather in *Once Were Samoans*, Tipene's father Chris is supportive of the relationship but incapable of standing up to Ngaire. However, unlike the cases of Anaru and Tusi or Taihape and Moa, this prohibition is explained by a recent rupture in the family relationships (Ritchie's murder) rather than by a historically derived sense of prejudice between the two families as Māori and Samoan people.

The series oscillates between previous connections and present disconnections, which points to the proximity and familiarity of the families—and perhaps the communities—beyond the sphere of the market. For example, when Ngaire meets Sef for coffee, she finds it difficult to extricate the past five years from a deeper, longer sense of being another mother to Sef for all the years of the boys' friendship. Similarly, when Ngaire visits Ina to attempt a truce, the two women recall their earlier close friendship. Indeed, it is tempting to propose that these multiple connections "outside the market" suggest the possibilities for Māori and Pasifika communities to recognize forms and histories of connection outside the market (capitalism), outside the economic struggle that I argue has underpinned and exacerbated much of the prejudice between the communities.

Despite the fatal fight being the immediate source of the feud, neither family lives outside of broader narratives about Māori and Pasifika communities. Indeed, the unveiling and waiata of the first scene are interrupted by a confrontation between the two matriarchs of the Lima and Johnson families when the Limas come to pay respects. When Ngaire realizes that the Limas have turned up, she is angered, and Tu'u reassures Chris that they will not stay for long. These men have little impact on the sequence of events, however, because Mike bowls over, yelling, "You've got a lot of cheek," and Ina starts yelling at Ngaire, who responds in kind:

> "You think you're so high and mighty aye—you're not the only victims here. . . ."
>
> "You murderers—get back to your own country where you belong—go murder your own. . . "
>
> "You bloody Maulis might have the foreshore—but these jandals will go over any part of the market they f— damn well please. . . ."

Ina's comment that "you're not the only victims here" pertains to Ritchie's death and Sef's incarceration, and Ngaire takes exception to the idea that the Limas should seek to compare their experiences. At this moment of extreme stress, however, Ngaire and Ina draw not on personal attacks or references to the situations of Sef and Ritchie but on broader racism, referring to each other in the plural as members of their ethnic collectivities ("you murderers," "you bloody Maulis"). Specifically, Ngaire extends a racist appeal for repatriation of Pasifika families, telling the Limas to "get back to your own country where you belong," implying that they do not belong in New Zealand. Ina replies to this generalized racism with some of her own ("you bloody Maulis") and refers to the prominent issue of the Seabed and Foreshore Legislation, which suggests an additional layer to the earlier comment "you think you're so high and mighty."

After Ina and Ngaire shift the frame of reference to national concerns (migration, Indigenous rights), Ina brings the focus back to the space of the market itself. By doing this, she sets up the market as the microcosm for the negotiation of national questions and, significantly, reframes the nation because this space is dominated by Māori and Pasifika communities.[20]

However, if the nation is allegorized by the market, their shared proximity is also accompanied by shared experience: "you're not the only victims here." Indeed, Ina could be suggesting that Māori are not the only victims to have suffered at the hands of the New Zealand government; Sāmoa was under the colonial power of New Zealand for much of the twentieth century, and Pasifika communities suffer economically and socially as a result of overt and institutionalized racism in New Zealand. Ngaire's desire to expunge the family is played out in further allegorical form when she directs Chris to arrange for the Lima family to be banned from the market. Chris, however, quietly responds, "That's a big thing . . . they've been here a long time," doubly acknowledging that the Lima family but also Pasifika communities have deep roots in Aotearoa.

The connection between the two young lovers Tipene and Julia appears to parallel Ritchie's and Sef's own earlier friendship, and the final episode clarifies the extent of this comparison. Although the entire series deserves far more thorough treatment of multiple strands that fall outside the scope of the immediate project, for the sake of the present discussion, we will fast-forward to the final episode. Chris is somewhat ineffective throughout the series, sidelined by his wife Ngaire's focus on her desire for revenge and alienated from his family after turning Mike over to the police for a particularly brutal street fight, and he has been emasculated both by his wife's affair and his own refusal to deal with matters head-on. However, in the final episode, Chris goes into the changing room to see Mike and starts, "This ain't a fight. It's a death match," underscoring the parallel between Ritchie's death at Sef's hands five years earlier and Mike's fight with Sef today.

In a dramatic twist, Chris reveals that Ritchie had come out to him a week before he died. Refusing to accept that his eldest son was gay, Chris had kicked Ritchie out and did not see him again until after his death: "I laughed at him. I laughed. The hurt in his eyes when I told him no son of mine is queer." Mike, who has pursued a fight with Sef to gain retribution for his brother's hypermasculine reputation as a fighter, on which he had been modeling himself, rethinks the terms of the fight after hearing that his adored bother was gay. He replies, "Is that why he bashed him? 'Cause he was a poofter?" and continues, after a moment's further reflection, "He's still my brother." Although his loyalty to his brother after this revelation is impressive, it doesn't feel like it fits with Mike's characterization in the series. Regardless, Mike decides still to fight Sef to avenge his brother's death.

The fight starts with both men taking opportunities to show their talents in the boxing ring. This is illegal fighting, though, and both suffer bloody injuries as the fight goes on. Sef ends up pinning Mike to the floor and repeatedly bashing him, and just as it looks like he will inflict serious harm on Mike, he is distracted by his own father's yelling and looks back to Mike but sees Ritchie's face instead. The flashback causes Sef to withdraw and declare the end of the first round. While Chris tends to Mike, he talks more about his brother's final revelations:

> When Ritchie told me he was in love with someone he told me he was in love with Sef. It was Sef he was in love with—his best mate.

When the fighters return for the second round, Mike asks Sef directly, "Did you kill my brother 'cause he was in love with you?" Sef replies,

> It was an accident Mike. He went f— crazy when I rejected him. I loved your brother—but not in the way he wanted me to. Mike—come on man it was an accident.

At this point of climax, Mike and Sef both withdraw from the fight. Significantly, the person most upset that the fight has been discontinued is Alby, the white entrepreneur who organizes the fights (and other illegal money schemes throughout the series, including as a loan shark and a pimp), which emphasizes again the context within which Māori–Pasifika relations take place and suggests that refusing to operate as expected has the power to undermine that system's dependence on brown bodies to keep it running.

In the final scenes, Sef comes into Mike's changing room—this liminal space functions literally as a "changing" room, in which Chris tells Mike, and then Mike and Sef talk further, and Sef confirms that Ritchie had declared his sexual attraction to him that same week five years ago. Although Sef spurned his sexual overture, he did not retract his friendship, but Ritchie was embarrassed, and things got out of control. (It might be useful to note that Sef's heterosexuality is highly visible and thereby secured: throughout the series, his physical relationship with a woman he initially engages as a prostitute is boldly represented on-screen.) The cause of Ritchie's death during his fight with Sef is not ultimately clarified. It could have been a form of suicide—or assisted suicide—or a genuine accident in the context of heightened emotion. Whatever happened, Sef was so devoted to his friend that he preferred to go to prison for five years rather than reveal details that would have compromised Ritchie's privacy about his sexuality.

Indeed, Sef's commitment to Ritchie demonstrates a form of connection that we find in utopic representations of romantic love. When Ritchie confronts Sef in the changing room and asks, "How come you didn't say anything before?" Sef replies with a declaration of commitment:

> Ritchie made me promise. It's the last thing he said to me. Didn't want anybody to know. All he was worried about was how people—especially you, Mike—would remember him. I couldn't tell you.

Does this loyalty suggest that their connection, like that of the original Romeo and Juliet, is more pure than the limitations of social forces around them but ultimately compromised by those same forces so that central characters make rash choices—to the point of death—of their lovers? From the first episode of the series, fighting is linked to sex: in an early scene, Mike's fight at a local boxing ring is intercut with shots of Sef engaged in sex. This sets up an inverse relationship between Sef's process of regeneration and purification (by asking the prostitute to be his legitimate girlfriend, but perhaps also through sex itself) and Mike's regression from competitive boxing to illegal fighting. Furthermore, the images of the two men engaged in their respective physical activities resonate visually. If fighting is symbolically paired with sex, another reading of Ritchie's and Sef's previous friendship, based as it was on fighting together, is possible.

The real Romeo and Juliet of the series, Tipene and Julia, do not function as central characters, despite being vital to the marketing of the series. They are not essential to the emotional configuration of the series; they have little impact on the direction of the narrative; and rather than their innocence setting them above the grittier realities of the rest of the characters, it seems simply to set them aside. Their meeting at the Brown Brothers T-shirt stall in episode 1 is coincidental and brief, but Julia returns soon afterward because she realizes she has lost her favorite bracelet and goes to retrieve it, explaining that her big brother gave it to her. This link explicitly ties Julia and Tipene, who are supposedly the Romeo and Juliet figures, with the shadowy—and yet more central—pairing of Sef and Ritchie. From this perspective, it seems that Sef and Ritchie are the star-crossed lovers after all: star-crossed not because of a preexisting family feud but because of their variant sexual orientations.

It is difficult to be confident about the resolution of the series, especially alongside *Romeo and Tusi* and *Once Were Samoans*, which clarified their resolutions almost to an extreme.[21] Because the plot of *The Market* is driven by the mystery of Ritchie's final hours, it feels surprising—and maybe even misleading—that so few clues throughout had pointed to this explanation for the murder. Perhaps this resolution feels ambiguous because a revelation of homosexuality is unexpected within the logic of the plot, Pasifika cultural production, or, indeed, mainstream New Zealand television. Surely the revelation is at the service of politics, but which politics? Is Sef's cover-up a demonstration of mateship that has the capacity to override the limits imposed by homophobic individuals, families, or communities? Or is Sef's claim of loyalty to Ritchie a smoke screen for a deeply entrenched homophobia in which five years in prison is preferable to the risk that such a revelation would have implications for his own sexuality? Does *The Market* really suggest that the only possible outcome for a gay Māori man in Ōtara is the blurred line between suicide and murder? The final act of the series echoes the opening scene, and this time, Mike sprays paint over the portrait that memorializes Ritchie, which was unveiled in the first episode. As in the opening shots, the paint is finally applied to the camera–screen itself. When Mike covers his brother's portrait with fresh paint, is he finally allowing him to rest as a sign of recognition that it is time to move on? Or is he erasing Ritchie from public memory, now that his homosexuality has been revealed?

Whereas Māori–Pasifika *dis*-connection in *Romeo and Tusi* and *Once Were Samoans* was motivated by a fear of blood mixture, in *The Market,* the anxiety is around homosexuality and, perhaps, masculinity. In some ways, *The Market* does not fit as easily with the two live performances *Romeo and Tusi* and *Once Were Samoans*. Indeed, one could argue that *The Market* does not thematize Māori–Pasifika relationships at all. However, this series trades on, extends, and reinforces existing discourses about Māori–Pasifika connections through its deliberate use of Romeo and Juliet as a shorthand for the family tension between the Johnsons and Limas. Much of the advertising material about the series foregrounded the innocent relationship between Tipene and Julia and the rift between their respective Māori and Samoan families, even if the series itself did not focus on disconnection between Māori and Pasifika communities apart from the opening moment in which Ngaire and Ina attack each other. Perhaps, echoing Grace-Smith's

"Te Manawa," rather than failing to deliver on a promise of exploring disconnections between Māori and Pasifika communities, *The Market* opens up space for elaboration of complex, nuanced, and multilayered connections between the communities, connections which take place on the basis of physical and experiential proximity.

When Romeo Met Tusi

There are questions to be asked about genre here. Because all of the texts on which this chapter focuses are performed, they are already necessarily collaborative and are fixed in place and time; if you do not attend the theater at the right time (or know how to source a play script) or watch the television show (or have access to a DVD copy), the representation is inaccessible. Interestingly, I have struggled to find references to Māori–Pasifika disconnections in written forms like poetry or fiction, and this might be because poets and fiction writers are not aware of the disconnections, prefer to focus on something else, or are unable to bring texts about this disconnection through to publication. This could also be about generation, place, time; both Māori and Pasifika communities are different in various times and places. Karlo Mila has talked publicly about her experience growing up Tongan in the predominantly white town of Palmerston North, in which the only brown people to whom she could gravitate were Māori. She has wondered if her experience of Tonganness would have been different had she been raised in Auckland, and I wonder if her experience of Māoriness would have been different too. Each of these texts can be understood as liminal, and this could explain how their creators have gotten away with representing disconnection as well.

The politics of gender demand consideration here. Surely it is no coincidence that the major instigators of these family feuds are the mothers. While the fathers are both present in *The Market,* Tu'u Lima and Chris Johnson are effectively emasculated by their wives (Ina and Ngaire, respectively) and powerless to stop them. When Ngaire is having a talk with her son Mike one day, she comments, "We're lucky that Tu'u Lima's as spineless as your father. What is it with the men around here?" In the midst of this clear statement about a crisis of Polynesian masculinity in this urban space, Mike attempts to assert himself as an exception: "Not all of us." Ngaire reminds him that she is his mother, which disallows Mike from simply assuming his father's position and secures her own position as matriarch.[22] In all three texts—*Romeo and Tusi, Once Were Samoans,* and *The Market*—the mothers could be understood in several ways: they could be strong characters, recognizing the inherently powerful role of women in Māori and Pasifika families; they could be strong characters by default, recognizing the very high proportion of Māori and Pasifika families that are solely headed (or financed) by women; or they could be caricatures of hysterical, unreasonable, ignorant, bitter women.

As long as Māori and Pasifika communities insist that their primary relationship is with the New Zealand nation-state, relationships between these communities will struggle to function beyond the narrow parameters that state provides. Tāngata whenua may well subsume Pasifika communities into the broad category of "not Indigenous": these communities are not Indigenous to the current configuration of the nation-state. (Although the cases of Tokelau, Niue, the Cook Islands, and, historically, Sāmoa are a little complicated here because while they are not Indigenous to the North and South Islands, they are Indigenous to land areas under the political control of New Zealand, in some ways a parallel, for example, to American Samoan and Chamorro Indigeneity in the U.S. empire. Another parallel with that empire in this regard is the Moriori, a community that is perhaps comparable to Hawaiians in the U.S. context: not the dominant Indigenous communities of the nation-state and yet Indigenous to land that is no less part of the nation-state than that with which American Indians are connected.)[23] Conversely, migrant communities can tend to focus on their relationship with the visa-granting nation rather than other, Indigenous, coexisting nations that occupy the same land. In the light of these mutual failures to render each other visible, it is difficult to reconcile the rapturous response to the arrival of tapa and the moments of present-day prejudice and suspicion treated in these Romeo and Juliet texts. Yet merely focusing on acts of collaboration and connection would silence many of the stories that demand to be told in the realm of the koura.

The Realm of Koura

THIS IS THE REALM OF KOURA, of Māori, of Aotearoa. Located at the center of the Kelburn campus of Victoria University of Wellington, Te Herenga Waka was the first university marae in Aotearoa New Zealand when it opened in 1986. The marae complex includes an ornately decorated house that was largely carved under the guidance of Takirirangi Smith. The carved pou[1] around the walls of the house were strategically selected to ensure that every Māori student and staff member would have at least one tupuna represented there.[2] In a conventional carved meetinghouse, at least one post in the center of the room supports the large ridgepole that runs down the middle of the house and thereby maintains the separation between Ranginui and Papatūānuku.[3] Te Herenga Waka is a tūrangawaewae of a particular kind. As well as being a home place in which the Māori world is centered, the whare is also a manifestation of Māori knowledges: library, map, encyclopedia, and periodic table in one. When you enter through the main front door, the first poutokomanawa[4] you see is Pacifically themed: Te Rangihiroa (yes, Te Rangihiroa from earlier in this book) on the bottom, with Pacific carvings reaching above him to the roof. It is not entirely unusual to represent non-Māori people in carved pou in whare, but what is interesting about the Pacific poutokomanawa at Te Herenga Waka is that rather than simply reading the figures as non-Māori, we recognize them as Pacific; they are there as our relatives and, more specifically, as our tuakana. This is the realm of koura, where, after two centuries of interacting with colonialism, Māori continue to recognize that our place is in the Pacific. If this is the case, though, why are we—Māori—not talking about this dimension of what it is to be Māori in New Zealand, and why aren't our writers producing more texts that explore this part of our experience? Where are the novels and short fiction and poetry and plays by Māori that are set in the brown suburbs of Auckland, Wellington, and Christchurch and that include mixed

Māori–Pasifika families and friendships? If there is a prominent Pacific supporting post in Te Herenga Waka, why is Māori not considered to be Pacific? Is it something to do with Aotearoa that defaults "Pacific" out? Is it something to do with the Pacific that cannot imagine Aotearoa?

Although the Māori village has been a permanent and durable feature of the Pacific represented at the Polynesian Cultural Centre (PCC) in Hawai'i, the presence of Māori in the Pasifika Festival, a celebration of Pacific culture, food, arts, and language that is the largest single event held in Auckland and the largest single Pacific event in the world, has been remarkably unstable. Over the course of two days—the one-day event was expanded because the crowds could not fit into the Western Springs Park venue—an estimated 250,000 Pacific and non-Pacific people gravitate to this huge event each year.[5] At times the festival, which started in 1993, has included Māori as a part of the Pacific in the same way as other Pacific communities (Sāmoa, Tonga, Niue, Cook Islands, etc.) by allocating a stage or village to "Aotearoa," and at times the festival has included Māori as tāngata whenua through processes of consultation and the use of tikanga for opening ceremonies and related events. Pasifika '93 had three performance stages—"Main," "Community," and "Contemporary"—which were joined by a collection of food vendors, information tents, displays, and stalls. Pasifika '95 included a "cultural village" to better organize the cultural aspects of what had already become a huge event, and the village structure changed again in 1999 to include several villages organized by distinct Pacific communities for the first time. The shift from a whole festival to a tribal or island village structure took some working out, and the configuration of the villages for the 1999 Pasifika Festival was finally confirmed by early February. The informational pamphlet distributed at the 1999 Pasifika Festival read,

> The NIU millennium. Pasifika 99 encompasses the NIU as the past, present and future for all things Pacific. The introduction of villages will bring you even closer to experiencing the uniqueness and diversity that is Pasifika, and with the many highlights and associated events leading up to the festival this will surely be the biggest and best Pasifika yet.[6]

Because of the hegemonic national configuration of the Pacific ("all things Pacific") at events such as Pasifika, in New Zealand, one would be surprised to find an iteration of the Pacific that did not include Sāmoa or the Cook Islands and yet has permission to be surprised to find communities from Kiribati, Wallis and Futuna, Papua New Guinea, Nauru, or, indeed, Aotearoa. At the bottom of a list of typed considerations for the Festival Komiti[7] to consider in February 1999 is a handwritten question: "What does NZ village mean?"[8]

The question "what does NZ village mean?" is ostensibly about a specific "village" in a specific time and place, but it is a question with which the organizers of the Pasifika Festival have grappled over the course of successive festivals. What, indeed, is a New Zealand village? What is a "village" when it is in New Zealand? As the crowds attending the Pasifika Festival grew, so, too, did the urgency of questions around the event: what counts as Pasifika? The formal evaluation of Pasifika '98 argued,

> Pasifika AND Maori should be a combined festival. We are a part
> of the culture and heritage of the Pacific afterall [sic].[9]

A note in the late 1999 minutes of the festival committee reads, "Aotearoa/ NZ village—change to Aotearoa."[10] Pasifika 2000 was themed "Dawn of the New Millennium," and the Aotearoa village, like the others, focused on culture in the forms of food, art, and performance:

> Watch young and elderly Maori weavers produce incredible art
> such as Kete (bag), Kono (food basket) and Potae (hat) woven
> from flax. Enjoy tasting traditional hangi food (meat and vegeta-
> bles). Listen and watch Kapa Haka (Maori cultural performance)
> groups entertain you while you explore this village.

Had the Aotearoa village been included in the Pasifika Festival each year, there would have been sufficient material to conduct an interesting comparison between the festival and the PCC in and of itself. However, another transition was yet to take place: the village previously named "Aotearoa" was renamed "Niu Sila," signaling a shift at Pasifika in which the Indigenous (and Pacifically) imagined "Aotearoa" vanished and the diasporic host "Niu Sila" appeared. In minutes of a Komiti meeting in late 1999 about the 2000 villages, we read,

> Content of this [Aotearoa] village is to be all inclusive of Maori
> and NZ born Pacific people.[11]

Certainly New Zealand–born Pasifika presence and representation at the Pasifika Festival deserves its own discussion, and yet the appearance of this new Niu Sila village apparently required the removal of an Aotearoa village. Reflecting a struggle to account for the specificities of Māori experience *and* the specificities of Pasifika experience in New Zealand, the question "what does NZ village mean?" could apparently only have one answer, and Indigenous and diasporic Pacific communities are forced to compete to represent the national space.

Jumping forward to Pasifika 2004, Aotearoa had completely left the building. Nine villages were dotted around Western Springs Park for the festival (Tonga, Fiji, Sāmoa, Kiribati, Niu Sila, Tokelau, Cook Islands, Niue, and Tuvalu), each of which was represented by a national flag on materials handed to Pasifika Festival visitors. As in 1999, the pamphlet included an appropriate greeting, information about specific events, and features of that village over the course of the day. How, one might wonder, would the Niu Sila village be described? The first sign that Aotearoa is definitely gone is the greeting "Welcome to Niu Sila Village," where a formal English "welcome" (unusual in New Zealand, where a Māori greeting is common in almost all such spaces) is offered in place of "Kia ora." The cultural dimension of Niu Sila is "showcasing New Zealand businesses from academic institutions to small business." According to the pamphlet, the details about specific features of the 2004 Niu Sila village include the following:

Performances [not elaborated]
Fresh BBQ-flamed mussels, prawns, crabs and mussel fritters
Information stalls from Ministry of Fisheries, Department of Labour, Pacific Pulse, the University of Otago, and Tenancy Services for Housing New Zealand
Handcrafts and Pacific Island Food

I wish this were a joke. No aspect of the Niu Sila village makes any reference to Māori, making those Pasifika communities involved complicit with the removal of tāngata whenua from the national imaginary. Furthermore, the "information stalls" of these government agencies and businesses are a stereotypical lineup for a Pasifika crowd. Since the first Pasifika Festival, there had been a range of educational, cultural, political, and governmental agencies and representatives in various tent sites and stalls. Now there was Niu Sila: the government (and business and education) had a village through which it could sell its wares. Although the difference between an Aotearoa and Niu Sila village had been intended to make room for New Zealand–born Pacific communities—Pasifika, indeed—the Niu Sila village is not a rich and complex diasporic space but simply a settler nation.

In 2005 at the Pasifika Festival, the Niu Sila village again greets visitors in English and again emphasizes its position as the settler host state. On the program, the Niu Sila village is set slightly apart in its own text box. Whereas Aotearoa was able to pass as an island village, Niu Sila has trouble mixing in with the rest:

> Welcome to Niu Sila Village. Come and visit our great craft and food stalls or speak with people from the government and tertiary institutions.
>   Whether you want to learn, or just lie around and listen to the DJ, there is something for you in Niu Sila.[12]

In this short introduction to the village, long-held configurations of the settler metropole and diasporic subject loom large. On one hand, Niu Sila village renders the local Indigenous community illegible and untraceable, while extending a beckoning hand with promises of the "great craft and food stalls" found in originary homelands, with the added bonus of governmental and educational opportunities. This is, indeed, a place to come and experience a better life. On the other hand, we find the eternally precarious division between worthy and unworthy diasporic subjects: those who take advantage of particular kinds of opportunities "to learn" and those who are content to passively consume, to "just lie around and listen to the DJ." The special event at the Niu Sila village in 2005 is a competition:

> Jump up on our village stage during one of our dance-off competitions and you could win a Pasifika Festival T-shirt to remember your day by.

It is tempting to read this allegorically rather than literally. Beckoning with stores of resources and infrastructure, the settler metropole entices the diasporic subject to engage in competition—capitalism, the forces of the market—in which, while it is unlikely, you may just win. (Presumably those who choose to "lie around and listen to the DJ" are the least likely to win in this competition.) Niu Sila village uses identical wording in 2006 and adds a Fijian singer and an open microphone at which people can perform if they so wish: "See our village MC and we might give you your 15 minutes of fame . . . or 15 seconds!" The "we" who have the power to "give" space for people to be heard in "Niu Sila" are unnamed, anonymous, hegemonic.

"Kia ora" is back in 2007, although it is paired with "welcome," and there is no other sign of Aotearoa:

> Kia ora and welcome to the Niu Sila Village. Come and visit our great craft and food stalls or sit for a spell in Aunty's house (themed by Cargo Cultures), and learn about the New Zealand Pacific Island experience.[13]

The Niu Sila village has taken on a more deliberate New Zealand–born Pasifika theme and has also more clearly targeted non-Pasifika attendees. Significantly, by 2010, the villages had become more diverse (and the number of villages increased to ten) and "Aotearoa" had come back, albeit by another name. Alongside Sāmoa, Tonga, Fiji, Tokelau, Tahiti, Niue, Tuvalu, Kiribati, and Tahiti is a Tangata Whenua village, a space designated by the Indigenous position of the people rather than by the name of a collective (or perhaps a nation).[14] In this book, I argue that we once were Pacific; in the Pasifika Festival, at least until we came back as tāngata whenua, we once were Aotearoa.

In the realm of koura, the Pacific is dynamically present within the boundaries of the nation-state of New Zealand, and despite the earlier roots of Pasifika communities in rural labor and the presence of Pacific people in rural and provincial schools from the early twentieth century, the story of Māori and Pasifika connections is largely an urban story. To put it plainly, the relation between Pasifika and Māori communities is more likely to be a salient day-to-day experience for Māori in the major metropolitan centers and, indeed, in the brown (often lower socioeconomic) neighborhoods of those centers such as Maaka's beloved Ōtara or my own beloved Glen Innes.[15] Curiously, even though the overwhelming proportion of Māori live in urban centers, including the majority of Māori writers, the balance of interest is not mutual between published Māori and Pasifika texts. While many Pasifika people are talking about their relationship with Māori, very few Māori—or at least Māori whose texts are widely distributed—are talking about the same relationship.[16] (The obvious, and complex, exceptions to this are the creative people like Miria George and Che Fu who are of mixed Māori–Pasifika descent.) Furthermore, there would seem to be a compelling connection between the liminality of these (marginalized, disenfranchised, stereotyped) neighborhoods in the national space and the liminality of the literary genres within which an Aotearoa-based Pacific is most often articulated. Although some scholars and writers have engaged with the particular space of the city, much of this work codes the city as a not-Māori space, and this undermines Māori articulations of urban-centered perspective or experience and erases Indigenous presence from the land on which the cities are located.

Finding ways to critically analyze this urban work is an important task for Māori literary studies. One possible place to turn for analysis of urban Indigeneity is the Indigenous studies work coming out of North America, and a specific parallel with the relationships between Indigenous people from the United States and Mexico seems a particularly promising prospect. In both cases, Indigenous communities experienced the region in specific spaces but had an ability to move according to a series of negotiated practices of encounter but an incoming colonial system, and specifically, the imposition of state boundaries restricted movement and produced rather different economic and political situations for people on either side. From the perspective of land-based people, I can imagine that the U.S.–Mexico border and the border between New Zealand and the rest of the Pacific could seem implausibly different because a border on continuous land (such as a continent) seems more arbitrary than borders drawn around islands that are already separated by ocean. Wendt and Hau'ofa remind us, though, that ocean is territory rather than empty space, and so surely, imposed national borders are no less arbitrary when they separate some places (such as American Sāmoa and independent Sāmoa) and join others (such as Kiribati or French Polynesia or the Cook Islands, all of which sprawl across a vast range of islands, many of which are geographically closer to islands that are now part of the next-door nation-state than islands with whom they share a capital, flag, and colonial language). Certainly the inclusion of Alistair Te Ariki Campbell in an anthology of Māori writing is less surprising when we recall that people from the Cook Islands are Māori too. A further similarity between these two cases is the marked economic differences that results in vastly uneven migration between the two places. Communities Indigenous to the U.S. side end up hosting yet more manuhiri on their already stretched and often alienated lands, and similarly, the members of Pacific communities who migrate to New Zealand because of the economic differences in this region end up on Māori land without anything but cultural and genealogical impulses to compel their recognition of tangata whenua.[17] Given all these similarities and resonances, one next step for scholarship that engages with Māori urban experiences, including interactions with Pasifika communities, could be to further extend this comparison.[18]

I said in the introduction to this book that talking about disconnection and misconnection is hard. Treating disconnection between Māori and Pasifika communities is tricky because analysis risks lapsing into a discussion of "Natives behaving badly," in which a moral position is asserted along with instructions for ideal interactions and reproaches for those failing to measure up. It falls on the critical scholar to be aligned with and contribute to the struggle for justice by carefully historicizing and contextualizing present predicaments, paying attention wherever possible to the role of power in the production of narratives and countering dominant configurations of power by ensuring that disempowered and marginalized voices have an opportunity to speak as well. The road from Tupaia's conversations with Māori at Uawa when the Tahitian tapa was first seen to the present day, in which Harris and Sione are friends (chapter 5), Mila is manuhiri (chapter 6), but Romeo meets Tusi (chapter 7) is a long road that all Māori and Pasifika people experience a little differently. Certainly there is a stark difference between reconnecting with Pacific people from Hawaiki as emissaries from an originary home (perhaps like the carved post in Te Herenga Waka) and negotiating relationships with Pasifika manuhiri with whom you compete for scarce resources.

In another context, Hawaiian historian Kealani Cook reflects on the seemingly paradoxical position in which some Hawaiians venerate the Micronesian navigator Mau Piailug for the knowledge he has generously shared to inspire and reignite Kanaka Maoli (and, in turn, Polynesian) voyaging and navigation and, at the same time, hold strongly prejudiced attitudes about Micronesians living in Hawai'i in the present day. Cook argues that Hawaiians engage with Piailug not as a Micronesian—indeed, *despite* his Micronesianness—and instead as an originary Hawaiian. It is worth quoting Cook at length on this point:

> In the current effort to revive Hawaiian ties to other islanders, the scars of history, particularly of the twentieth century, must be

examined. European and American discourses that define islanders as primitive, uncivilized, and pre-modern remain strong, even
among many Islanders. Hawaiians revere Mau, but unfortunately
many do so because they see him not so much as what a modern
Islander can be, but what ancient Hawaiians were. It is not that far
a conceptual leap between praising Mau as a cherished remnant
of the Hawaiian past and denigrating Marshallese immigrants as
primitive and ignorant.[19]

Cook draws our attention to the uncomfortable connection between contemporary antagonisms and a form of cultural parochialism, neatly sketching
a possible explanation for how communities and individuals are capable of
making this conceptual leap.

However, in his writing about the Hawaiian context, Kealani Cook cau-
tions us to recognize the hand of colonialism in any interaction between
Pacific people:

So in these contemporary efforts to reconnect, we must be aware
of how the discourses we are engaging in have been shaped by history, and make conscious choices about how we use and reshape
them.[20]

Cook does not imagine a world in which genuine Pacific–Pacific engagement is impossible or foreclosed, and he does not limit the "history" that has
"shaped" "the discourses we are engaging in" to colonial history, and thereby
he leaves room for (and in his work, he deliberately pursues) an enlarged
sense of the "history" in the Pacific. He argues that this engagement with
other Pacific people is possible when we "make conscious choices" about
the discourses available to us. It is not that we once were Pacific and now we
are not but instead that the ways in which we articulate ourselves in relation
to the Pacific are deeply inflected by the past two centuries.

Such a conceptual leap was made in the documentary *Made in Taiwan:
Oscar and Nathan's Excellent Adventure,* fronted by Oscar Kightley (of
Brotown and *Sione's Wedding* fame[21] and the cowriter of *Romeo and Tusi*)
and Nathan Rarere (popular Māori youth show TV presenter) and aired in
early 2006.[22] The pair had their genes tested by Oxford University and went
on a trip through the Pacific from Aotearoa to the Cook Islands to Sāmoa
to Vanuatu to Taiwan to trace histories of migration across the Pacific as

"proven" by this genetic research. In each destination, Nathan and Oscar spent some time learning about the local place, and the journey also included "big reveals" to their family members in New Zealand and Sāmoa about their "real" origins. This is a fascinating and multileveled documentary, and yet it refuses to acknowledge either the very old and ongoing explanations of the peopling of the Pacific (the film is essentially a film of first encounters) or the connections between Māori and other Pacific people in a national as well as regional space. *Made in Taiwan* sidesteps the complicated histories of Pacific migration, and the various configurations of power, connection, and violence bound up in those histories, by simply repatriating people to their "home" islands throughout the film. While one has certain conversations on the road or at home, it is disappointing that, while they were engaged in what Cook would describe as a "contemporary effort[ ] to reconnect," Nathan travels all the way to Rarotonga to discover the similarities between the New Zealand Māori and Cook Island Māori languages. Certainly there are Cook Islanders in Rarotonga, but whose purposes does it serve to simultaneously erase the long (albeit quiet) history of Cook Islander presence in New Zealand and reinforce the idea that Cook Islanders are not members of New Zealand's contemporary national community but merely predecessors to Māori?

A careful negotiation is required to invoke claims of connection between Pacific people and at the same time recognize Indigeneity in a particular place. In some ways, this is a matter of balancing the realm of tapa—and its aspirational Pacific vision—with the national, local, specific realm of koura. In *Rongo* in 1973 Will 'Ilolahia called on Polynesian people to unite on the basis of shared cultural backgrounds and political experiences of oppression ("POLYNESIANS [Maori and non-Maori Polynesian] have the same problem—That is racism") and yet he leaves room to recognize that Māori are marked differently in this national space:

> It is granted that land is strictly a Maori–Polynesian crisis and the non-Maori Polynesian can only take a stance of solidarity and support.[23]

Recognizing the question of land brings the role of the state right into the middle of the Māori–Pasifika relationship, and rather than privileging originary regional connections or flattening out all oppressions so a

"land . . . crisis" is unable to be differentiated from any other form of racism, 'Ilolahia names and calls for action to witness the specific experience
of Māori in relation to New Zealand. His call is underpinned by his belief
that "Polynesian" is a sufficiently robust identification to provide the basis
for *just* struggle against injustice, and he refutes the idea that Māoriness is
challenged or assimilated by Polynesianness:

> This *doesn't* mean that the Maori lose their Maoritanga and replace
> their Maoriness. No it means that opposite, because by obtaining
> and using one's own Maoritanga, Maori way of life, Maoris become
> more Polynesian. A basic principle of Polynesian culture is what
> Maoritanga is all about. Communal living is Polynesia. Having
> AROHA is as much a part of Samoan or Tongan culture as it is to
> the Maori people.

This, after all, is the realm of koura, and we have had enough narratives of
assimilation here. Māori filmmaker and philosopher Barry Barclay describes
Māori filmmaking as the "camera on the shore," as opposed to the camera
on the boat arriving from across the sea, and this concept of perspective
and place can be extended beyond filmmaking. 'Ilolahia's arguments do
not require Māori to relinquish our position on the shore to understand
ourselves as Polynesian—as Pacific—but, instead, he suggests that through
our connection to the shore, we reaffirm our connection to the ocean. Con-
ceptualizing "Polynesian" as something Māori achieve by going through
Māoritanga rather than by departing from it provides the opportunity for
Māori and Pasifika communities to connect on the basis of shared experience
of racism, yes, but shared cultural values—"communal living," "AROHA"—
as well. 'Ilolahia's turn to Polynesianness as a basis for connection is later
echoed in texts like *Romeo and Tusi* and by Nesian Mystik (who extend it
to Nesianness and thereby include the whole Pacific).

If the Pasifika Festival forces Māori and Pasifika communities to compete
for representational space at the level of region, and if *Made in Taiwan* prefers Māori relationship with the Pacific to be ancient and migratory rather
than present and proximate, and if 'Ilolahia calls for shared experiences
of racism and shared cultural practice to form the basis of a "we are all
Polynesians" stance that still has room to acknowledge Indigeneity, what,
then, do we do with Daniel Maaka? Does Te Papa demonstrate a commitment to recognizing Māori as distinct from Pasifika in the context of New

Zealand when it downgrades Maaka's presence on Pacific branding? *Once Were Pacific* does not have a perfect answer to the question of whether the image of Daniel Maaka should have been used in the branding of Te Papa's exhibition, but part II has teased out the context in which this decision was made and why it matters.

In the realm of koura, many of the articulations of Māori and Pasifika connections have taken place in liminal spaces, and yet this is where these things are worked out. Participants in a discussion thread on the HiphopNZ.com site responded to the Daniel Maaka story in ways that demonstrate how and whether these questions matter. At first, the story that Te Papa was hoping to identify the man in the photo was posted on the site, to which one response read,

> I wonder what would happen if they found the guy and discover a downward spiralling story of gang, drugs and jail. Not that thats what im hoping but ah, so much expectation for the guy, be interesting to see what then happens to marketing etc. Would he get money for his image being used like that too? Hmm ch-ching!![24]

In the image, "Ōtara" is used to stand in for "Pacific," but it cannot help but also stand in for poverty, and this person pairs observations about Ōtara and its reputation, including the range of possible futures for a young Polynesian man growing up in a racist and marginalized environment, with questions around the property of the image and, in turn, Te Papa's economic interests in a photo that is significant for its representation of an economically impoverished space. A later post by another person—"as though wearing ŌTARA on ya t shirt means you're down with the brown . . . pffffft"— cynically challenges the easy association on which Te Papa relies between the place of Ōtara and a particular set of experiences or political commitments. Once the update to the story was available, which explained that the photo of Maaka was no longer to be used as the "hero image" for the exhibition, people posting to the site were quick to respond. Some people preferred to emphasize the place of Te Papa in this negotiation:

> Good shit they found him though . . . suxx that a mueseum with a Maori name wants to change their front man of the exhibition.

It is a pacific island exhibition though, and they have said he will still be a major focal point.

For goodness sakes get ya shit togehter Te Papa!

Echoing 'Ilolahia, but also echoing *Romeo and Tusi* and more besides, one comment brings together the intersecting strands of nation, origin, and racism in the realm of koura:

Maoris ,Tongans Samoans Cook Islanders, Theyre all Polynesians.
Irish Scottish Welsh English, Theyre all european.
Far No wonder nz is so racist so much sepratism.

Still others focused on the underlying question of whether Māori are Pacific, recognizing that Māori articulation of being Pacific is inextricable from the category "Polynesian" and the specificities of place. The discussants are adamant and engaged in this discussion, affirming the ongoing and diverse range of ways in which Māori articulate connections with the Pacific, and confirming that these questions matter:

But yeah, when are c— gonna recognize Maori are pacific islanders

True. aotearoa is in the *pacific*. there's a nth *island* and sth *island*.

Thats what I thought! Or are Maori only considered Polynesians not Pacific Islanders? f— knows

E Kore Au e Ngaro

It is tempting to try to imagine what Tupaia was thinking as he painted one specific moment of trade between an Englishman bearing tapa and a Māori man bearing seafood in 1769. Yet Robert Sullivan's poetry about Tupaia and Mai in *voice carried my family* reminds us of the tension between desiring to extol such historical figures and knowing that this itself is a form of representation that could unwittingly "take the middle of [their] throat[s]":[1]

> Who am I to extol Tupaia? Star navigator. Great Chief.
> Cartographer of a chunk of the Pacific Cook claimed his own?
> Loving Tupaia of the Arioi? Who am I to say these things?[2]

Sullivan carefully distinguishes between "bring[ing]" Tupaia's and Mai's "Polynesian eyes" for his own project of reframing (as he has described in the poem "The Great Hall," discussed in chapter 2) and presuming to speak from their perspective: "Your story. Your story and your eyes are yours." Indeed, most of Sullivan's poem "Tupaia" recounts Sullivan's own whakapapa and recalls Māori responses to Tupaia rather than attempting to tell Tupaia's story. Without attempting to presume Tupaia's thoughts and motivations, then, we can reflect on the act of painting in which he was engaged and the relationship between the painting itself and the world in which he painted.

In a 2008 exhibition at Pataka Museum in Porirua titled First Contact, Michel Tuffery both reproduced and extended Tupaia's work. Tuffery, who is of Samoan, Tahitian, and Cook Islands descent, is a prolific and eminent Pasifika artist and has enjoyed many solo and group exhibitions: his iconic sculptural pieces which create life-sized cattle out of tins of corned beef are highly suggestive but also highly recognized in New Zealand. After engaging with Tupaia's story, this Pacific—and Pasifika—painter of the twenty first century has been intrigued, in turn, by the eighteenth-century interactions between Polynesians and Europeans. The curator Helen Kedgley writes that "Tuffery, who identifies strongly with Tupaia, wants to raise awareness of the pivotal role Tupaia played in the history of first contact."[3] She cites personal communication with Tuffery in which he explicitly accounts for the twinned continuities of perspective (Pacific) and medium (paint) between himself and Tupaia:

> Omai and Tupaia were here when it was all happening, the first Polynesians witnessing all this business. I am trying to carry on with what Tupaia would have done if he had the materials I have now.[4]

In particular, Tuffery reworks the painting to which this book has paid close attention into a diptych: *Tupaia's Chart, Cook and Banks—Tupaia and Parkinson's Paintbox* (2004), which appears on the cover of this book. In her essay in the exhibition catalog, Karen Stevenson underscores the significance of the connections between Tupaia and Tuffery:

> The circumstances behind this image [Tupaia's painting] become a catalyst for Tuffery's imagination spurring him both to reflect upon and acknowledge not only the exchange of physical objects, but the experiences and interactions that were of overwhelming significance to all involved.[5]

It is significant that Tuffery reframes Tupaia's piece in a diptych: one pairing (Banks and the Māori man as represented in the original) is framed by another pairing (the diptych itself), which holds the original alongside another pairing (Tupaia and Parkinson sharing a paint box) and gestures to the ultimate intergenerational pairing (Tupaia and Tuffery). These layers of pairing and relationship—exchange that is represented, frame of representation, medium of representation—emphasize not only the relationships inherent to the moment of encounter but also the relationships and elements inherent to the framing and moment of creative production. Indeed, having a Tahitian painting on the cover of this book echoes this layering in the present day and—certainly—in the present project.

Although the painting shows the tapa and koura, three items were being held at the moment depicted by Tupaia—tapa, koura, and paintbrush—and Tuffery reminds us about the paintbrush. In the case of his painting, Tupaia was working in an unfamiliar medium, which brought its own conventions and possibilities of expression. The paintbrush suggestively gestures toward the physical embodied act of textual production as well as the ways in which the medium of textual production both explicitly and subtly shapes representation. The paintbrush foregrounds perspective and kaupapa. In this final part of the book, it is time to examine the stakes and implications of the project itself. These will be approached through three specific strands: a reflection on the written, English-language, scholarly, university context of the present discussion; a brief consideration of the redrafted chronology of published writing in English, particularly of writing by colonized and previously colonized people; and an exploration of the potentially precarious situation in which a project such as this could be understood to reframe an Indigenous community as a migrant community. This is the realm of the paintbrush: the possibilities and stakes of representation when the means of representation is held in Indigenous hands.

Cook's Ship, Tupaia's Ship, Maui's Ship

Hau'ofa's and Wendt's vision of Oceania, to which we have returned over and over in these pages, decenters the relationship between colonizer and colonized in favor of local constructions of the region as a space overwritten by multiple crisscrossings and navigational histories. Why, then, would I hold a description of first contact between Cook and a Māori community as a beginning point for this book? The answer for me is clear. It is because of how, and where, this conversation is taking place: in the English language, between the pages of a book. This book may well travel beyond the university—and indeed, I hope it does—but I am mindful that it has emerged from an aspect of my doctoral research and that I write (and am funded) as a practicing academic in a university. I refuse *not* to acknowledge the context of this conversation, and I propose that the story of Cook's trade with Māori, which resulted in his astonished observation that Māori valued Tahitian tapa cloth far more highly than European trinkets, provocatively plays out in allegorical form the relationship between Māori, the Pacific, and the academic context of the university.

When the Indigenous—in this case, Māori—scholar approaches (or, to echo the allegory of European voyaging more closely, is approached by) the university (or the specific discipline of literary studies), it may seem that the most useful and productive trade will be between Indigenous and European knowledges. I will contribute some aspect of Māori knowledge to academia, and in return, academia will allow me access to its carefully guarded and bounded European knowledge. The Western academy, setting out in an age of European exploration into new waters with a colonial presumption to "know"[6] the Other as well as to improve modes of European resource extraction, recognizes that it will need to set up reciprocal relationships with those from whom it needs fresh produce and prepares the trinkets and nails for trade. (Interestingly, the very products Cook hoped to acquire from the Māori trading communities—fish and sweet potatoes—are both metaphors for knowledge within various Māori cultural contexts.)[7] Specifically, Cook sought to acquire cultivated, prepared, and fished foods; European explorers were inherently dependent on the application of Indigenous labor. Unexpectedly, these fish and kūmara were traded for tapa, a material acquired through colonial trade and perhaps a touch of souveniring, on which, from Cook's perspective, Māori placed an "extraordinary" value. I have suggested throughout this book that this tapa obtained at Tahiti stands in for the Pacific, given the flourishing of the paper mulberry plant from which tapa is produced throughout the Pacific region, except for most of Aotearoa, and like the kūmara and fish of Aotearoa, tapa is a product of Indigenous knowledge and expertise. The university seeks, at least on the more recent stretches of its journey, not simply natives as *objects and informants* but also Native *knowledges and scholars*.

So, then, one of the most exciting things the academy currently offers Māori literary analysis (and perhaps Māori scholarship more broadly) is the opportunity for Māori to connect with the Pacific: to engage with a vast regional comparative context that has the capacity to reaffirm the whakapapa and historical links between the Māori community and our Pacific relatives. While the (at least nominal) inclusion of Māori literature within Pacific literary horizons is an aspect of Pacific studies outside Aotearoa, the (sense of) cultural distinctiveness developed over centuries of no contact with the rest of the Pacific, and the contemporary emphasis on an Indigenous–non-Indigenous bifurcation, means that, at least in New Zealand, Māori and Pacific are not as productively or consistently linked as one might hope or expect. Māori *did* have remnant forms of tapa, accompanied by complementary oral traditions about much larger and sturdier sheets elsewhere in earlier homes, before they set out on their journey to Aotearoa, which enabled them to recognize, contextualize, and value the tapa they were offered centuries later.[8]

In our story about the exchange of tapa and food, the university is the ship, a constructed and mobile site for trade.[9] This is a productive and complex space, yet it is neither neutral nor egalitarian. The university has become a part of the crisscrossing—the histories, the relationships, the boundaries—of the Pacific and takes its place alongside the many watercraft fashioned by Indigenous and non-Indigenous people. Although the university performs an important role, this should not be understood to eclipse, counter, override, or undermine the reasons why people of the Pacific consent to trading in the first place or, indeed, where we might decide this kind of trade can take place. It might be the university, but it might be the Takitimu Festival, the paepae, the stage, online, or around family kitchen tables. We come with our own motivations and have our own systems for determining the value of various products. Sometimes we most desire the thing the university did not set out to acquire, let alone trade, and yet it is what *we* might have decided to come for. Of course, there are limits to this metaphor of the Good Ship University. Equating this kind of academic space with a story of first contact problematically reinscribes (even insists on) the antiquity or purity of the Indigenous body. Likewise, universities (like Cook's ship) tend to be inhabited by more Indigenous people from around the Pacific than we popularly give them credit for or than this metaphor allows,[10] and there is a problem with a story in which mobile universities meet landlocked Pacific people or trading middlemen (gender bias intended) meet passive, consuming Natives. Yet this metaphor of ships might be a start, at least for getting the conversation going.

Some time around the early 1850s, Te Arawa writer Wiremu Maihi Te Rangikaheke met a man, Maui Tione, from elsewhere in the Pacific. In an unfinished letter he evidently intended to send "home" to Hawaiki with Maui, who had identified himself "Nō Hawaiki ke ahau,"[11] Te Rangikaheke expresses his concern that Māori may have forgotten aspects of cultural practice and philosophy since their migration from tropical Polynesia, and especially since the range of interactions with Europeans that century. Identifying this chance meeting as an opportunity to determine the extent to which Māori had strayed from their roots, he opened the letter as follows:

Ana he korero Maori atu enei naku ki a koutou ki nga tangata o Hawaiki, kia mohio mai koutou ki ena korero.[12]

He anticipated that "nga tangata o Hawaiki" would be mutually interested in their connection with Māori and able to read the Māori language. Directly addressing "nga tangata o Hawaiki" in this way, Te Rangikaheke demonstrates his own belief that Māori historical accounts of migration from Hawaiki were accurate but also that the people of Hawaiki would reciprocate with generosity according to the conventions of a long-standing relationship.

Although Maui Tione had come to Aotearoa working on a European ship, he advised Te Rangikaheke that his relatives in Hawaiki have a ship of their own. Recognizing that Hawaiki potentially held knowledges and histories away from which Māori had navigated through migrations and more recent cultural change, Te Rangikaheke directly asked for this ship to be sent back to Aotearoa:

> A, mea atu ahau ki taua tangata nei, 'Ki te tae koe ki tou kainga, ki Hawaiki, ina hoki i rongo atu nei au i tau korero he kaipuke ano to koutou: a, ki te tae koe ki reira, mea atu ki ou whanaunga kia homai to koutou kaipuke hei uta kai mai maku, kia kai atu au i nga kai o te kainga i heke mai nei o tatou tupuna o mua.[13]

Food is literally nourishing, but in this instance, it is also tied up with history ("eat the food of the place from which our ancestors came"). Te Rangikaheke's request for the people of Hawaiki to send a ship full of food extends our metaphor about ships bringing knowledge to Aotearoa from around the Pacific, an extension that fits the wider context of his letter, which seeks clarification around tikanga and philosophy, and we can imagine his anticipation that knowledge from Hawaiki would provide a kind of nourishment too. Reading Te Rangikaheke's request as a shipment of knowledge suggests the possibilities and urgency of intellectual discovery through relationship, mutual hospitality, and exchange. Like the Māori people at Uawa instantly recognizing the tapa on Cook's ship as a manifestation of a bigger picture beyond the here and now, Te Rangikaheke desired to engage in a visceral and personal way with "the place from which our ancestors came in former times."

Pacific ownership of ships enables an alternative series of travels: journeys and opportunities for trade that are under the control of Pacific people and for Pacific purposes. Later in his life, Banks recalled that "Tupia [sic] the Indian" drew Banks himself "exchanging a nail" with the Māori man at Uawa rather than exchanging tapa, as Tupaia recorded it:

Tupia the Indian who came with me from Otaheite Learnd to draw in a way not Quite unintelligible. The genius for Caricature which all white people Possess Led him to Caricature me and he drew me with a nail in my hand delivering it to an Indian who sold me a Lobster but with my other hand I had a firm fist on the Lobster determined not to Quit the nail till I have Livery and Seizin of the article purchased.[14]

Banks misremembers the trade which took place but clearly recalls his own anxieties about the moment of trade and his strategy to retain control in the situation. Likewise, the university may misremember or fail to recognize the extent of Māori–Pacific interaction that takes place in its hallowed halls, and even where its memory is prodded, it may, like Banks, falsely recall that exchange as one that it assumes has taken place (the nail, trinkets) rather than the one that has (tapa). Banks and the university have their memory, but we, thanks to Tupaia, have ours. Te Rangikaheke's request resonates with Hau'ofa's observations about the history and capacity of mobility around Oceania, reminding us that although Tupaia arrived on Cook's ship, and Maui on someone else's, this is not the only possible configuration of how vessels and people—and knowledge—can move around these waters. At the end of the day, much to Cook's astonishment, Māori—those "Pacific" people that we are—have the power and knowledges to determine the measurement of value for various cargoes, and this power is a mechanism of trade by which we can continue to rhetorically as well as physically navigate around the Pacific, recementing the ties from long ago.

Titaua's ship (for Titaua, in your time of transition)[15]

Alice Te Punga Somerville

another time we saw you:
you arrived on your ship
loaded with tapa and other gifts
from your home

you spent time talking genealogy:
catching up and trading stories

with relatives you hadn't seen
for generations

you came with tapa in sheets of impossible size:
proof of what we'd thought were grandparents' myths
about our shreds of paperbark
stories of Hawaiki.

we knew you'd brought the ship to come and find us:
next time Cook came
we asked him where you were—

we've waited for your return.

this time,
your ship was shaped like a lecture theatre—
once again it was loaded with things from your home

though they all spoke with confidence about the cargo in their hold,
and I couldn't understand a word you said,
I know this is
titaua's ship

one day, girl,
this won't be a ship anymore:
one day
this will be our waka

New Literary Genealogies

The interdisciplinary approach of this book should not detract from its implications for the specific disciplinary concerns of Anglophone literary studies, including accounts of postcolonial, Indigenous, Commonwealth, and New Zealand writing in English. The majority of scholars in these fields do not engage deeply with Māori, the Pacific, or Indigeneity, and the field of literary studies has not paid attention to most of the texts and critical claims contained in this book. Many scholars have called for expanding the exploration of Indigenous writing both back in time and in terms of genre, publication site, and status of publication. Although one remedy is to outline the gaps and limits of previous and ongoing work, this section is called "New Literary Genealogies" to foreground the potentially collaborative, additive effect of the present discussion. Like genealogies, these lines of discussion do not limit but add to existing conversations. In the first published novel by a Māori woman, *Mutuwhenua,* the central character, Linda, makes an argument for charting a new course (she is going to marry a Pākehā man) by reciting whakapapa: "I began to recite the old names to her, the ones from the wall and the ones from before then, and the ones before that."[16] Recounting genealogies affirms genealogical and historical place, and this project has provided an opportunity to talk about the writers already known ("from the wall") as well as utter the names of writers from "before then."

The conventional narrative that links Māori writing and publishing in English to the 1970s, when the first single-author publications of fiction appeared, is convenient but also misleading. When Chadwick Allen and Powhiri Rika-Heke independently argue that a better starting point is the first publication of creative work in the magazine *Te Ao Hou* in the early 1960s,[17] they affirm that although writers such as Ihimaera, Tuwhare, and Grace fronted a literary dimension of the so-called Māori Renaissance of the mid-1970s, several Māori writers were already in print.[18] Beyond New Zealand, literary scholars have undertaken and modeled major reconsiderations of Indigenous histories of writing. About the Australian context, for example, Penny van Toorn argues that

> by adjusting the theoretical lens through which Indigenous writing is perceived, a new history of Aboriginal writing comes into view. It becomes possible to see that when David Unaipon published his first book in 1929, Koori peoples in the Sydney region had been reading and authoring written texts for 140 years.[19]

Similarly, Abenaki literary scholar Lisa Brooks reminds us that texts by early Indigenous writers are manifestations of vibrant critical conversations happening in other forums rather than evidence of individual alienation or cultural rupture:

> The texts of the north-eastern Native tradition emerged from within this indigenous space of exchange, not, as is often portrayed,

from displaced Indian individuals reflecting on the state of their lives in relation to the colonial world. Occom, Brant, Aupaumut and Apess weren't individuals "caught between two worlds;" they were Native thinkers who inhabited many spaces of interaction, just as we do today.[20]

There will always be more Māori writing than we think, beyond books for sale at bookshops and post-1970s publications. To produce a "new history of [Māori] writing," we need to conduct careful and ongoing searches of the archive, broadly defined, and seek unpublished as well as scarcely and distantly published works. Although it could be fairly argued that there are insufficient interested scholars and students even to treat those Māori texts that appear on the shelves of mainstream bookshops, there remain a massive number of Māori texts and related paraphernalia in archives around Aotearoa, the wider Pacific region, and the rest of the world.[21]

Perhaps the most obvious contribution this book makes to chronologically expanding the scope of Māori writing in English is its inclusion of Vernice Wineera and Evelyn Patuawa-Nathan, whose collections from 1978 and 1979 are a significant achievement for Māori and Pacific literary history. Indeed, their collections place Wineera and Patuawa-Nathan in the rather small group of nonwhite women poets anywhere who enjoyed single-author publication before the 1980s. Furthermore, Patuawa-Nathan contributes another kind of earlier written text: the spectral presences of unpublished Māori writing in English. A note at the beginning of Evelyn Patuawa-Nathan's book of poetry mentions an earlier writing project:

> Twenty years ago she wrote a historical novel which the publishers, Collins of London, were interested in publishing. The manuscript for correction went astray in the mail. Evelyn "Didn't have another copy nor the staying power to stick with it."[22]

A collection of poetry in 1979 is a very impressive thing; an historical novel in 1959—the year after Achebe's *Things Fall Apart* and five years before Ngugi wa Thiong'o's *Weep Not Child*—would have been extraordinary. (The first novel to make it to publication in the Pacific was Papua New Guinea writer Vincent Eri's *The Crocodile* [1970].)[23] Interestingly, Patuawa-Nathan had elected to work in the specific mode of an historical novel, whereas the first published single-author New Zealand–based Māori fiction (novels and short story collections) all focused on contemporary themes.[24]

Still earlier than Patuawa-Nathan's mystery novel, while researching the figure of Te Rangihiroa for this project, I happened on—in a barely indexed file at the Bishop Museum in Honolulu—a single handwritten short story he had composed.[25] We already know that Te Rangihiroa was an immensely prolific writer, leaving behind theses, letters, books, articles, speeches, and notes, and the papers could have conceivably been field notes, or a letter, or just thick description. However, the opening lines—"The rain pelted down on the corrugated iron roof that had replaced the old time thatch on the tribal meeting house at Taumarunui"—feel like something else. Lines have been crossed out and replaced by words for stylistic rather than semantic reasons, and the text self-consciously works at a symbolic as well as descriptive level. As far as I know, this short story only exists in this handwritten draft. Although my current typed version of the story contains some gaps for words I am unable to decipher, "The Historian Who Lost His Memory" is currently around four thousand words in length.[26] Unfortunately, these files at the Bishop are not consistently organized in chronological order, which means that one cannot assume that undated material is of the same vintage as the materials around it, and yet Te Rangihiroa's death in late 1951 provides a latest possible date for its creation.

Continuing back in time, there are more spectral texts to which we do not (currently) have access, including those of our first published Māori writer, Mowhee. Tommy Drummond was the English name given to Mowhee (Maui; Māori spelling had not yet been standardized), who was born around 1796 in Aotearoa and who, after leaving Aotearoa as a child of nine or ten years old, lived in Norfolk Island and Australia. On Norfolk Island he went to school and learned how to read and write, and in Australia he attended Marsden's Māori Seminary in Parramatta. Although he was returned to his home in 1814, in 1815 he signed up as a common sailor and traveled to London, where he was taken to the Church Missionary Society and placed under the care of Reverend Basil Woodd.[27] Before he passed away in December 1816, Mowhee produced a recollection of his life of which the Reverend Woodd published a paraphrased version in several formats, including as *Memoir of Mowhee: A Young New Zealander Who Died at Paddington*[28] and as articles for various missionary publications.

There are, beyond Patuawa-Nathan, Te Rangihiroa, and Mowhee, many references to manuscripts and first drafts of books in letters to editors and publishers,[29] and yet we need not look to the furthest extremes of first poets, lost novels, and unpublished stories. We might also, for example, expand our sense of Māori writing in the 1980s. With the exception of Keri Hulme, the most well known Māori writers of today continue to be those who were already publishing in the 1970s: Ihimaera and Grace, but also Tuwhare, despite his earlier date of first publication. After these firsts, the next big bubble of writing is often perceived to have come about in the 1990s, when writers such as Duff and Sullivan appeared, Huia publishers started making a different kind of Māori voice accessible, and the major multivolume anthology *Te Ao Mārama* was released. However, in between this first crop of single-author publications in the 1970s and the new writing of the 1990s, a number of important and prolific writers started to publish. Taylor and Hinewirangi are treated here because of their mutual engagement with the Pacific, but their presence in *Once Were Pacific* makes visible their absence from many other discussions about Māori writing in English. Perhaps a revisioning of the 1980s Māori literary scene is an important next step as well.

Genealogies are more like webs than just straight lines, and after she finished reciting the names back in one direction, Linda, in *Mutuwhenua,* broadened her reach:

> "But that's only the trunk of the tree," I said, "the length." And she
> nodded, waiting for me to go on. "Now these are the branches
> that spread everywhere," and I continued the recitation, linking
> every name with every name until there were no more. "And every
> branch reaches out," I said. "Touches every other."[30]

A key intervention of this book has been to name writers in the Māori literary line, but discussions about Māori literary histories are complemented by other discussions, and I will gesture here toward some other possibilities for Māori literary studies and, indeed, because "every branch . . . touches every other," for literary studies more broadly.

Once Were Pacific has returned over and over again to place. My own lived experience in the urban centers of Auckland and Wellington and outside Aotearoa, and the position of my iwi as urban because of occupation by a large city rather than because of migration from a rural homeland, has compelled me to look for texts produced by urban and diasporic Māori writers. Although the more prominent Māori writers in English are mostly based in the cities, much of their writing continues to focus on stories that either center on or look toward the rural space. Similarly, although much of Ihimaera's fiction and Sullivan's poetry, to name two examples, have been produced outside New Zealand's borders, few discussions or collections of Māori writing treat the Māori diaspora. As long as 80 percent of the New Zealand–based Māori community lives in urban spaces and up to 20 percent of the Māori community lives overseas,[31] it seems remiss to not include this other writing too. Although many contemporary Māori texts do site their narratives either fully or partly in urban areas, the scholarship on these texts has yet to develop nuanced, specific, and theorized approaches to thinking about the urban space. Furthermore, dominant treatments of Māori engagements with urban space tend toward melancholic or problem-oriented discussions; Māori in cities are understood more in terms of the *distance* between themselves and their utopic rural homelands than through their *proximity* to other urban people, including Pasifika people.[32] Once we pay attention to Māori engagements with Pasifika communities, then, sidelined histories and spaces and creative forms become visible.

Once Were Pacific extends literary genealogies beyond conventional narratives of time and space but also beyond the conventional forms treated in literary studies: hip-hop, children's literature, film, television, visual art, and cultural ephemera take their place here beside poetry, fiction, and theater. Certainly some sites already expect this formal range to count in literary studies, but in Aotearoa New Zealand and much of the Pacific region, literary studies is formally conservative and often, because of the poor resourcing and limited value placed on Pacific literature, stretched just to teach and research the available texts that are conventionally literary. Furthermore, the discussion of genre and form throughout this book draws attention to the related considerations of publication, production, funding, distribution, and circulation.

Finally, the development of scholarship about Māori writing in English must not take up the space of, and yearns for the intellectual company of, parallel development of scholarship about Māori writing in the Māori language. Taking a broader view of Māori-language writing, there is work on Māori-language newspapers,[33] but literary studies work on other written Māori texts, both historical and contemporary, is needed, and that which is undertaken has tended to languish in theses and unpublished papers. Arini Loader's master of arts thesis on the prolific nineteenth-century writer Te Rangikaheke and doctoral research on nineteenth-century writing in Ōtaki,

Krissi Jerram's master's research on contemporary Māori-language short fiction in the Huia anthologies, Jillian Tipene's work on literary translation of Māori-language texts, and the work of organizations such as Te Reo o Taranaki, which have specialist archivists working directly with communities as well as with depositories, are but four examples of the possible directions in which this strand of scholarship will continue.[34] Linda reminds us that "every branch reaches out" and "touches every other." No single scholar can be proficient in all these areas of research, and no scholar needs to be. At the same time, it is too easy to focus only on one genealogical line and forget about the branches between. Instead, I am advocating here a collaborative, interdependent, "reaching out" approach to the ongoing development of the field of Māori literary studies and beyond.

Māori: Indigenous versus Pacific?

If Māori once were Pacific, what of our unique ties to the specific place of Aotearoa New Zealand? Is it possible to be Pacific and Indigenous at the same time? In a certain light, this book could, at its extreme, be shorthanded as "migrant" versus "Indigenous." To be more direct, according to the logics of Indigeneity and migration as those concepts tend to be articulated at present, claiming that we once were Pacific does not easily sit alongside a simultaneous claim to Indigeneity. Indeed, on some levels, this book risks—through its focus on Māori as a *Pacific* identification—being construed as undermining the political imperatives and possibilities of Māori as an *Indigenous* identification. Returning to the specific space of Matiu/ Somes Island, which was introduced at the beginning of this book, allows us to think about this problem in another way: can we understand ourselves as "always-having-been-theres" (Matiu in the mouth of the fish) and as "arrivals" (Matiu named by Kupe) at the same time? Is this contradictory? How, indeed, does this book project maintain, assert, and/or practice sovereignty? Is it possible that *Once Were Pacific* could inadvertently undo or threaten sovereignty?

When I went to a conference in Taipei in November 2005 at the invitation of an Indigenous Taiwanese scholar, Dr. Pu, I was struck, as are many Māori people who make that trip, by the unbelievable physical likeness between the people I met and my relatives at home. I'd been invited because there is an ongoing and growing interest in connections between Māori (the babies of the Pacific) and Indigenous Taiwanese communities (the place from which many people believe we originally come), and I got to play the somewhat bizarre game of "how do you say . . . ," in which I spoke English and they spoke Chinese and the only language we shared was the one with which my relatives had left Taiwan over five thousand years ago. However, I was not the only person exploring Māori–Indigenous Taiwan links in 2005. So was the New Zealand mainstream media. Indeed, mainstream coverage of the news of Māori genetic links with the Pacific appeared in newspapers in 2005, even though much of this information was not very new. (For example, the hip-hop group Nesian Mystik refers to mitochondrial DNA in their 2003 album *Polysaturated*.) Meanwhile, at the Native American Literary Symposium in 2006, Hokulani Aikau talked about the implications of always starting discussions of Hawai'i with explanations of "the peopling of the Pacific." Aikau argued that centering the narrative about the arrival of Hawaiians to Hawai'i ultimately serves the desire of the U.S. state to incorporate Hawaiian people into the discourse of "a nation of immigrants" against which claims to Indigeneity are pitted.

What is the link between genetic research about Indigenous people in Aotearoa and Taiwan and national discourses of a nation of immigrants? Is there a connection between these links and the relationship between Indigeneity and migration? Well, 2005 was election year in New Zealand, and election years here are known as Māori-bashing years. Everyone wants cheap votes, for which we pay the price: either Māori are ridiculous and need to be stopped from getting all the extra privileges, or Māori are ridiculous and, luckily, someone knows how to save us from ourselves. The 2005 election was particularly nasty because of the 2004 Seabed and Foreshore issue, which was heightened when Don Brash, leader of the opposition National Party, kicked the election season off with his now infamous Orewa speech in early 2004.[35] Brash's major platform was on the complete erasure of Māori status as Indigenous people with special (he called them "race-based") rights or positions. The specific phrase of "a nation of immigrants" started to turn up in his campaign speeches. How curious, then, that suddenly the mainstream media wanted to focus on Māori histories of migration from Taiwan. I'm not the only person to have connected some of these dots; Alec Hutchinson's 2006 journalistic essay "Worlds Apart" explores Indigenous resistance to the use of DNA for the purpose of making grand claims about Pacific migration. Drawing attention to the documentary *Made in Taiwan,* discussed in the conclusion to part II, which aired on mainstream television in early 2006, Hutchinson cites Paul Reynolds, who described the politics of this genetic research:

> Indigenous people aren't stupid. We've been here before. We've had centuries of exploitation by non-indigenous people. This is highly political. It's race-based research, and therefore it can be manipulated and used for political benefit. . . . This could link straight into what Don Brash wants to hear: that everybody comes from the same place.[36]

Neither Reynolds nor I dispute the genetic research itself or the idea that Māori are the descendents of Polynesian navigators who may ultimately have come from present-day Taiwan. What is at issue here is the politics of research and the potential "manipulation" of that research by those in power to reinforce their own positions by diminishing Māori claims to Indigeneity.

Following Kealani Cook's observation that "contemporary efforts to reconnect" are irrevocably "shaped" by ongoing histories of interaction, including interaction with colonialism, it is striking to recognize that the discourse of a nation of immigrants is central to *Made in Taiwan*. In this documentary, *our* stories (and indeed any other explanations, linguistic, anthropological, botanical, etc.) are marginalized by the so-called scientific evidence supplied by genetic research.[37] The opening comment is voiced over a shot of people walking on the footpath of a cosmopolitan Auckland street: "In New Zealand we all come from somewhere else." Although Māori navigation histories and non-Māori immigrant histories can be read in such a way that this is *technically* true, "all coming from somewhere else" problematically smoothes out any distinctions between the relative positions of Māori and non-Māori in the contemporary nation-state. In the context of reactionary but dominant mainstream concerns about Māori getting special treatment, especially as land and other claims are worked through and as strategies such as quotas for educational institutions and Māori-run social services are set up to counter the damage that has been done by general provision of these services, a documentary that provides scientific evidence that Māori are "from somewhere else" in the same way as all other New Zealanders are cannot help but participate in affirming particular political positions. This is about the third—Somes—story of our little island called "Matiu." The national narrative plays these two first narratives (the fish one and the Kupe one) against each other to achieve this. To assimilate the Indigenous into the nation, a narrative of shared immigrantness is foregrounded.

Whether one can be a migrant and Indigenous at the same time is particularly pressing in the context of a state that articulates itself as a nation of immigrants. Unlike nations in which the majority of citizens trace their descent from people who have "always" lived in the specific place, or thereabouts, settler nations like Canada, the United States, Australia, and New Zealand depend on a different logic to connect themselves to territory. Non-Indigenous claims to affective connection with particular landscapes mimic Indigenous connections with land, and yet the mimicry is never sufficient. The settler claim is never as deep or long or complex as that of the Indigene, and so the figure of the Indigene always threatens to trump settler claims of an emotional or historic connection with place. Although invisibilizing, nullifying, or coopting ongoing Indigenous presence is one settler strategy, where Indigenous presence is unavoidable or incontrovertible, the concept of a nation of immigrants links citizenship to immigration instead of autochthony. Rather than New Zealanders sharing a common connection with place, they share a common experience of mobility.

In a nation of immigrants, migration is framed as an equally disconnecting and reconnecting experience, despite the historical and ongoing inequities of mobility. To a large extent, of course, this makes perfect sense. Non-Indigenous New Zealanders share the experience of arrival rather than connection with land back into antiquity or genealogical (or cultural or linguistic) connection with each other. Once everyone becomes an immigrant and nationhood thereby becomes inseparable from an experience of movement away from an earlier home, everyone gets to claim a history of removal, disconnection, adjustment. Crucially, this configuration connects one with the land by permitting access to the nation-state and not vice versa, which neatly sidesteps any involvement in historical (and ongoing) acts of state violence against Indigenous communities. The idea of a nation of immigrants can have some positive outcomes; according to its logic, my nephew's father (born in Eritrea) has the same rights and access to citizenship as my own father (a Pākehā New Zealander). (Of course, it's always more tricky than this: I suspect that my nephew's father gets asked where he's "really" from more often than my nephew's grandfather does.) When the access point of the nation is (quite literally) the journey rather than the destination, the settler occupies the center of the national narrative, and a claim of belonging is granted to the non-Indigenous New Zealander through the systems of connection and ownership bestowed on a citizen.[38] In this way, the haka, for example, is the property not of those whose dance and martial form it may be but of the nation. It stands in for New Zealandness not because Māori have an elevated status in New Zealand or because this is a way of "showing respect" for a particular dimension of the nation but because the haka is one of the commodities one receives along with the passport, national anthem, and permission to get teary eyed about central Otago during *The Lord of the Rings*, whether or not one has actually been there. It's not that narratives of connection do not feature—but the narratives are the property of citizens rather than the basis of citizenship.[39]

But what about the Indigenous New Zealander? Once the link between connection with land and membership of the nation is ruptured, the Indigene's primary connection with land no longer threatens the ability of dominant settlers to understand themselves to be at home in New Zealand. (Indeed, ongoing Indigenous connection with land is understood to be presumptuous and unjust: if all New Zealanders are New Zealanders in the same way, why should Māori get special treatment? In this formulation, Māori who articulate ongoing connection are framed as disloyal subjects, the "community" is disrupted by "protestors," or "haters and wreckers," as they were called by a prime minister.)[40] Because Indigeneity is usually expressed as a claim of historic connection to specific place, the Indigenous subject doesn't easily fit into a nation of immigrants, and migration is posed as a shared experience that flattens out other forms of connection. The difference between Māori and non-Māori migration to these islands is thereby articulated as temporal rather than as a difference of kind. Like Taylor's character Sione in "Pa Mai," the only difference between Māori arrival on canoes and Pasifika arrival on Air New Zealand is timing.[41] In this context, the recognition of lawful immigrant status is framed as a generous and inclusive act of the state, to the extent that evidence of migration actually forces incorporation into the nation and undermines a possible claim of difference on the basis of Indigeneity. Discursively, at least, rather than the settler becoming quasi-Indigenous to articulate connection with landscape or nation, the Indigene becomes quasi-settler.[42]

How, then, might we reconcile these simultaneous designations of migrant, Indigene, and citizen, and what does it all mean for this book? Māori don't have a defense when we're accused of being immigrants because we *are*, in fact, in Aotearoa on the basis of a series of migrations. Why would we want to defend ourselves against being *migrants*? Because this status is used as proof that we're *not Indigenous*. *Indigenous* need not open up so much that it includes all migrants, but the danger of not carefully uncoupling migrant from not Indigenous is that some communities will continue to have our Indigenousness challenged in ways that currently feel indefensible. We need to be smarter than the logic of these arguments. I do not want to suggest that it is unethical or problematic to explore Māori–Pacific connections per se. The risk of the project of this book is therefore not the research itself but the historical, racial, political, legal, and scholarly contexts within which the research is conducted. Merely engaging with the Pacific and regionalism is risky business for communities that rely heavily on claims around Indigeneity—without the room to clarify the complexities of that term—for political, legal, and sometimes physical survival. Does being Pacific—being migrants from across Te Moananui-a-Kiwa—default us out of conventional modes of articulating ourselves as Indigenous? Does identifying strongly as Indigenous default us out of conventional modes of understanding ourselves as Pacific? If we as Māori have decided to wrest back the conversation so we get to talk about what matters to us, rather than being paralyzed by or dismissive of these possible implications, we need to work our way through them on our own terms.

Returning again to our island of Matiu/Somes, when do we get to ask these questions about Matiu if we still spend so much time focusing on the relationship between Matiu and Somes for our survival? Indeed, it is hard to stop talking about the third story of the island (Somes; the colonial–national dimension), especially when we need to constantly correct people who, despite "Matiu" being reinstated as a (half) name in 1997, insist on calling the island "Somes." Constant vigilance about making our very presence visible can distract us from the multiplicity inherent in our understandings about the autochthonous and migratory stories connected to the island's name "Matiu." When we stand on Matiu, we are both these things: our people have always been there, and we arrived there. That's the place to start.

Once Were Pacific

Once were Hawaiki. Tupaia's first encounters with Māori in 1769 were marked by curiosity, engagement, and the establishment of relationship. Beads and nails were less "valued" by Māori on first contact than lengths of tapa recently obtained from Tahiti because Māori oral traditions had retained a memory of the existence of such large pieces of tapa, even though the temperate environment in Aotearoa made production of even scraps of tapa all but impossible for a thousand years. A century later, Te Rangikaheke's concern about changes to Māori cultural practice and philosophical understandings, both because of recent colonialism and because of isolation from the wider Pacific region prior to European arrival, compelled him to respond in very specific ways when he met a man he identified as coming from "Hawaiki." Writing a letter to the people of Hawaiki to affirm tikanga and seek correction may seem a little strange, but there is a logic of connection and reciprocity that underpins Te Rangikaheke's decision to write. Years later, in 1920, Rewiti Kohere, writing as "RTK" in the Gisborne newspaper *Te Kopara,* explored the topic of cross-Pacific connections in his article "Kei Hea Hawaiki."[43] He argued that European knowledge of the Pacific region was able to help Māori answer the question about where Hawaiki is located, and he argued that Hawaiki is a multiplicity rather than a singular site: "Kua ki ake au kahore i kotahi te Hawaiki."[44] In RTK's articulation of Hawaiki, each of the sites around Polynesia is a Hawaiki of sorts, and this configuration produces room for connection as well as room for specificity. Certainly "Hawaiki" can suggest a Polynesian-centric notion of the Pacific region, although Uncle Rawiri from *The Whale Rider* reminds us through his sojourn in Papua New Guinea that the possibilities of connection extend beyond our closest Polynesian relatives to elsewhere in the Pacific too.

In 2008, Ngahiwi Tomoana echoed RTK's argument for the potential of reengaging Hawaiki to articulate contemporary connections when he described a distinctly political—and pro-Indigenous—kaupapa for the Takitiumu Festival:

> Ngāti Kahungunu will be hosting the inaugural Takitimu Festival to give effect to the United Nations Declaration on the Rights of Indigenous Peoples. This festival will be a celebration and development initiative in the rebuilding of relationships of indigenous peoples across Aotearoa, the Pacific and the Hawaiiki nation. We encourage all families and communities to celebrate our past, our present and our future in Aotearoa and the Pacific by participating in the festival.[45]

Tomoana proposes a particular configuration—a "Hawaiiki nation"—by which specific Indigenous communities can agitate for their rights in the context of the United Nations Declaration. Just as the scientific gathering of genetic data can be used for certain purposes, so, too, can the gathering of "indigenous peoples across Aotearoa, the Pacific and the Hawaiiki nation." Rather than articulating Indigenous rights in terms of a relationship with the colonizing nation-state, however, Tomoana quietly sidesteps New Zealand altogether: "our future" is in "Aotearoa and the Pacific." The historical Hawaiiki nation centered on Taputapuātea, a space whose underlying purpose was to provide the governmental, diplomatic, artistic, spiritual, and scientific basis for the continued flourishing of the various specific communities contained within its sweep. As a vision for self-determination, sovereignty, tino rangatiratanga, mana motuhake[46]—as a vision for Aotearoa, for Māori, for the Pacific—this one gets my vote. After all, e kore au e ngaro; he kākano i ruia i Rangiātea.

A Time and a Place

IN AUGUST 2008, a deed of settlement was signed between the Port Nicholson Block Claim and the Crown.[1] At Pipitea, marae leaders from Taranaki whānui spoke on behalf of the whānau, including my own family, who had been repeatedly mistreated by successive New Zealand governments. In response, ministers representing the Crown offered an apology and the promise to pass the legislation, which would give effect to the compensation package that had taken over twenty years—and in some ways, 169 years—to negotiate. One of the details of the package was that the "harbor islands," including Matiu/Somes and Mākaro, would be returned to those from whom they had been wrongly taken.

For my own part, I have a particular relationship to Matiu/Somes through my involvement in refurbishing the Whare Mahana, our iwi house on the island, and the extension of this into an ongoing role connected to the kaitiakitanga[2] of the island. In very real ways, I, having been raised outside of the Wellington region, have been literally "painting my way home" to meaningful connection with my broader iwi through my physical labor in renovating the house. Given my active research in this area of Māori–Pacific connection, the significance of this specific involvement with Matiu/Somes is not lost on me. I moved back to the Wellington area from the United States in early 2005, and coming home to Te Ātiawa and to Te Whanganui a Tara has meant a homecoming to Matiu and, in turn, to Kupe's prophetic act of naming. Ngugi wa Thiong'o has talked about the act of naming as an act of memory. Any new name brings a memory that is overlaid on top of existing memories and induces a process of forgetting and amnesia that foregrounds one particular narrative and diminishes another.[3] Quite rightly, the focus for our iwi has been on the relationship between "Matiu" and "Somes"—between specific Indigenous communities and the Crown in all of its institutional manifestations. Now that Matiu has been returned to us, we have the opportunity to renotice the other pairing of names in our harbor: Matiu and Mākaro. In that pairing, we find another series of relationships and another framework of history. We might turn to the opening of Wineera's 1978 poem "Hokule'a," which, reflecting on a key moment of the resuscitation of Polynesian voyaging, articulates this sense of possibility:

> We have all watched
> with some misgiving
> the ocean of possibilities
> beyond our doors,
> wondering, in our complacency,
> whether we had courage enough
> to chart a course
> to farther islands.[4]

Regaining Matiu represents an opportunity to reframe relationship with the Crown but also with the Pacific. We find another mode and motivation for our articulation of who we are.

The final writing and editing of this book is taking place on Matiu. There's a big table here, pushed up against the window of the dining room of the iwi house, and this table is where a great deal of connecting and reconnecting takes place for many of us associated with the island. I am sitting at the dining room table, looking out at our harbor, surrounded by water and recalling the tears cried by my own relatives as we fought and pleaded and negotiated and waited for our islands to be returned. Now that we can stand on these islands again, we have both an opportunity and a responsibility to shift our gaze to another place. From the top of Matiu, there is a clear view of Wellington city and New Zealand's parliament buildings. However, if you turn a little to the left, from the peak of Matiu, you can see all the way past Mākaro and out to the channel between the harbor and the open sea. Beyond the channel stretches Te Moananui a Kiwa.

As they did for Kupe, these islands provide a temporary refuge for a tired people, but they can also impel and symbolize a broader picture of connection and migration. While the island was Somes, the government decided to lop off the top of its head to install gun emplacements during World War II: the peak of Matiu is now several meters shorter than it once was. Colonialism and our necessary period of introspection and struggle may have diminished our view of Te Moananui a Kiwa, then, but we can still see enough to remember who we are and to whom we're connected. Spending time here, reflecting on Kupe's naming of our island, the relatively more recent visit from Tupaia makes a different kind of sense. No wonder the "fondness" shown toward the large sheets of tapa that day when Tupaia and Cook dropped by in 1769 was described as "extraordinary." Standing on Matiu, knowing that there are koura in the waters around and tapa in the waters beyond, and holding a paintbrush—or laptop—in hand, we articulate who we were and who we are: we once were Pacific, and along with our numerous other identifications, we will continue to be so.

Notes

Introduction

Māori is used by New Zealand Māori and Cook Islands Māori communities. I acknowledge that the unmarked *Māori* could refer to either of these communities; however, in this book, *Māori* should be understood as New Zealand Māori, unless otherwise indicated.

Please note that the Māori language (and several other Polynesian languages) uses the macron to indicate a long vowel (ā, ē, ī, ō, ū). Because this convention is not used universally (it is rather recent and does not appear in older sources but also does not always appear in contemporary texts), throughout this book, the Māori language is left in direct quotes as it appears in the original and in names as the person would have spelled his or her own name: Te Rangihiroa instead of Te Rangihīroa, for example. (This also applies to the names of organizations; I have left Nga Tamatoa without a macron because this is the proper name of a specific group, and the macron was not used at the time.) Also, where words have been Anglicized by adding a suffix not present in the original language (e.g., the *n* at the end of *Sāmoa* to create the word *Samoan*), I follow the convention of recognizing that the word has become English and therefore has no macron. Also note that the Māori language does not identify the plural in the noun or adjective itself, and so it is accepted convention to avoid adding an *s* to indicate a plural. For example, *Māori* could refer to the singular or plural, as inferred from the surrounding sentence. The plural can also be indicated by a shift to a longer vowel: *tangata whenua* is singular, whereas *tāngata whenua* is plural.

The convention of italicizing foreign words is tricky in the place of Indigenous languages, and there are various schools of thought around whether Māori should be italicized in this kind of English-language text. Although I recognize the argument that italicizing Māori prevents it from being incorporated into the English language as a set of loanwords rather than retaining its integrity as a quotation from a distinct language, I prefer to follow the convention of leaving the Māori language in roman type as a recognition that, for this writer, and for many of the readers of this book, Māori is not a foreign (or to use the term of the *Chicago Manual of Style,* "unfamiliar") language. In this way, the Māori language is unmarked in the same way as, for example, Latin is unmarked in other predominantly English texts. English and Māori sit side by side as center languages in this book, neither capable of fully rendering the other as Other, foreign, or unfamiliar.

Finally, three original poems appear in this book (in chapter 1, chapter 6, and the conclusion), which were written by the author. These are intended to extend the critical engagements undertaken in the prose text and therefore are not themselves critically analyzed or discussed.

1. Ra'iatea is known in the Māori language as Rangiātea and is referred to in the epigraph: "e kore au e ngaro; he kākano i ruia i Rangiātea," literally, "I can never be lost for I am a seed sown at Rangiātea," which confirms that any descendent of the voyages from tropical Polynesia can never be extricated from her place in the networks of Māori identification and relationship. Because this whakataukī, or "proverb," asserts the impossibility of absolute separation from whakapapa, it is often mobilized in contemporary times as an affirmation for Māori whose knowledge of their own genealogies, language, or tikanga has been lessened or ruptured by the impact of colonialism. Rangiātea is also the name of a spiritual realm (one of twelve heavens).

2. Nicholas Thomas spends some time reflecting on this map in his introduction to *On Oceania: Visions, Artifacts, Histories* (Durham, N.C.: Duke University Press, 1997).

3. In North America, lobster.

4. Harold B. Carter, "Note on the Drawings by an Unknown Artist from the Voyage of HMS *Endeavour*," in *Science and Exploration in the Pacific*, ed. Margarette Lincoln (Woodbridge, UK: Boydell Press, 1998), 133–34. Carter identified this as Tupaia's work in 1997 on the basis of a letter written by Banks to Dawson Turner dated December 12, 1812. Banks (1743–1820) was a scientist who traveled extensively in regions we now know as the Americas, Africa, and the Pacific. He desired to take Tupaia to London "as a curiosity, as some of my neighbours do lions and tigers at greater expense that he will ever put me to," but Tupaia passed away in Batavia (now Indonesia) before Banks was able to carry out this fantasy. Instead, "Omai," a younger man picked up in Tahiti during Cook's second voyage around the Pacific, was the Polynesian who accompanied Banks to London.

5. Keith Vincent Smith, "Tupaia's Sketchbook," *eBLJ*, article 10 (2005), http://21citizen.org.uk/eblj/2005articles/pdf/article10.pdf.

6. British Library Department of Manuscripts, Add. MS 15508. The Māori man pictured holding the crayfish is unknown; the European pictured is Joseph Banks.

7. "Aotearoa" is commonly used as the Māori name for New Zealand, although I recognize that historically, this name has referred to the North Island only.

8. Sidney M. Mead, *Landmarks, Bridges, and Visions: Aspects of Maori Culture: Essays* (Wellington, New Zealand: Victoria University Press, 1997), 7–8.

9. *Kōkiri,* "Te Hono Ki Rarotonga," 2009, http://www.tpk.govt.nz/en/in-print/ kokiri/kokiri-13-2009/te-hono-ki-rarotonga/ (accessed March 21, 2009).

10. Peter Adds makes this argument in his teaching about the peopling of Polynesia at Victoria University of Wellington.

11. Please note that Hawaiki is spelled "Hawaiiki" in some sources; I have left the original spelling in quotations but otherwise follow the convention of a single *i.*

12. Waitangi Tribunal, *Te Whanganui a Tara me ona Takiwa; Report on the Wellington District* (Wellington, New Zealand: Waitangi Tribunal and Legislation Direct, 2003), 110.

13. The return of "Matiu" as a part of the name after years of the island being "Somes" is testimony not only to the Indigenous–Māori context of the island but also to the ongoing struggle on the part of the Indigenous people to maintain links to that island.

14. Alan Duff, *Once Were Warriors* (Auckland, New Zealand: Tandem Press, 1990). The feature film based on Duff's novel was released four years later. *Once Were Warriors,* VHS, directed by Lee Tamahori (1994; Auckland: Communicado Film, 1995).

15. *Indigenous* is a terrifically complex word, and it can do its best work when it is allowed to be as supple and flexible as possible. Its meaning is either slightly or dramatically different each time it is produced, whether at the United Nations, on the contents page of an anthology, on the guest list of an academic conference, and so on. Although the word is engaged across a range of spatial, temporal, and cultural contexts to describe the predicament of (usually minority) communities who are the original inhabitants of an area, *Indigenous* most often refers in a rather limited sense to those communities over whose lands the four (largely) Anglophone settler nations of Australia, Canada, New Zealand, and the United States are presently spread. Often described as the fourth world, this particular group of Indigenous communities shares originary claims of a unique and primary connection to specific land; historical experiences of British imperialism; demographic marginalization in which non-Indigenous communities make up the majority of citizens in the settler nation-state; and an ongoing struggle to retain linguistic, cultural, spiritual, governmental, resource, intellectual, and creative sovereignty.

16. Vernice Wineera, *Into the Luminous Tide: Pacific Poems* (Provo, Utah: Centre for the Study of Christian Values in Literature, 2009).

17. Māori make up an increasing proportion of the New Zealand population because of the relative youth of the community.

18. Competition for recognition by the state is a corollary of this situation, as when some Māori questioned Prime Minister Helen Clark's willingness to formally apologize to Sāmoa on behalf of New Zealand for its colonial exploits, despite being reluctant to engage with Māori in the same way.

19. The boundaries of the New Zealand state are understood conservatively here: Tokelau is a dependent territory and could conceivably be considered part

of New Zealand's territory (the "Realm of New Zealand"). At a further remove, Niue and the Cook Islands remain in political free association with their former colonial power, and a proposal that New Zealand should formally recolonize those nations comes to light with surprising regularity.

20. Further information about these original journeys is plentiful. For example, see K. R. Howe, ed., *Vaka Moana, Voyages of the Ancestors: The Discovery and Settlement of the Pacific* (Auckland, New Zealand: David Bateman, 2006).

21. The paepae is the space from which orators speak.

22. Ngāti Kahungunu Iwi Inc., "Supporting Indigenous Rights through Takitimu Fest," *Scoop: Independent News,* October 9, 2008, http://www.scoop.co.nz/stories/CU0810/S00114.htm.

23. I am using the term *Anglophone literary studies* in place of *English* because of the slippage between English the language (and the literary tradition of texts written in that language) and English the culture–nation (and its own literary tradition). The production of an English literary canon has naturalized the slippage between a literary tradition of English-language texts and the English culture–nation because the vast majority of texts in the English canon are produced by ethnically English writers. Gauri Viswanathan observes that the discipline of English *itself* was in fact produced in India as a specific tool of the colonizing project. *Anglophone,* by contrast, means English language, but its refusal to naturalize a mutual relationship between English language and English culture produces an entirely different configuration between English language, specific literary forms, English culture, British imperialism, and the colonial project. Gauri Viswanathan, *Masks of Conquest: Literary Studies and British Rule in India* (New York: Columbia University Press, 1989).

24. Thomas King, *The Truth about Stories: A Native Narrative* (Toronto, Ont.: House of Anansi Press, 2003).

25. I align myself with the dominant contemporary view that a text's production of meaning (linguistic, visual, aural, movement, or otherwise) is the outer limit of the scholar's reach. This means, for example, that I am less interested in conducting a forensic evaluation of a Wineera poem to deduce what she *really* thinks than I am in focusing on the poem as a poem, as a text that produces meaning about those connections through its use of language and which, I may argue, suggests some things whether or not Wineera intended that meaning or whether her intention at the time of writing is accessible by me or, indeed, by her. One cannot entirely remove the figure of the writer and her lived experience; if it were possible to do so, there would be no such thing as Māori writing in English because the whakapapa of the writer would be irrelevant, but this does remove an obligation to link or limit claims about a text to the perceived or stated deliberate intentions of the person who produced the text [x].

26. Rewiti Tuhorouta Kohere, *The Autobiography of a Maori* (Wellington, New Zealand: A. H. and A. W. Reed, 1951).

27. Chadwick Allen, *Blood Narrative; Indigenous Identity in American Indian and Maori Literary and Activist Texts* (Durham, N.C.: Duke University Press, 2002); Otto Heim, *Writing along Broken Lines: Violence and Ethnicity in Contemporary Maori Fiction* (Auckland, New Zealand: Auckland University Press, 1998); Evan Rask Knudsen, *The Circle and the Spiral* (Amsterdam, Netherlands: Rodopi, 2004).

28. Tracy McIntosh, "Hibiscus in the Flax Bush," in *Tangata o te Moana nui: The Evolving Identities of Pacific People in Aotearoa New Zealand,* ed. C. Macpherson, P. Spoonley, and M. Anae (Palmerston North, New Zealand: Dunmore Press, 2001); Donna Awatere, *Maori Sovereignty* (Auckland, New Zealand: Broadsheet, 1984).

29. A U.K.-edited collection of essays about the topic includes some good material. Graham Harvey and Charles D. Thompson Jr., eds., *Indigenous Diasporas and Dislocations* (Aldershot, U.K.: Ashgate, 2005).

30. Tony Ballantyne, "Race and the Webs of Empire: Aryanism from India to the Pacific," *Journal of Colonialism and Colonial History* 2, no. 3 (2001), http://muse.jhu.edu/login?uri=/journals/journal_of_colonialism_and_colonial_history/v002/2.3ballantyne.html.

31. Many mixed Māori–Pasifika people are active in Māori and Pasifika communities, including artistic and literary communities. Perhaps among the most prominent would be Che Fu (a Niue–Māori hip-hop practitioner) and Miria George (a Cook Islander–Māori playwright and poet).

32. Anne Salmond, *The Trial of the Cannibal Dog: Captain Cook in the South Seas* (Auckland, New Zealand: Penguin, 2004).

Introduction to Part I: Tapa

1. Some early European references spell this "aouta."

2. Māori are included in various incarnations of the Pacific outside New Zealand. For example, Māori have participated in the Pacific Arts Festival since its inception. Bill Kerekere writes about his experience in the inaugural festival in "South Pacific Festival of Arts," *Te Ao Hou* 72 (1973): 43–48. In the arena of visual arts, three international exhibitions of contemporary New Zealand–based Pacific art have included Māori artists (Pasifika was curated by Melissa Chu at the Canberra Contemporary Art Space; Pasifika Styles was curated by Amiria Henare and Rosanna Raymond at Cambridge University, 2006–8; and AnneMarie Tupuola brought a Pacific art exhibition to New York City in 2002). Likewise, courses on Pacific literature in North America, Europe, and around the Pacific usually include Māori writers and texts.

3. Thanks to April Henderson and Teresia Teaiwa for vivid and enthusiastic discussion around this point.

4. Albert Wendt, "Towards a New Oceania," *Mana* 1, no. 1 (1976): 49–60. The essay has been reprinted often; in some key collections and essays, reprints are given as the source, and this implies that the essay is from that year. For example,

the bibliography of Borofsky's *Remembrance of Pacific Pasts* notes its publication date as 1983, when it appeared in *A Pacific Islands Collection (71–85) Seaweeds and Constructions: Anthology Hawai'i 7*. Robert Borofsky, *Remembrance of Pacific Pasts: An Invitation to Remake History* (Honolulu: University of Hawai'i Press, 2000).

5. Epeli Hau'ofa, "Our Sea of Islands," in *A New Oceania: Rediscovering Our Sea of Islands*, ed. Eric Waddell, Vijay Naidu, and Epeli Hau'ofa, 22–16 (Suva, Fiji: University of the South Pacific, 1993).

6. Of course, *Oceania* is still in the language of the colonizer (or at least one of the colonizers), and some scholars are engaging Indigenous terms, such as Tevita Ka'ili's preferred *Moana*, which is a pan-Polynesian term but not, unfortunately, pan-Pacific.

7. Wendt, "Towards a New Oceania," 71.

8. In this chapter, page references will be to the 1999 reprint of the essay. Epeli Hau'ofa, "Our Sea of Islands," in *Inside Out: Literature, Cultural Politics, and Identity in the New Pacific*, ed. Vilsoni Hereniko and Rob Wilson (Lanham, Md.: Rowman and Littlefield, 1999).

9. Ibid., 31.

10. Ibid., 30.

11. Ibid., 32.

12. Producing a detailed overview of Pacific studies and Pacific literary studies is not the purpose of this introduction. However, I will note, perhaps as a caveat, that Pacific studies itself is neither monolithic nor understood monolithically. Like many other fields of area studies and Indigenous studies, its boundaries are endlessly contestable and are not determined by topic or content alone.

13. This was crystallized for me at the workshop titled "Future Directions in Pacific Studies" at the University of California, Santa Cruz, in May 2004, in which several of the scholars working in interdisciplinary fields drew on Wendt's "Tatauing the Post-colonial Body," an essay that comes explicitly out of literary studies.

14. Steven Edmund Winduo, "Unwriting Oceania: The Repositioning of the Pacific Writer Scholars within a Folk Narrative Space," *New Literary History: A Journal of Theory and Interpretation* 31, no. 2 (2000): 599–613. A correlation between the production and criticism of Pacific literary works is widely recognized; literary scholars from the Pacific tend also to be writers. It is possible to imagine a pragmatic connection, in which writers seek employment opportunities in a related field, but we might also consider the high value placed on reciprocity that underpins many Pacific ontologies.

15. What counts as Pacific literary studies? Is Paul Lyons's and Michelle Elleray's very productive work on writing *about* the Pacific by non-Pacific people a part of this field?

16. In this essay, Wendt models Pacific literary criticism that invokes a Pacific-centered metaphor—the tatau (Samoan body tattoo)—to approach Pacific

literature, recasting the conventional (Western–institutional) notions of literature, literariness, and criticism by assuming that the tatau belongs in its scope both as text and as theory. Because his essay focuses on the pe'a/malu that is specific to Sāmoa, he does not advocate moving from cultural specificity toward a squishy and pan-Pacificness but rather suggests that this literally embodied specificity is itself one way to apprehend the whole region. Albert Wendt, "Tatauing the Post-colonial Body," *SPAN* 42–43 (April–October 1996): 15–29.

17. Subramani, *South Pacific Literature: From Myth to Fabulatio* (Suva, Fiji: University of the South Pacific, 1908), xi. Subramani does not elaborate on these so-called common motifs, and given that Māori and Indigenous Australian writing has tended to assert a distinctive voice, it is difficult to argue with confidence that Māori and Indigenous Australian writing uncomplicatedly "belongs" to the mainstream of either country.

18. Vilsoni Hereniko elaborates the significance of 1994 to Pacific literary studies in his foreword to Nicholas J. Goetzfridt, *Indigenous Literature of Oceania: A Survey of Criticism and Interpretation*, Bibliographies and Indexes in World Literature 47 (Westport, Conn.: Greenwood Press, 1995).

19. Paul Sharrad, ed., *Readings in Pacific Literature* (Wollongong: New Literatures Research Centre, University of Wollongong, 1993); Goetzfridt, *Indigenous Literature of Oceania*; Hereniko and Wilson, *Inside Out*.

20. Te Rangihiroa, "The Evolution of Maori Clothing," *Journal of Polynesian Society* 33, no. 129 (1924): 31.

21. Ibid., 31. Indeed, Te Rangihiroa had attended school at Te Aute, which derives its name from the local area, Te Aute, where aute plants previously thrived before their extinction.

1. Māori People in Pacific Spaces

1. Te Rangihiroa was also known by the name of Peter Buck, or Sir Peter Buck after his knighthood. I am following the convention of using the name "Te Rangihiroa" when I refer to him because this was his preferred name under which to publish. ("Te Rangihiroa" also appears as "Te Rangi Hiroa" in some sources.)

2. J. B. Condliffe, *Te Rangi Hiroa: The Life of Sir Peter Buck* (Christchurch, New Zealand: Whitcombe and Tombes, 1971), 39.

3. Te Rangihiroa's publications are fully listed in ibid.

4. "Te Rangi Hīroa," *Wikipedia*, http://en.wikipedia.org/w/index.php?title=Te_Rangi_H%C4%ABroa&oldid=404458547 (accessed January 10, 2011).

5. "Te Rangi Hīroa," Wikipedia, http://en.wikipedia.org/wiki/Te_Rangi_Hiroa (accessed December 2008).

6. Te Rangihiroa, *The Coming of the Maori* (Wellington, New Zealand: Maori Purposes Fund Board and Whitcombe and Tombes, 1949).

7. Des Kahotea has written about Te Rangihiroa's phase as an anthropologist. Des Kahotea, "Rebel Discourses: Soclonial Violence, Pai Marire Resistance, and Land Allocation at Tauranga," PhD diss., Waikato University, 2005.

8. Condliffe, *Te Rangi Hiroa*, 158.

9. Ibid., 228. A heiau is a Hawaiian temple.

10. For an excellent treatment of the impact and methods of these disciplines, look at Martin Nakata, *Disciplining the Savages, Savaging the Disciplines* (Canberra, Australia: Aboriginal Studies Press, 2007).

11. The only book-length biography of Te Rangihiroa was written by Condliffe after Eric Ramsden and then Ernest Beaglehole (both prominent popular scholars and writers of the time) passed away while working on earlier drafts. Condliffe's biography is popular rather than scholarly but is a valuable resource. He outlines the relationship between Yale and the Bishop Museum in the chapter "Yale in Polynesia." Condliffe, *Te Rangi Hiroa*, 169–85. By the time Te Rangihiroa arrived at Yale in 1932, Yale students and alumni had had a deep historical connection with the Pacific, and especially Hawai'i, since the early nineteenth century. Several alumni had worked as whalers, merchants, and missionaries, which resulted in a group of Hawaiian men (most notably Opukahaia) traveling to New Haven. Yale alum missionaries based in Hawai'i sent their sons back to Yale, and a close connection was forged that ultimately linked the Bishop Museum in Hawai'i and Yale in New Haven. The Bishop would send scholars to Yale on year-long lectureships to provide specialist Pacific teaching capacity, and the director of the museum would be a member of the faculty of the Graduate School at Yale, appointed by the museum trustees but funded by Yale. Te Rangihiroa's original connection to Yale in 1932 was in this capacity. Kehaulani Kauanui has written about Opukahaia in J. Kehaulani Kauanui, "Diasporic Deracination and 'Off-Island' Hawaiians," *Contemporary Pacific* 19, no. 1 (2007): 138–60.

12. A close friend to Te Rangihiroa, Ramsden, was a Pākehā–white scholar based in New Zealand.

13. Te Rangihiroa to Eric Ramsden, May 5, 1948, Alexander Turnbull Library, Wellington, New Zealand.

14. *Senate Journal,* Territory of Hawaii 22nd Legislature, Regular Session, 1943, 945.

15. Ibid., 946.

16. Ibid.

17. Ian F. Haney Lopez, *White by Law: The Legal Construction of Race* (New York: New York University Press, 1996). At the end of the Civil War, Senator Sumner unsuccessfully attempted to expunge the legacy of the 1857 case *Dred Scott v. Sandford,* in which the Supreme Court ruled that no one of African descent could claim U.S. citizenship, "by striking any reference to race from the naturalization statute"; ibid., 4. Naturalization is the relevant law because Te Rangihiroa was already a citizen elsewhere; reference to race was removed from U.S. birthright citizenship legislation in 1940.

18. Ibid., 2.

19. Ibid., 28.

20. Quoted in ibid., 71.

21. In the New Zealand context, perhaps the most prominent argument for an elevated racial understanding of Māori was made by Tregear, who drew on comparative mythology and linguistics. Edward Tregear, *The Aryan Maori* (Wellington, New Zealand: G. Didsbury, 1885).

22. As a result of this case, not only was Thind's application for citizenship declined but at least sixty-five people of Asian Indian origin who had been naturalized between 1923 and 1927 were stripped of their citizenship.

23. Much of the work about these issues assumes that all noncitizens approach the United States for citizenship from the same position. It would be interesting to research arguments for citizenship on the basis of residence (jus soli) and on the basis of blood (jus sanguinis) in the specific case of Hawaiian and Samoan Polynesians living in U.S.-controlled territory. Kehaulani Kauanui's work is an important starting point for this project. J. Kehaulani Kauanui, *Hawaiian Blood: Colonialism and the Politics of Sovereignty and Indigeneity* (Durham, N.C.: Duke University Press, 2008).

24. Certainly "Caucasian origin" is not the same as "white," although this public document relies on a slippage between "Irish" and "Caucasian," and because the "Caucasian origin" of "Polynesians" is offered as a counter to an exclusion from citizenship on the basis of race, one could argue that "Caucasian" is supposed to be (mis)understood here to stand in for "white."

25. In June 1946, Te Rangihiroa got a better offer: a knighthood. I have written about this in more detail elsewhere: "I belong to that stock: Te Rangihiroa's application for US citizenship," in Barbara Baird and Damien Riggs, eds., *The Racial Politics of Bodies, Nations, and Knowledges* (Newcastle upon Tyne, U.K.: Cambridge Scholars Press, 2009).

26. Te Rangihiroa to Eric Ramsden, May 5, 1948, Alexander Turnbull Library, Wellington, New Zealand.

27. Although the American Samoan community experiences disproportionately high mortality and injury rates out of all ethnic communities in the U.S. military, American Samoans are not accorded citizenship as a right. Being born in American Sāmoa makes one a U.S. national rather than a U.S. citizen.

28. This "Asian Pacific" is still the configuration in formal American racial categories, as foregrounded in the scholarly context of debates about the naming of the Association for Asian American Studies.

29. In the poem that follows, a waiata tangi is a song of lament or mourning, a whare is a house, whakairo are carvings, a karanga is a woman's chant, and wairua is the spirit.

30. Terry Webb, "The Temple and the Theme Park: Intention and Indirection

in Religious Tourist Art," in *An Anthropology of Indirect Communication,* ed. Joy Hendry, 128–42 (New York: Routledge, 2001).

31. Polynesian Cultural Center, "Frequently Asked Questions," http://www.polynesia.com/faqs.html#purpose.

32. Terry Webb, "High Structured Tourist Art: Form and Meaning at the Polynesian Cultural Centre," *The Contemporary Pacific* 6, no. 1 (1994): 80.

33. A whakataetae is a competition; in this case, competition itself is referred to by the name "Whakataetae." Kapa haka are Māori performing arts.

34. Matthew Kester, "Race, Religion, and Citizenship in Mormon Country: Native Hawaiians in Salt Lake City, 1869–1889," *The Western Historical Quarterly* XX (2009): 51–76.

35. Vernice Wineera, "Selves and Others: A Study of Reflexivity and the Representation of Culture in Touristic Display at the Polynesian Cultural Centre," PhD diss., University of Hawai'i at Manoa, 2000.

36. Hokulani Aikau, "Polynesian Pioneers: Twentieth Century Religious Racial Formations and Migration in Hawai'i," PhD diss., University of Minnesota, 2005.

37. R. Lanier Britsch, *Moramona: The Mormons in Hawaii* (Laie, Hawai'i: Institute for Polynesian Studies, 1989).

38. Ibid., 15.

39. In turn, these pre-Indian communities are understood to be remnants of the original tribes of Israel, which, as well as conceptually providing an historical basis for the LDS Church, also literally provide the written foundation of the church by having produced the Book of Mormon, an ancient text buried by that community before it disappeared.

40. Robert O'Brien, *Hands across the Water: The Story of the Polynesian Cultural Center* (La'ie, Hawai'i: Polynesian Cultural Centre, 1983), 73.

41. Ibid.

42. Ibid.

43. Te Rangihiroa, *Arts and Crafts of Hawaii* (Honolulu, Hawai'i: Bishop Museum, 1957).

44. Barney Christie, interview by Kalili Hunt, PCC Oral History Program, Brigham Young University–Hawai'i Joseph F. Smith Library Archives and Special Collections, 1982.

45. Māori scholar Robert Joseph is very active in this area of research.

46. A marae is a courtyard space used for meeting and ritualized encounters; it has acquired a conventional meaning to refer to the complex (including meetinghouses, dining room, etc.) and is often understood as the ultimate space in which Māori protocols are paramount.

47. Polynesian Cultural Centre, *Polynesia in a Day* (La'ie, Hawai'i: Polynesian Cultural Centre, 1969), 14. Haere mai means "welcome."

48. Ibid., 14.

49. Ibid.

50. Polynesian Cultural Centre, *This Is Polynesia* (La'ie, Hawai'i: Polynesian Cultural Centre, 1982), 11.

51. The entwined fates of Indigenous groups and colonial nation-states are never far from view. This brochure includes information about "Special Cultural Days at the Polynesian Cultural Centre" and notes Waitangi Day ("Maori cultural day") and Bastille Day ("Tahitian cultural day") along with two Hawaiian holidays.

52. Robert Sullivan, Albert Wendt, and Reina Whaitiri, *Whetu Moana* (Auckland, New Zealand: Auckland University Press, 2003); Selina Tusitala Marsh, *Niu Voices* (Wellington, New Zealand: Huia, 2006); Kareva Mateata-Allain, Frank Stewart, and Alexander Mawyer, *Vārua Tupu* (Honolulu: University of Hawai'i Press, 2006); Ku'ualoha Ho'omanawanui, *'Ōiwi 3* (Honolulu, Hawai'i: 'Ōiwi Press, 2005).

53. Frank Stewart, Kareva Mateata-Allain, and Alexander Dale Mawyer, eds., *Vārua Tupu: New Writing from French Polynesia* (Honolulu: University of Hawai'i Press, 2006), front cover.

54. Witi Ihimaera, "Kaupapa," in *Te Ao Mārama 1: Te Whakahuatanga O Te Ao*, ed. Witi Ihimaera (Auckland, New Zealand: Reed, 1992), 15.

55. Barbara M. Benedict, "The Paradox of the Anthology: Collecting and Difference in Eighteenth-century Britain," *New Literary History* 34 (2003): 236.

56. Wendt, "Towards a New Oceania," 71.

57. J. C. Sturm was the first Māori writer included in a collection of New Zealand fiction in 1966.

58. Paula Morris, *Words Chosen Carefully: New Zealand Writers in Discussion,* ed. Siobhan Harvey (Auckland, New Zealand: Cape Catley Books, 2010), 186.

59. Bernard Gadd, *Pacific Voices: An Anthology of Writing by and about Pacific People* (Albany, N.Y.: Stockton House, 1977).

60. C. K. Stead, ed., *The Faber Book of Contemporary South Pacific Stories* (London: Faber, 1994).

61. Vilsoni Hereniko and Sig Schwarz, "Four Writers and Once Critic," in *Inside Out: Literature, Culture, Politics, and Identity in the New Pacific,* ed. V. Hereniko and R. Wilson, 55–64 (Lanham, Md.: Rowman and Littlefield, 1999).

62. Witi Ihimaera and D. S. Long, eds., *Into the World of Light: An Anthology of Maori Writing* (Auckland, New Zealand: Heinemann, 1982).

63. Several other editors had already demonstrated deep commitment to, and familiarity with, literature in the Pacific, e.g., Paul Sharrad, Richard Hamasaki, and Don Long.

64. And, perhaps, the recognition of the field *as a field* such that Faber's book would have a potential readership.

65. E.g., anthologies and collections from the Solomon Islands, Niue, and Sāmoa. Julian Maka'a, Hilda Kii, and Linda Crowl, eds., *Raetem Aot: Creative Writing from Solomon Islands* (Honiara: Solomon Island Writers Association/USP Centre

Solomon Islands/South Pacific Creative Arts Society/Institute of Pacific Studies, 1996); Larry Thomas, *Musings on Niue* (Suva: Pacific Writing Forum, 1997); Sina Va'ai and Asofou So'o, eds., *Tofa Sasa'a: Contemporary Short Stories of Samoa* (Apia: National University of Samoa, 2002).

66. Regional distribution is extremely variable. The Pacific is crisscrossed by various publishing networks, including the major split between North American and Commonwealth English language publishing (e.g., which affects my decision to publish with Minnesota), as well as the idiosyncrasies of small distribution networks. It can be much easier to purchase a text written hundreds of miles away than one from the next island. This is further complicated in the case of non-English-language publications in Indigenous languages and in other colonial languages of the Pacific, notably French.

67. I am grateful to Vilsoni Hereniko, who encouraged me to think more carefully about my claims of Māori exclusion. Certainly Māori writers have better access to publishing (and related circulation) than most other Pacific writers, and so in a certain light, Māori texts can seem to stand in for (or even dominate) Pacific literature.

68. All these nations are also the hosts of universities. Publication at the University of the South Pacific has been crucial to the dissemination of much Pacific writing through the distribution of single-author and multiple-author collections and the production of literary journals, of which *Mana* is preeminent. Unfortunately, the Institute for Pacific Studies Press at USP, which produced most of this work, has been closed down by that university; Vilsoni Hereniko is involved in establishing a replacement.

69. As the biographies in Pacific anthologies demonstrate, Pacific writers live all over the world and, particularly, all around the region.

70. There is a very strong bias for Polynesian texts in Pacific literary studies. Yet Polynesia itself is unevenly represented because Francophone and Hispanophone Polynesia are often excluded. Furthermore, texts from Papua New Guinea texts are dominant over other Melanesian material, and Micronesian material is particularly light. Emelihter Kihleng and Craig Santos Perez are actively engaged in bringing more Micronesian writers to publication, and a Guam-based journal, *Storyboard*, has published some Micronesian writers.

71. Danielle O'Halloran and Felolini Maria Ifopo, *Fika: First Draft Pasifika Writers* (Christchurch, New Zealand: First Draft Pasifika Writers, 2008).

72. Witi Ihimaera, "Kaupapa," in Ihimaera, *Te Ao Mārama 1*, 18.

73. Albert Wendt, *Lali: A Pacific Anthology* (Auckland, New Zealand: Longman Paul, 1980), xiii; emphasis added.

74. Ibid., xii; emphasis added.

75. Albert Wendt, *Nuanua: Pacific Writing and English since 1980* (Auckland, New Zealand: Auckland University Press, 1995), 3.

76. Ibid., 1.

77. Benedict, "Paradox of the Anthology," 242.

78. Wendt, *Nuanua*, 3.

79. Additionally, diasporic writers are able to take their place as Pacific (or at least Polynesian) writers because the order of writers does not forcibly (and potentially restrictively) repatriate them to homelands.

2. Pacific-Based Māori Writers

1. Evelyn Patuawa-Nathan is also known as (and published under) Evelyn Finney.

2. Rewiti Kohere, *The Autobiography of a Maori* (Wellington, New Zealand: Reed, 1951). Hone Tuwhare, *No Ordinary Sun* (Auckland, New Zealand: Blackwood and Janet Paul, 1964). Witi Ihimaera, *Pounamu Pounamu* (Auckland, New Zealand: Longman Paul, 1975). Patricia Grace, *Waiariki* (Auckland, New Zealand: Longman Paul, 1975).

3. Indeed, I bumped into Vernice's book for the first time on the open-stack shelves in a library in Hawai'i (at Brigham Young University–Hawai'i [BYU-H]) when I was working on my PhD.

4. Residence and citizenship do not always remove a writer from the New Zealand literary scene; e.g., Paula Morris, who lives outside New Zealand, and Sia Figiel, who is not a New Zealand citizen and lives outside New Zealand, are both celebrated as New Zealander.

5. Vernice Wineera Pere, *Mahanga: Pacific Poems* (La'ie: Institute for Polynesian Studies, Brigham Young University–Hawai'i, 1978). The preface is written by Robert D Craig, Publications Editor, Institute for Polynesian Studies (this was later renamed Pacific Studies), BYU-H. *Mahanga* was published under the name Vernice Wineera Pere, although the poet now uses the name Vernice Wineera.

6. Vernice Wineera Pere, *Ka Po'e o La'ie* (La'ie, Hawai'i: Polynesian Cultural Centre, 1979). The collection, published by the Polynesian Cultural Centre, comes out of the writing group Wineera helped establish in La'ie. Because La'ie has a Mormon undergraduate university and temple, the surrounding community is both transnational and multicultural. This collection certainly deserves greater attention in a separate project.

7. Wineera Pere, *Mahanga*, 57.

8. A tekoteko is a carved ancestor located at the apex of a meetinghouse.

9. Although this comparison falls outside the scope of this book, I am working on a longer version of it elsewhere.

10. Wineera Pere, *Mahanga*, 28.

11. Wineera, *Into the Luminous Tide*. This poem circulated as an unpublished text for a number of years before it was published in this collection.

12. A pipi is a small shellfish, and paua is Māori for abalone.

13. Whakapapa is genealogy; as a verb, it literally means "to layer."

14. The relationship between tattoo and writing has been explored in various places around the Pacific. Hanlon reflects at length on the idea of writing as a form of tattoo in an essay about writing and history in the region. David Hanlon, "Beyond the English Method of Tattooing: Decentring the Practice of History in Oceania," *The Contemporary Pacific* 15, no. 1 (2003): 19–40. Robert Sullivan, "The English Moko: Exploring a Spiral," in *Figuring the Pacific: Aotearoa New Zealand Cultural Studies,* ed. Howard McNaughton and John Newton, 12–28 (Christchurch, New Zealand: Canterbury University Press, 2005). Rawinia Higgins and Ngahuia Te Awekotuku have produced excellent work on tā moko. Rawinia Higgins, "He tānga ngutu, he Tūhoetanga te Mana Motuhake o te tā moko wāhine: the identity politics of moko kauae," PhD diss., University of Otago, Dunedin, 2004. Juniper Ellis, *Tattooing the World: Pacific Designs in Print and Skin* (New York: Columbia University Press, 2008).

15. Whether the reader is included in the "we" is ambiguous in the English language (unlike, e.g., in Māori).

16. Emphasis added.

17. Evelyn Patuawa-Nathan, *Opening Doors: A Collection of Poems* (Raiwaqa, Fiji: South Pacific Creative Arts Society, 1979).

18. Ibid.

19. Within a Māori context, dawn is a highly symbolic and charged moment in which the relations between things are reconfigured and reconfigurable.

20. A waka is a vessel or canoe or, contemporarily, the dominant mode of transport.

21. Patuawa-Nathan, *Opening Doors,* 11–12.

22. Interestingly, the location of Australia is upstaged by a distinctly Aotearoa-based cartographic sensibility: from the perspective of Sydney, "Northerners" are more easterly, and yet the "Northerners" retain their identification with regard to the geography of Aotearoa.

23. Maoriness is signaled here by an obviously Māori name; the change would not be marked in the same way if Louise Santos used to be called "Lucy Smith."

24. Robert Sullivan, "A COVER SAIL," in *Star Waka* (Auckland, New Zealand: Auckland University Press, 1999), inside cover.

25. Sullivan's *Captain Cook in the Underworld* is described in a subtitle as a "libretto of Orpheus in Rarohenga."

26. I am using the term *originary* to refer to the ideas that the English language describes variably as history and mythology, but these words have their own connotations and limits, and I am describing something that falls between the two.

27. Chris Prentice, "'A knife through time': Robert Sullivan's Star Waka and the Politics and Poetics of Cultural Difference," *Ariel: A Review of International English Literature* 37, nos. 2–3 (2006): 111–35. Jon Battista, "Robert Sullivan's 'waka 100': Inscribed by the Stars," *Graduate Journal of Asia Pacific Studies* 5, no. 1 (2007): 58–70.

28. Robert Sullivan, personal communication, 2004.

29. A karakia is a prayer.

30. The right of occupation as maintained by the continual keeping of fires in a particular place, now often used for people who reside in a tribal center or homeland.

31. Emphasis added.

32. Robert Sullivan, *voice carried my family* (Auckland, New Zealand: Auckland University Press, 2005), 29.

33. Ibid., 28.

34. I acknowledge that some Māori communities claim to be in Aotearoa as a result of earlier migrations or through processes of autochthony.

35. Lapita is a pottery form identified by archaeologists as an indicator of technological expansion (and thereby patterns of human expansion) around the Pacific.

36. Sullivan, *voice carried my family,* 29.

37. Ibid., 40.

38. Vernice Wineera, preface to *Ka Po'e o La'ie* (La'ie, Hawai'i: Polynesian Cultural Centre, 1979), vii.

3. Aotearoa-Based Māori Writers

1. Elizabeth DeLoughrey's class at Cornell, The Transoceanic Imaginary, provided an opportunity for me to reflect on this dimension of the text.

2. Hinewirangi, *Kanohi ki te Kanohi* (Wellington, New Zealand: Moana Press, 1990).

3. Hone Tuwhare, *Sapwood and Milk* (Dunedin, New Zealand: Caveman, 1972).

4. Apirana Taylor, "The Fale" and "In Samoa at Solaua Fatumanava," in Sullivan et al., *Whetu Moana,* 213.

5. Cathie Dunsford, *Cowrie* (North Melbourne, Australia: Spinifex, 1994).

6. Cathie Dunsford, *The Journey Home* (North Melbourne, Australia: Spinifex, 1997).

7. Cathie Dunsford, *Manawa Toa/Heart Warrior* (North Melbourne, Australia: Spinifex, 2000).

8. Ambury Hall, *Below the Surface: Word and Images in Protest at French Testing on Moruroa* (Auckland, New Zealand: Vintage, 1995).

9. *Whale Rider,* DVD, directed by Niki Caro (2002; Auckland, New Zealand: South Pacific Pictures, 2003).

10. Witi Ihimaera, *The Whale Rider* (Auckland, New Zealand: Reed, 1987).

11. The film was partially funded from German sources, a fact which may or may not have anything to do with Porourangi ending up with a blonde German partner instead of the Māori wife he marries in the novella.

12. Two widely distributed major feature films depict Māori: *Once Were Warriors* and *Whale Rider;* perhaps *The Piano* would be another contender. If Māori had,

as white Americans do (to take an extreme counterexample), multiple images of themselves in multiple medias, single films would not have to hold up to the amount of scrutiny to which we hold *Whale Rider*.

13. Although the international and domestic press announced *Whale Rider* as a "Māori" story (all the speaking characters are Māori, the film's narrative is based on a book by a Māori writer, and the mythological and cultural context of the narrative is purportedly "Māori" too), there are a number of compelling arguments that this is not, in fact, a Māori film. A number of other Māori scholars have engaged with the film, including Brendan Hokowhitu, Jo Smith, Tania Ka'ai, and Charise Schwalger.

14. This discussion refers to the original 1987 edition of the novella. Subtle changes to the novella in the postfilm International edition detract from these aspects of the book.

15. Atomic and nuclear testing is a major strand of pan-Pacific identity that structures *The Whale Rider*. Weapons testing by Euro–American powers in Pacific waters catalyzed both a renewed orientation of many Māori toward their Pacificness and an increasing realization in New Zealand about its Pacific location.

16. In this case, "metropolitan" includes New Zealand.

17. John Hovell's illustrations mark the beginning of each of the parts of the novella: prologue, "Spring," "Summer," "Autumn," "Winter," and epilogue. These illustrations suggest a Pacific sensibility by drawing on the arts of various cultural groups: Rapanui, Aotearoa, Sāmoa, and Fiji.

18. This is removed from the 2003 U.S. edition of the text. Instead, that detail is removed to a foreword in which Ihimaera describes the New York context of his decision to write the story.

19. Separate italicized chapters are narrated from the perspective of the whales themselves.

20. Ihimaera, *Whale Rider*, 50.

21. Ibid.

22. Ibid., 52.

23. Ibid., 54.

24. Although in the U.S. and some other contexts, *native* is used interchangeably with *Indigenous*, in the Antipodes, *Native* is an almost exclusively derogatory term.

25. Despite its proximity to the Pacific region, Australia is often excluded from "the Pacific" because of the cultural and linguistic distinctiveness of Aboriginal communities from Melanesian–Micronesian–Polynesian communities. Torres Strait Islanders are a distinct case and do share links with Melanesians in Papua New Guinea.

26. The duty owed a father by his son finds its parallel in the film, where Porourangi struggles against his father's demands for him to stay home. (Porourangi in the novella is already committed to staying at home, and does so.)

27. Ihimaera, *Whale Rider*, 54.

28. Ibid.

29. Ibid., 68.

30. Ibid., 56.

31. Emphasis added.

32. Ibid.

33. Reading the father's disability in this way opens up possibilities for rethinking his "illness." Could this physical ailment echo Seri Luangphininth's claims about colonial madness? Seri Luangphinith, "Tropical Fevers: 'Madness' and Colonialism in Pacific Literature," *The Contemporary Pacific* 16, no. 1 (2004): 59–85.

34. Ihimaera, *Whale Rider*, 56.

35. Ibid.

36. Ibid., 56–57.

37. Ibid., 57.

38. Ibid., 56.

39. Ibid.

40. Ibid., 57. "Their reo was spoken in a thousand different tongues" suggests that a unitary language ("reo") is divided into different "tongues," which naturalizes the inherent singularity of the "national identity" in question. Problematic metaphors of "fracture" are frequently used to speak about multilingual nation-states in Melanesia.

41. Iwi, literally bone, is usually translated as tribe; an iwi is a group of people who share an eponymous ancestor. Reo is language.

42. The idea of so many years "in one lifetime" is alluded to in the title of the Papua New Guinea writer Albert Maori Kiki's autobiography *Ten Thousand Years in a Lifetime*. Albert Maori Kiki, *Ten Thousand Years in a Lifetime: A New Guinea Autobiography* (Melbourne, Australia: Cheshire, 1968).

43. Ihimaera, *Whale Rider*, 59.

44. Ibid., 57.

45. Ibid.

46. Ibid., 59.

47. Ibid. The sea is telling Rawiri to return to his homeplace.

48. Ibid., 60.

49. Ibid.

50. Ibid.

51. Ibid.

52. Ibid.

53. Ibid., 60–61.

54. Ibid., 61.

55. Ibid.

56. Ibid.

57. Ibid.

58. Ibid.

59. Ibid.

60. Hinewirangi, *Kanohi ki te Kanohi,* 5. Various people (including, in Hinewirangi's case, some Māori people) have various alternative reasons for their beliefs about Māori migration, and these narratives have truth value for their adherents.

61. Ibid., 4–5.

62. A kuia is an elderly woman; tikanga is protocols or conventional practices.

63. Hinemoana Baker, *Koiwi Koiwi* (Wellington, New Zealand: Victoria University Press, 2010), 45.

The Realm of Tapa

1. Chantal Spitz, *Island of Shattered Dreams,* trans. Jean Anderson (Wellington, New Zealand: Huia, 2007).

2. Ibid., 121.

3. Kaupapa is a foundation, principle, or motivation.

4. Okalani is the Tongan transliteration of two major sites of the Tongan diaspora: Auckland and Oakland. The slippage between these two transliterations has been noted by several commentators.

5. Aukilani is a generic Polynesian transliteration for Auckland. Tāmaki-makau-rau is the original Māori name for the area now known as Auckland (and as Aukilani).

6. Ty P Kāwika Tengan, *Native Men Remade: Gender and Nation in Contemporary Hawai'i* (Durham, N.C.: Duke University Press, 2008), 201–2.

7. I am lumping together Māori who travel as individuals, Māori migrants who intend to return home, and Māori communities with roots in new places and acknowledge that this use of the word *diaspora* moves beyond the usual use of the word as it is found in scholarly work. A symposium at Victoria University of Wellington on this topic in November 2010 posed *manurere* as an alternate term for these experiences.

8. Diasporic Māori writers are not restricted to their diasporic experiences; their works can be productively brought into existing and emerging conversations about Māori writing in English. For example, Vernice Wineera's poem about apprehending an ancestral house after time away resonates with specific poems by Apirana Taylor and Katerina Mataira.

9. Susan Davis and Russell Haley, eds., *The Penguin Book of Contemporary New Zealand Short Stories* (Auckland, New Zealand: Penguin, 1989).

10. Māori have been traveling to—and living in—Australia since the early 1800s, when young men and women would board whaling and trading ships and put down roots across the Tasman. A new vocabulary arose, including the transliteration Poihākena for Port Jackson (Sydney) and Ahitereiria (Australia). "Loanwords Used in Māori-Language Newspapers" lists seventeen different transliterations for "Australia," suggesting the extent of contexts in which the place was discussed.

Jenifer Curnow, Ngapare K. Hopa, and Jane McRae, *Rere Atu, Taku Manu! Discovering History, Language, and Politics in the Maori-Language Newspapers* (Auckland, New Zealand: Auckland University Press, 2002). I am working elsewhere on the Māori individuals who stayed with Marsden at his seminary in Parramatta, as are Kuni Jenkins and Alison Jones.

11. Ihimaera, *Whale Rider*, 51. Kia ora is an informal greeting. (It can also express thanks, agreement, or support.)

12. As well as Māori individuals and whānau scattered around the globe, Māori communities such as Ngāti Rānana (London), the Māori Anglican Fellowship Te Wairua Tapu in Newtown (Sydney), long-standing Māori families in Parramatta (Sydney), and the Mormon enclaves in Hawai'i, Las Vegas, and Utah have long historical roots in their new homes.

13. Jean Riki, "Te Wa Kainga: Home," in *Waiting in Space: An Anthology of Australian Writing*, 18–24 (Annandale, NSW: Pluto Press, 1999). Kelly Joseph, "Transient," in *Huia Short Fiction 5*, 147–149 (Wellington, New Zealand: Huia, 2003).

14. Craig Womack, *Red on Red: Native American Literary Separatism* (Minneapolis: University of Minnesota Press, 1999).

15. *Transactions of the New Zealand Institute* XLV (1912): 375–84.

Introduction to Part II: Koura

1. "Otara Mystery Man Stars at Te Papa," *Manukau Courier*, September 3, 2007, http://www.stuff.co.nz/auckland/4188503a6016.html.

2. "Te Papa Mystery Man Revealed," *Manukau Courier*, September 5, 2007, http://www.stuff.co.nz/auckland/46279.

3. Ibid.

4. *TV3 News*, http://www.tv3.co.nz/.

5. Māori men are rendered ethnically identifiable in Polynesian Cultural Centre publicity by the application of a facial tattoo.

6. Dave Burgess, "Now You See Him, Now You Don't," *Dominion Post*, September 25, 2007, http://www.stuff.co.nz/entertainment/arts/21689.

7. The phrase "someone who is Pacific Island" indicates the lack of familiarity with rather basic codes of reference. "Pacific Island" is not usually used in this way in New Zealand: one would expect adjectival forms such as "Pacific Islands," "Pacific Islander," or "Pacific," or perhaps one of the various spellings of "Pasifika."

8. This is also true for Māori with citizenships other than New Zealand. (New Zealand citizenship is rather more complicated in Sāmoa, Niue, the Cook Islands, and Toklelau, where New Zealand has been, and in some cases continues to be, an explicit colonial power.)

9. Louise Mataia, "'Odd Men from the Pacific': The Participation of Pacific Island Men in the 20th Maori Battalion 1939–1945," MA thesis, University of Otago, 2007.

10. Alongside Campbell's poetry, we might consider *Haviliviliaga Manatu*, a collection of poems from Niue that recalls relatives signing up for deployment in World War I, although none of the poems mentions a Māori presence in that war. *Haviliviliaga Manatu* (Alofi, Niue: Tohitohi Nukutuluea, 1999).

11. Thanks to my cousin Hawea Tomoana for affirming this insight.

12. Gina Tekulu, "Te Aute College," *Te Ao Hou* 64 (September 1968): 56–57. Tekulu's article describes the history and present standing of the school but does not mention the presence of Pacific students. An article by another Te Aute student in the same issue reports on Gina's accomplishments in athletics: "This year's winner is Gina Tekulu. He stands there concentrating and looking seriously at the bar as if to say, 'I'll tell you who's master.' Unfortunately he doesn't break that record, but equals it. In a way *I'm glad, because that record still belongs to a Maori*." Frank Heperi, *Te Ao Hou* 64 (September 1968): 52; emphasis added.

13. Teupoko I. Morgan, *Vainetini Kuki Airani Cook Islands Women Pioneers: Early Experiences in Aotearoa New Zealand* (Tokoroa, New Zealand: Anau Ako Pasifika, 2001), 20.

14. Ibid., 15.

15. Linda Nikora treats some of this history in her PhD dissertation. Linda Waimarie Nikora, "Māori Social Identities in New Zealand and Hawai'i," PhD diss., University of Waikato, 2007.

16. Morgan, *Vainetini Kuki Airani*, 20.

17. The place of Pasifika and Māori in New Zealand national identity is earnestly discussed in the realm of sports, especially with regard to rugby union and rugby league (e.g., the appearance of Pasifika and Māori rugby players in Island Nation teams, New Zealand teams, and non-Pacific teams such as Wales, Australia, Italy, and France).

18. "Tokelauans Welcomed to New Zealand," *Te Ao Hou* 58 (March 1967): 32–33.

4. Māori–Pasifika Collaborations

1. *South Sea Island Festival: His Majesty's Theatre, Sat Dec 18th, 1943* (Auckland, New Zealand: Auckland Service Print, 1943).

2. Look to David Chappell's and Keith Vincent Smith's work for elaboration of this history. In Albert Wendt's novel *The Mango's Kiss*, Arona leaves his family in Sāmoa around the turn of the twentieth century to work on boats around the Pacific and beyond; he ends up being involved in criminal activities and lives in hiding in early-twentieth-century New Zealand. David Chappell, *Double Ghosts: Oceanian Voyagers on Euroamerican Ships* (Armonk, N.Y.: M. E. Sharp, 1977). Keith Smith, "Mari Nawi (Big Canoes): Aboriginal Voyagers in Australia's Maritime History, 1788–1855," PhD diss., Macquarie University, 2008. Albert Wendt, *The Mango's Kiss* (Auckland, New Zealand: Vintage, 2003).

3. Although some individual writers in Polynation are well known, the group itself is not.

4. Hau'ofa, "Our Sea of Islands," 34. Note that Hau'ofa uses the Māori term *tangata whenua* in this configuration.

5. *Burn This CD* was a collaboration of music, poetry, a radio play, and interviews about the police raids of October 15, 2007, that was not formally published. All the people involved signed away their rights so that no one holds copyright to the material.

6. Radio New Zealand, *Te Ahi Kaa Programme Catalogue,* November 4, 2007, http://www.radionz.co.nz/national/programmes/teahikaa3/20071104 (accessed September 8, 2008).

7. Roma Potiki, the main organizer, spoke about this fund-raiser at the 2005 Stout Centre symposium, which commemorated the twentieth anniversary of Hulme's Booker Prize.

8. Likewise, TVNZ produces the program *Tagata Pasifika,* and it airs on that channel late on a weeknight, whereas Māori TV replays the show at prime time on Saturday evenings.

9. Huinga Rangatahi o Aotearoa, *Rongo* (Auckland, New Zealand: Brian McDonald, Ngahuia Volkerling, and John Miller, 1973).

10. Ibid., 2.

11. In 1978, the same organization that produced *Rongo* produced a document *Maori Language Week Hepetema 14–22* with the Department of Education.

12. Whina Cooper led the now famous Hīkoi, or Land March, in 1975. A direct outcome of this massive feat of peaceful protest was the Treaty of Waitangi Act 1975, which established the Waitangi Tribunal.

13. Chadwick Allen includes *Rongo* in the chronology that forms an appendix in his book *Blood Narrative.*

14. "The Islands of the Pacific."

15. Huinga Rangatahi o Aotearoa, *Rongo,* 2.

16. Kōrero means to speak, discuss, or talk.

17. Huinga Rangatahi o Aotearoa, *Rongo,* 14.

18. Ibid.

19. Thanks to Richie Tuhipa and his anonymous cousin for confirming this point for me.

20. I am grateful to Arini Loader for this insight.

21. Because of the limits of my language skills, I have not worked with the Tongan-, Samoan-, or Niuean-language parts of *Rongo* but look forward to supporting scholars and students who have the capacity to work with this publication. One effect of this limitation is that the treatment of *Rongo* is somewhat lopsided here.

22. Huinga Rangatahi o Aotearoa, *Rongo,* 5.

23. Melani Anae, with Lautofa (Ta) Iuli and Leilani Burgoyne, *Polynesian Panthers:*

The Crucible Years, 1971–74 (Auckland, New Zealand: Reed, 2006), 73.

24. The orality of hip-hop interrupts the supposed binary between tradition–orality and modernity–print. Often the emergence of new written forms of Māori—and Pacific—cultural production are inadvertently contextualized by a progress narrative that relies on a linear historical shift from oral to written literatures.

25. Nesian Mystic, *Polysaturated,* compact disc, Bounce Records, 2002.

26. "Lost Visionz," ibid.

27. I am using "urban Māori" very broadly here to include people whose home-lands have been concreted over by cities as well as people who moved from rural to urban areas. The existence of the former group is undermined when the dominant use of the term refers only to the latter.

28. Note the repeated use of the indefinite article: "*a* Polynesian" is as achievable an identification as "*a* Tongan."

29. Similarly, Losttribe's track "Summer in the Winter," *Aotearoa Hip Hop 1,* compact disc, BMG, 1998, repeats the refrain "Don't let the sun go down / Polynesians all around the world." Foregrounding the experiences of Pacific diasporic communities is a feature of much Pasifika hip-hop.

30. Doug Poole, *Polynation—Queensland Poetry Festival,* compact disc, August 23, 2008.

31. Doug Poole, "Polynation at the Queensland Poetry Festival," unpublished, September 15, 2008.

32. Ibid.

33. The report by Dr. Greg Clydesdale, a Massey University economics academic, which concluded that Pacific people have a negative impact on the New Zealand economy, gained widespread media attention in 2008.

34. Poole, "Polynation at the Queensland Poetry Festival."

35. Repeating this claim—"we are Polynation"—brings its truth into being. Furthermore, when the word *polynation* is repeated aurally, it seems to slip into *Polynesian.*

36. Poole, *Polynation.*

37. Poole, "Polynation at the Queensland Poetry Festival."

38. This idea of a space between anxiety and confidence is drawn from Roma Potiki's essay of a similar title, "The Journey from Anxiety to Confidence," in Ihimaera, *Te Ao Mārama 2,* 314–19.

5. "It's Like That with Us Maoris"

1. Apirana Taylor, *He Rau Aroha: A Hundred Leaves of Love* (Auckland, New Zealand: Penguin, 1986).

2. Apirana Taylor, *Eyes of the Ruru* (Wellington, New Zealand: Voice Press, 1979).

3. Ibid., 81.

4. Ibid.

5. Ibid.

6. Ibid.

7. Ibid. Indeed, this cliché is sometimes mobilized to sideline Māori claims of exceptionalism on the basis of Indigeneity. This is treated more fully in the concluding section of this book.

8. Ibid., 82.

9. Ibid.

10. Ibid.

11. Ibid.

12. Ibid.

13. Ibid., 83.

14. Fa'asāmoa is "the Samoan way"—the cultural practices and values of Sāmoa.

15. Taylor, *Eyes of the Ruru,* 83.

16. Ibid.

17. Ibid.

18. Patricia Grace, *Watercress Tuna and the Children of Champion Street* (Auckland, New Zealand: Puffin, 1985).

19. "Tuna" is the Māori name for an eel; it is not the same as the tuna you find in tins at the supermarket.

20. New Zealand school journals and similar school-targeted publications treat these communities too. One prolific contributor to the journals for many years was Johnny Frisbie, originally from Pukapuka (Cook Islands), who is credited as the first Pacific writer in English. Florence Frisbie, *Miss Ulysses from Pukapuka* (New York: Macmillan, 1948).

21. The existence and influence of entities from preurban Wellington landscapes (here, a tuna with the "magic throat" in the late-twentieth-century neighborhood of Cannon's Creek) is a feature of Grace's adult fiction too. In her first novel, *Mutuwhenua,* a Māori woman is unsettled by spiritual entities in the Wellington landscape to which she moves. Patricia Grace, *Mutuwhenua: The Moon Sleeps* (Auckland, New Zealand: Longman Paul, 1978). In *Cousins,* Wellington-based institution-raised Mata is less sensitive to the spiritual dimension of the cityscape than her cousin Makareta, who was raised with their whanau. Patricia Grace, *Cousins* (Auckland, New Zealand: Penguin, 1992). The Māori spiritual dimension of urban areas could be attributed to Grace's Te Ātiawa and Ngāti Toa ancestry (these iwi have tūrangawaewae in Wellington–Porirua) and challenges the assumption that rural = Māori and urban = Pākehā.

22. Grace, *Watercress Tuna,* n.p. Although "Champion Street" is the name of a real street, in the Māori translation of the book, this is translated ("te Tiriti Toa") rather than transliterated or left in English.

23. Ibid.

24. Likewise, no children clearly come from a mixed family. Perhaps this can be attributed to the moment in which Grace wrote the book and the politics around language retention and maintenance at the time. After all, this book was published around the time the first Kōhanga Reo were being set up!

25. Hokulani Aikau's work on the Polynesian diaspora in Utah undertakes a fascinating consideration of the relationship between patterns of displaying decorative cultural objects and class. Poutama is a design from traditional decorative tukutuku panels, and wakahuia is a carved treasure box.

26. Porirua, and in particular Porirua East–Cannons Creek, is marked in mainstream discourse as one of the notorious urban neighborhoods in New Zealand.

27. Houses owned by the government and rented to low-income families.

28. Grace's former career as a schoolteacher, and her frustration with the books available for her students, is significant here.

29. Briar Grace-Smith, "Te Manawa," in *The Six Pack*, 17–33 (Auckland: New Zealand Book Month, 2006).

30. Ibid., 17.

31. Ibid., 18.

32. Ibid.

33. Ibid., 19.

34. Ibid.

35. Ibid., 22.

36. Ibid., 23.

37. Ibid.

38. Ibid., 26.

39. Ibid.

40. Ibid., 30.

41. Ibid.

42. Ibid.

43. Ibid.

44. Ibid., 19–20.

45. Another contemporary writer who could be included in this discussion is Paula Morris. *Queen of Beauty* (Auckland, New Zealand: Penguin, 2002), for which she won the New Zealand Society of Authors Hubert Church Best First Book Award in 2003, included one minor Pasifika character, after which Morris created a more central and complex Pasifika character in Siaki, one of the key people in her 2005 novel *Hibiscus Coast* (Auckland, New Zealand: Penguin, 2005). Finally, there is a kindly older man called Uncle Suli in her short story "Red Christmas" who lends his van to some young Māori siblings who go out looking through household rubbish and furniture that has been left outside for collection. Paula Morris, "Red Christmas," in *Forbidden Cities*, 127–40 (Auckland, New Zealand: Penguin, 2008).

6. Manuhiri, Fānau

1. Karlo Mila, *Dream Fish Floating* (Wellington, New Zealand: Huia, 2005).

2. Albert Wendt, *The Songmaker's Chair* (Wellington, New Zealand: Huia, 2004).

3. Nofo, a Samoan cognate of the Māori noho, means to sit or live or remain in a specific place.

4. Wendt, *Songmaker's Chair*, 96.

5. While I am not directly treating his work here, in a later project, I look forward to carefully considering his work in this regard. To mention but a few of his relevant works, in *Ola,* the central character forms a close friendship with a Māori woman and her whanau and partly locates her own story in (parallel or entangled) relation to them; in the historical novel *The Mango's Kiss,* a key Samoan character lives undercover in New Zealand and marries a Māori woman; finally, in his recent magnum opus *The Adventures of Vela,* he includes references to Aotearoa in his epic treatment of Samoan deities and history. Albert Wendt, *Ola* (Auckland, New Zealand: Penguin, 1991). Albert Wendt, *Mango's Kiss.* Albert Wendt, *The Adventures of Vela* (Wellington, New Zealand: Huia, 2009). Niuean writer John Pule also peoples his urban Auckland landscape with Māori families. John Puhiatau Pule, *The Shark That Ate the Sun = Ko E Mago Ne Kai E La* (Auckland, New Zealand: Penguin Books, 1992).

6. Alistair Te Ariki Campbell, *Island to Island* (Christchurch, New Zealand: Whitcoulls, 1984).

7. Ihimaera, *Into the World of Light.*

8. Robert Sullivan, "Savaiki Regained: Alistair Te Ariki Campbell's Poetics," MA thesis, University of Auckland, 2006.

9. Alistair Te Ariki Campbell, *Maori Battalion: A Poetic Sequence* (Wellington, New Zealand: Wai-te-Ata Press, 2001).

10. Ibid., 5.

11. Ibid., 101–3.

12. Campbell, *Island to Island,* 83.

13. Alistair Te Ariki Campbell, "A Childhood in the Islands," in *Just Poetry,* 7–8 (Wellington: HeadworX, 2007).

14. This poem responds to the racist term *darkie,* which Paul Holmes used on a nationally broadcast radio breakfast show in 2003 to refer to Kofi Annan, then head of the United Nations.

15. Karlo Mila, "Eating Dark Chocolate While Watching Paul Holmes' Apology," in Mila, *Dream Fish Floating,* 43–45.

16. Tauiwi is a term sometimes engaged to mean "all who are not Indigenous" and sometimes to refer only to Pākehā.

17. Jo Smith, "At the Limits of the Seeable and Sayable: Identity Politics and New

Zealand Film Studies," paper presented at the MediaNZ Conference, Wellington, February 8, 2007.

18. Karlo Mila, "On One Tree Hill Falling," in Mila, *Dream Fish Floating*, 57.

7. When Romeo Met Tusi

1. Politically, some Pasifika communities and organizations have formally acknowledged the Indigenous position of Māori in the nation-state of New Zealand. McIntosh, "Hibiscus in the Flax Bush."

2. Indigenousness (this word is an unusual construction in the Māori language too).

3. Miria George's *And What Remains* uses this convention to great effect with the relationship between a Māori and a Pākehā character. Miria George, *And What Remains* (Wellington, New Zealand: Tawata, 2007).

4. Certainly Albert Wendt's *Sons for the Return Home* (Auckland, New Zealand: Longman Paul, 1973) presents the story of a young man whose intimate relationships with a Pākehā woman and a Sāmoan woman parallel his relationships with their respective cultures.

5. Wendt's *Sons for the Return Home* explores the mutual prejudice of Māori and Pasifika communities through a Samoan–Palagi couple, and that text is certainly part of the background of this exploration.

6. Oscar Kightley, as cited in Michael Neill, "From the Editor," *Shakespeare Quarterly* 52, no. 4 (2001): iii.

7. Although I am reading these as Māori–Pasifika relationships, in all these cases, the pairing is specifically of a Māori boy with a Samoan girl.

8. Erolia Ifopo and Oscar Kightley, *Romeo and Tusi* (Wellington, New Zealand: Playmarket, 2000). The play was also performed in Auckland in 1999.

9. Vilsoni Hereniko, *Woven Gods, Female Clowns, and Power in Rotuma* (Honolulu: University of Hawai'i Press, 1995).

10. Caroline Sinavaiana-Gabbard, "Where the Spirits Laugh Last: Comic Theater in Samoa," in *Inside Out: Literature, Cultural Politics, and Identity in the New Pacific*, ed. Vilsoni Hereniko and Rob Wilson (Lanham, Md.: Rowman and Littlefield, 1999), 183.

11. Ibid., 183–84.

12. The New Zealand police raids of October 15, 2007, add another layer here.

13. E.g., the dance company Black Grace was also known to engage directly with the audience.

14. New Zealand audiences often find themselves racially misreading the Māori actor Cliff Curtis to engage with the logic of overseas films in which he portrays Arabic, Mexican, and black characters, a phenomenon that the *Brotown* episode "A Maori at My Table" satirizes and that Jani Wilson treats in her thesis, "The Cinematic Economy of Cliff Curtis," MA thesis, University of Auckland, 2006. In *No.*

2, the film based on the play of the same name by Toa Fraser, audiences engaged in the opposite process, needing to believe that well-known Māori, Tongan, and Samoan actors were all members of the same Fijian family, whose matriarch was the African American actor Ruby Dee. The struggle to override this proved impossible for many. *No. 2*, DVD, directed by Toa Fraser (2007; South Yarra, Australia: Buena Vista Home Entertainment, 2007).

15. *The Market*, first broadcast September 15, 2005, by TVNZ. Directed by Rene Naufahu, Damon Fepulea'i, and Geoff Cawthorn and written by Rene Naufahu, Brett Ihaka, and Matthew Grainger.

16. T-shirt logos have been used dynamically in Pasifika communities as a marker of identity, often using Pacific-centric language and images and humor that subvert or extend mainstream or commercial logos. Many such small businesses sell their wares at the Ōtara flea market (and elsewhere), and artists such as Shigeyuki Kihara and Siliga David Setoga have brought the Pasifika subversion of brand names, logos, and capitalism into other spaces. Daniel Maaka's locally produced sweatshirt is an important forerunner of this phenomenon.

17. The words were composed by Hirini Melbourne.

18. I am grateful to Teresia Teaiwa for sharing this insight with me.

19. Uncle Ronnie sells rotten fish at his fish shop in the Ōtara town center, a detail that reinforces his moral decay and his dealings with the line between life and death. Significantly, his space of decay and bodily disintegration is where he and Ngaire carry out their sexual affair.

20. There are also minor Asian characters in the series.

21. Note *Romeo and Tusi's* talk show and the final item of *Once Were Samoans* set in Samoa, which was already narratively implied by the last scene set in New Zealand.

22. Later, Mike taunts his father for his passivity and calls him "disgusting."

23. Damon Salesa's arguments for a reading of a New Zealand empire are useful here. Damon Salesa, "New Zealand's Pacific," in *The New Oxford History of New Zealand,* ed. Giselle Byrnes, 149–72 (South Melbourne, Australia: Oxford University Press, 2009). Because of New Zealand's colonial role in the Pacific, Samoan, Niuean, Cook Islander, and Tokelauan people have had access to New Zealand citizenship. These communities, along with Moriori, are an Indigenous presence within New Zealand's political territory; however, although the state's boundaries have included these places at specific times, the communities have not occupied space understood to be "New Zealand" in the dominant imaginary.

The Realm of Koura

1. A pou is a carved figure; these line the inside walls of a carved house.

2. Tupuna (in some places, tipuna) is an ancestor.

3. Ranginui and Papatūānuku are the Sky and Earth, respectively.

4. The supporting post of the house.

5. *Spasifik Magazine,* http://www.spasifikmag.com/latestupdates_13feb09pasifikafestival/ (accessed March 13, 2009).

6. *Pasifika 1999* (Auckland, New Zealand: Auckland City Council and Festival Komiti, 1999), Auckland City Archives AKC310/11m.

7. Komiti is a Polynesian transliteration for "committee."

8. Auckland City Council and Festival Komiti, loose paper Festival Komiti notes, Auckland: Council Organised Events/Pasifika Events/vol 17, February 1999, Auckland City Archives.

9. Pasifika '98 Evaluation, 1998, Auckland City Council and Festival Komiti, Auckland City Archives AKC307/132g .

10. Pasifika Festival Komiti, minutes, November 4, 1999, Auckland City Archives AKC307/134a.

11. Ibid.

12. *Pasifika 2005* (Auckland, New Zealand: Auckland City Council and Festival Komiti, 2005), Auckland City Archives AKC310/11ae.

13. *Pasifika 2007* (Auckland, New Zealand: Auckland City Council and Festival Komiti, 2007), Auckland City Archives AKC310/24s.

14. Auckland City Council, "Pasifika," http://www.aucklandcity.govt.nz/whatson/events/pasifika/default.asp.

15. Someone like me, for example, has a very different sense of these connections than would someone whose experiences have been in predominantly Māori or Māori-and-Pākehā places. See Māori scholar Tracey McIntosh's pertinent essay "Growing South," http://www.alumni.auckland.ac.nz/2497.html (accessed October 15, 2007).

16. Alice Tawhai's short stories and Paula Morris's fiction are important urban voices, as are many of the writers included in the Huia collections.

17. We might also consider the resonances between Hawaiki and Aztlan as an imagined homeland that exists outside of and yet in many ways coincident to the present space.

18. E.g., in her work on northern California, Renya Ramirez acknowledges the many Indigenous communities layered around a single urban space. Renya Ramirez, *Native Hubs: Culture, Community, and Belonging in Silicon Valley and Beyond* (Durham, N.C.: Duke University Press, 2007).

19. Kealani Cook, "Sea of Islanders: Non-local Pacific Islanders and Pacific History," paper presented at the Pacific Worlds and the American West Conference, Salt Lake City, Utah, February 9, 2008.

20. Ibid.

21. *Sione's Wedding* has been distributed as *A Samoan Wedding* outside New Zealand.

22. *Made in Taiwan: Oscar and Nathan's Excellent Adventure,* televised documen-

tary directed by Dan Salmon (2006; Auckland, New Zealand: George Andrews Productions).

23. Rangatahi o Aotearoa, *Rongo*, 5.

24. Back2Basics: HiphopNZ Forums, "Discussion Thread: Do You Know This Man?" http://back2basics.hiphopnz.com (accessed January 14, 2009). The quotes that follow in this section are all from the same thread. I have included all quotes verbatim; the irregularities in spelling and grammar are in the original versions. However, I have also used dashes in place of profanity in these quotations because of the range of sensibilities of a Pacific readership.

Conclusion

1. Sullivan, *voice carried my family*, 28.

2. Ibid., 27.

3. *Michel Tuffery: First Contact* (Porirua, New Zealand: Pataka Museum, 2007), n.p.

4. Ibid.

5. Karen Stevenson, "Michel Tuffery First Contact," in ibid.

6. The European "discovery" of the Pacific was a combination of scientific research (Cook had botanists, astronomers, etc., on board) and a desire to find a more economically agreeable method of extracting resources and bringing them to Europe. Of course, a fair amount of biblical "knowing" took place during these Pacific voyages too!

7. That kūmara (sweet potato) is tied to knowledge has already been discussed. Ika most commonly means "fish" (the noun, not the verb), but Te Ahukaramū Charles Royal suggests that fish is a metaphor for ideas; the appearances in the oral traditions of ika are therefore about the pursuit of understanding, innovation, knowledge acquisition, and theoretical debate.

8. Robert Sullivan pointed out to me that it appeared to Māori that Tupaia provided translation and navigational services to Cook. I wonder if this emphasizes the role of Pacific practitioners and scholars already operating within the university system whose ability to operate within many knowledge spheres earns them not only a place on the ship (Tupaia was highly respected by the Europeans on board, especially Cook) but also recognition of a place within the academic structure.

9. Special thanks to Brandy Nālani McDougall for pushing and encouraging me to explore this dimension of the metaphor.

10. I am talking about Pacific scholarly legacy here: the actual number of positions occupied by Indigenous Pacific people in universities worldwide and regionwide is sadly far less than it could or should be.

11. Margaret Orbell, trans., "Two Manuscripts of Te Rangikaheke," *Te Ao Hou* 62 (March 1968): 11. Original Source is GNZMMSS 45. The translation for this phrase is "I am from Hawaiki."

12. Ibid. "This is an account written in Māori to you, the people of Hawaiki, to acquaint you with these matters."

13. "You have told me that you and your relatives own a ship. When you return home to Hawaiki, ask for your ship to be loaded with food for me, so that I may eat the food of the place from which our ancestors came in former times."

14. Harold B. Carter, "Note on the Drawings by an Unknown Artist from the Voyage of HMS *Endeavour*," in *Science and Exploration in the Pacific*, ed. Margarette Lincoln (Woodbridge, U.K.: Boydell Press, 1998), 133–34.

15. Titaua Porcher is a Tahitian literary scholar I met in Auckland at the Cultural Crossings: Negotiating Identities in Francophone and Anglophone Pacific Literatures/A la croisée des cultures: de la négociation des identités dans les littératures francophones et anglophones du Pacifique conference, which was held in November 2008.

16. Grace, *Mutuwhenua*, 100.

17. Powhiri Rika-Heke, "Margin or Center? Let Me Tell You! In the Land of My Ancestors I Am the Centre: Indigenous Writing in Aotearoa," in *English Postcoloniality from Around the World*, ed. Radhika Mohanram and Gita Rajan, 147–64 (Westport, Conn.: Greenwood, 1996). Chadwick Allen, *Blood Narrative: Indigenous Identity in American Indian and Maori Literary and Activist Texts* (Durham, N.C.: Duke University Press, 2002).

18. By the time Ihimaera's *Pounamu Pounamu* was published in 1972, for example, Tuwhare was already on to his third collection of poetry, J. C. Sturm had been anthologized in a collection of New Zealand writing, and many writers had published creative work in *Te Ao Hou* and elsewhere.

19. Penny van Toorn, *Writing Never Arrives Naked: Early Aboriginal Cultures of Writing in Australia* (Canberra, Australia: Aboriginal Studies Press, 2006), 2.

20. Lisa Brooks, "Digging at the Roots: Locating an Ethical, Native Criticism," in *Reasoning Together: The Native Critics Collective*, ed. Craig S. Womack, Daniel Heath Justice, and Christopher B. Teuton, 234–64 (Norman: University of Oklahoma Press, 2008).

21. I am presently undertaking a project called "Ghost Writers," which explores the work of early Māori writers Mowhee, Teeterree, Kooley, etc.

22. Patuawa-Nathan, *Opening Doors*. I have started to think of this novel as a spectral presence, paving the way for Māori people writing in English.

23. Vincent Eri, *The Crocodile* (Milton, Australia: Jacaranda Press, 1970).

24. I am following up this story of Patuawa-Nathan's missing novel in another project.

25. Manuscript Notes of Peter H. Buck, MS SC BUCK Box 2.29, Bishop Museum, Honolulu, Hawai'i.

26. I have written about this in greater detail in "The Historian Who Lost His Memory: A Story about Stories," *Te Pouhere Kōrero* 3 (2009): 63–82.

27. David Chappell, *Double Ghosts: Oceanian Voyagers on Euroamerican Ships* (Armonk, N.Y.: M. E. Sharp, 1997). I am conducting further research on Mowhee in another project and acknowledge that Kuni Jenkins and Alison Jones are looking at him from the perspective of early Māori literacy.

28. Basil Woodd, *Memoir of Mowhee, a Youth from New Zealand Who Died at Paddington, December 28, 1816; Serious Thoughts on Eternity* (Cornhill, Mass.: Samuel T. Armstrong and Crocker and Brewster, 1821).

29. Another extension of Māori writing in English is that writing was self-consciously produced in European literary forms in the earlier twentieth century but has fallen out of memory either because of the venue in which it was published or because it exists only in prepublished forms. Chadwick Allen has meticulously researched Māori self-representation in the 1950s, and Jane Stafford has done some work on a single poem by Apirana Ngata. Jane Stafford, "Terminal Creeds and Native Authors," *Journal of New Zealand Literature* 24, no. 2 (2007): 153–84. With Jane Stafford and Mark Williams, *Māoriland: New Zealand Literature 1872–1914* (Wellington, New Zealand: Victoria University Press, 2006).

30. Grace, *Mutuwhenua*, 100.

31. It is difficult to be accurate about this number because information about Māori is collected differently in the different states within which they live; some census data collapse Māori into Pacific or New Zealand categories.

32. In her outstanding doctoral work on Māori experiences in the city, Melissa Williams explores the limits of conventional narratives about urban Māori.

33. Paul Meredith is an avid scholar of this material. See also work by Lachy Paterson and scholars included in Curnow et al., *Rere atu, taku manu!*

34. Arini Loader, "Haere Mai me Tuhituhi he Pukapuka: Reading Te Rangikāheke," MA thesis, Victoria University of Wellington, 2009.

35. Don Brash's speech was titled "Nationhood" and was presented at the Orewa Rotary Club on January 27, 2004.

36. Alec Hutchinson, "Worlds Apart," *New Zealand Listener*, March 4–10, 2006.

37. This genetic research "finally" providing "scientific evidence" about the peopling of the Pacific bears striking parallels to Te Rangihiroa's ethnographic work, which was also understood as scientific evidence. It is easy to forget that ethnography was considered a real science: indeed, one of Te Rangihiroa's honorary degrees is a DSc.

38. Aileen Moreton-Robinson's work on the possessive logic of whiteness is an important connection here.

39. Similarly, the ownership of water and the seabed and foreshore in New Zealand has been asserted as a taken-for-granted right of citizens against which Māori claims are then understood to impose, although the "ownership" of these had never been legally conferred in the New Zealand state. (This misunderstanding is the basis of the Seabed and Foreshore furore that began in 2003.) Similarly,

note recent protests against so-called foreign ownership of New Zealand farmland.

40. Prime Minister Helen Clark described the organizers of the peaceful Hikoi (march) against the proposed Seabed and Foreshore legislation as "haters and wreckers." "Helen Clark Slams Hikoi," *TVNZ.co.nz*, May 4, 2004, http://tvnz.co.nz/view/news_story_skin/424042.

41. Although this echoes the distinction Te Papa articulates between being "Pacific Island" and being "Pacific Island in origin," the Te Papa case is about Māori inclusion in the "Pacific," whereas this is about Māori inclusion in the state.

42. Sometimes this logic is extended so that Indigenous people are anachronistically described as "first" citizens of their particular nation-states—First Australians, First Canadians, First Americans—which assimilates the Indigenous communities into their respective occupying nation-states as always-already citizens of a settler-nation-to-come rather than as always-already nations invaded by a trespassing group.

43. Rewiti Kohere (RTK), "Kei Hea Hawaiki," *Te Kopara* 81 (1920), http://www.nzdl.org/cgi-bin/library?a=p&p=about&c=niupepa&l=mi&nw=utf-8.

44. "There is more than one Hawaiki." Translation Arini Loader.

45. Ngāti Kahungunu Iwi Inc., "Supporting Indigenous Rights through Takitimu Fest," *Scoop: Independent News*, October 9, 2008, http://www.scoop.co.nz/stories/CU0810/S00114.htm.

46. Tino rangatiratanga was used in the 1840 Treaty of Waitangi to describe what Māori retained and is often translated "sovereignty"; mana motuhake is a non-Treaty concept that includes sovereignty and is often translated as "self-determination."

Epilogue

1. Taranaki whānui ki te Ūpoko o te Ika is the name used for the purposes of the Port Nicholson Block Claim, which represents a group of Taranaki-derived iwi with links to the Wellington region: Te Ātiawa, Taranaki, Ngāti Ruanui, Ngāti Tama, and Ngāti Mutunga. Taranaki whānui is not itself an iwi.

2. Kaitiakitanga is stewardship or guardianship.

3. Ngugi wa Thiong'o, "Decolonising the Mind: A Conversation about Culture, Power, and Translation," roundtable, University of Hawai'i English Department, April 2008.

4. Wineera Pere, *Mahanga*.

Publication History

Portions of chapter 1 were previously published as "I Belong to That Stock: Te Rangihiroa's Application for US Citizenship," in *The Racial Politics of Bodies, Nations, and Knowledges,* ed. Barbara Baird and Damien W. Riggs, 211–27 (Newcastle upon Tyne, U.K.: Cambridge Scholars Press, 2009). Published with permission of Cambridge Scholars Publishing.

Portions of chapter 1 were previously published as "Not E-mailing Albert: A Legacy of Collection, Connection, Community," *The Contemporary Pacific* 22, no. 2 (2010): 253–70.

Portions of chapter 1 were previously published as "Our Sea of Anthologies: Collection, Display, and the Deep Blue Sea," in *Cultural Crossings: Negotiating Identities in Francophone and Anglophone Pacific Literatures,* ed. Raylene Ramsa, 217–34 (Brussels: P. I. E. Peter Lang, 2010).

Portions of chapter 2 were previously published as "'My Poetry Is a Fire': Wineera and Sullivan Writing Fire from Hawai'i," in *Indigenous Identity and Resistance: Researching the Diversity of Knowledge,* ed. Brendan Hokowhitu et al., 37–54 (Dunedin: University of Otago Press, 2010).

Portions of "The Realm of the Tapa" were previously published as "Maori Cowboys, Maori Indians," *American Quarterly* 62, no. 3 (2010): 663–85. Copyright 2010 The American Studies Association.

Portions of chapter 4 were previously published as "In the (Brown) Neighbourhood: An Aotearoa-Based Oceania," *Journal of the South Pacific Association for Commonwealth Literature and Language Studies* nos. 54 and 55 (2005): 68–76.

"Pacific Note" and the introductory poem in *Mahanga* (La'ie, Hawai'i: Institute for Polynesian Studies, Brigham Young University–Hawaii Campus, 1978) are reprinted with permission of the poet, Vernice Wineera.

"Toa Rangatira," "Heritage," "Hokule'a," and "this island" are reprinted with permission of the poet, Vernice Wineera, and from *Into the Luminous Tide: Pacific Poems* (Provo, Utah: Center for the Study of Christian Values in Literature, Brigham Young University, 2009), with permission.

The poems "he karakia timatanga" and "i" are reprinted with permission of the poet, Robert Sullivan, and from *Star Waka* (Auckland, New Zealand: Auckland University Press, 1999), with permission.

"Tupaia," "Ahi Ka—the House of Ngapuhi," "the crackling page," "For the Ocean of Kiwa," "The Great Hall," and "Pearl Harbour" are reprinted with permission of the poet, Robert Sullivan, and from *Voice Carried My Family* (Auckland, New Zealand: Auckland University Press, 2005), with permission.

"Hawaii noa" and "Kaho o lawe," in *kanohi ki te kanohi* (Wellington, New Zealand: Moana Press, 1990), are reprinted with permission of the poet, Hinewirangi Kohu Morgan.

"Letter from Stuart Maireriki" and the dedication are reprinted with permission of the poet, Alistair Te Ariki Campbell, and from *Maori Battalion: A Poetic Sequence* (Wellington, New Zealand: Wai-te-ata Press/Te Whare Tā o Wai-te-ata, Victoria University of Wellington, New Zealand, 2001).

"A Childhood in the Islands" is reprinted with permission of the poet, Alistair Te Ariki Campbell, and from *Just Poetry* (Auckland, New Zealand: HeadWorX, 2007), with permission.

"Manuhiri," by Karlo Mila, is reprinted from *Dream Fish Floating* (Wellington, New Zealand: Huia, 2005), with permission.

Index

ALICE TE PUNGA SOMERVILLE is senior lecturer at
Victoria University of Wellington, New Zealand.